The Rise and Fall
of the Third Reich
A History of Nazi Germany
by William L. Shirer

The Rise and Fall of the Third Reich

A History of Nazi Germany

by William L. Shirer

Based on an Abridgment Prepared by Reader's Digest

GALLERY BOOKS
An imprint of W.H. Smith Publishers Inc.
112 Madison Avenue
New York, New York 10016

Page 1: Dr Goebbels, chief propagandist of the Nazi
Party, addressing a meeting in 1930.
Page 2: 'Only Hitler' – a Nazi poster.
This page: Hitler and his generals watch a flypast of the
newly-established Luftwaffe, 1935.

Published by Gallery Books
A Division of W H Smith Publishers Inc.
112 Madison Avenue
New York, New York 10016

Produced by
Brompton Books Corp.
15 Sherwood Place
Greenwich, CT 06830
USA

ISBN 0-8317-7404-5

10 9 8 7 6 5 4 3 2 1

Printed in Hong Kong

Reprinted 1990

This abridgement of *The Rise and Fall of the Third Reich*
is composed of two elements: passages taken from the
original text and passages taken from the lengthy
condensation that originally appeared in *Reader's Digest*
magazine. The publisher gratefully acknowledges the
courtesy of the author and Simon & Schuster, Inc. and
Martin Secker & Warburg, Ltd., for permission to
reproduce the former and of The Reader's Digest
Association for permission to reproduce the latter.

Contents

161.

Introduction

S. L. Mayer

One of the best-selling books of all time, and certainly the best-selling historical work ever written in modern times, was William L. Shirer's *The Rise and Fall of the Third Reich*. Published in 1959 and reprinted scores of times in hardcover and paperback, the work has sold many millions of copies in the English language and millions more in translation in almost every European language and many Oriental ones. It is still in print, used by students of history and members of the general public alike as perhaps the best-written single volume covering the phenomenon of Nazi Germany. Publishers are often dazzled by boxcar figures of bestsellers, and often ponder over why one or another book has captured the public interest so completely while others fail. There can be little astonishment about why Shirer's book enjoyed such immediate success and still continues to be an immensely popular work. The author and the subject he covered were made for one another.

After World War II there was, and continues to be, a fascination about how and why a man like Hitler and a movement like Nazism could capture the imagination of the German people, and how such a man and such a movement could move a people to come as close as any nation has to dominating the world through force of arms. Shirer explained why and understood the movement and Hitler intimately. For one thing, he was there at the time. Fluent in German and married to an Austrian, he had lived for a time in Vienna. After a

period of assignment to India by his then-employer, *The Chicago Tribune*, Shirer took up a journalistic post in Berlin in 1934. From that time on, until December 1940, he remained in Berlin, working first as a journalist and subsequently as a radio commentator for the Columbia Broadcasting System, a post for which he was recruited in 1937 by the legendary CBS broadcaster, and later telecaster, Edward R. Murrow. From this vantage point, and with his fine journalistic skills, he reported to the American people on events which led to war in Europe, staying on in Berlin well over a year after World War II broke out. He met, knew, talked with and occasionally drank with all the leading Nazi figures of the time: Hitler, Himmler, Goering, Hess, Heydrich, Goebbels and von Ribbentrop. His *Berlin Diary*, an account of his Berlin years, was published soon after his return to the United States during the war and is in itself a modern classic. His broadcasts from Germany and throughout the war became as much a part of the history of the war as Murrow's eye-witness accounts of the Blitz in London.

The Rise and Fall of the Third Reich could be said to have been the culmination of a lifetime's work for Shirer. In fact it took roughly a decade of research to produce, but its origins were to be found in those grim days of appeasement in which Shirer's loathing of Nazism was born. It remains the best single-volume treatment of one of the most riveting historical periods in modern times.

Left: William L. Shirer broadcasting in 1939 from Rome on the occasion of the election of Pope Pius XII.

Below: A typical Nazi propaganda image; the Army, Air Force and Navy stand fast, ready to meet attacks.

Below right: "Victory over the Bolsheviks!" is the slogan on this Nazi poster.

Left: The author preparing to broadcast from Compiegne, 22 June 1940, when the French surrender to the Germans was signed.

Right: Fruits of the Nazi economic program in the 1930s. A stretch of autobahn near Munich is officially opened.

Below: Changed times. A German street is renamed by American soldiers, December 1944.

Inevitably the 1960s and 1970s produced a group of revisionist historians who challenged the anti-Nazi sentiments which Shirer epitomized. A.J.P. Taylor's *Origins of the Second World War*, the first among many of these, blamed the Western Allies as much as Hitler for bringing about the war, charging that the likes of Neville Chamberlain and Edouard Daladier only served to encourage Hitler, who, according to the argument, wanted no war, but only the fruits of victory without war. Subsequent historians have praised and blamed Hitler as a military strategist during World War II. Underlying these arguments is the principle that war and history are never simplistic, that nothing in life or in history is clear-cut, and that, by implication, the straightforward views of Shirer, a non-professional historian with a journalistic background, were in fact only the reflection of American and indeed Allied postwar attitudes which, in the fullness of time, could now be safely discarded.

Nevertheless, Shirer continues to be read and admired by readers in great numbers. The reason is clear. The public still believes Shirer's point of view. It reflects accurately the Anglo-American view of Hitler's War as a struggle between tyranny and democracy, between evil and good, in which the issues, for once, were clear-cut. Shirer's clarity of observation and explanation can be understood by anyone, not merely by a highly trained academic (and consequently small) audience. It is for that reason that this abridged and illustrated edition of his classic work appears now. It gives a new generation and a potentially even wider audience an opportunity to read a landmark of historical writing, a standard against which all subsequent interpretations of the history of the Third Reich must be measured. No one can read about this time or understand Hitler, Nazism or the Third Reich without first reading William L. Shirer. The publishers are, therefore, proud to present Shirer's classic in illustrated form in the hope that the facts about this dramatic period in history will never be forgotten. They hope also that the lessons taught by this sinister story may be studied by future generations in the knowledge that those who do not learn from history are condemned to repeat it.

1. How Hitler Rose to Power

Birth of the Third Reich

On the eve of the birth of the Third Reich feverish tension gripped Berlin. The Weimar Republic, it seemed obvious to almost everyone, was about to expire. Adolf Hitler, leader of the National Socialists, the largest political party in Germany, was demanding for himself the chancellorship of the democratic republic he had sworn to destroy.

The wildest rumors of what might happen were rife: there was talk of a Nazi putsch, of a general strike. On Sunday, January 29, 1933, workers crowded into the Lustgarten in the center of Berlin to demonstrate their opposition to making Hitler chancellor.

Throughout most of Sunday night Hitler paced up and down his hotel room. Despite his nervousness he was supremely confident that his hour had struck. For nearly a month he had been secretly negotiating with the leaders of the conservative Right. He had had to compromise. He could not have a purely Nazi government. But he could be chancellor of a coalition government whose members agreed with him on the abolition of the democratic Weimar regime. Only the aged, dour president, Field Marshal Paul von Hindenburg, had seemed to stand in his way. As recently as January 26, the grizzled old field marshal had stated that he had "no intention whatsoever of making that Austrian corporal chancellor of the Reich."

Yet under the influence of his son and other members of the palace camarilla, the president was finally weakening; he was 86 and fading into senility.

Shortly before noon on Monday, January 30, 1933, Hitler drove to the Chancellery for an interview with Hindenburg that was to prove fateful for himself, for Germany and for the rest of the world. From a window in the Kaiserhof hotel, Joseph Goebbels, Ernst Roehm and other Nazi chiefs kept an anxious watch on the door of the Chancellery, where the Fuehrer would shortly be coming out. "We would see from his face whether he had succeeded or not," Goebbels noted. For even then they were not quite sure. "Our hearts are torn back and forth between doubt, hope, joy and discouragement," Goebbels jotted in his diary. "We have been disappointed too often for us to believe whole-heartedly in the great miracle."

A few moments later they witnessed the miracle. This man with the Charlie Chaplin mustache, who had been a down-and-out tramp in Vienna in his youth, an unremarked soldier of World War I, a derelict in Munich in the first grim postwar days, the somewhat comical leader of the Beer-Hall Putsch, this spellbinder who was not even German but Austrian, and who was only 42 years old, had just been administered the oath as chancellor of the German Reich.

That evening from dusk until far past midnight delirious Nazi storm troopers marched in a massive torchlight parade to celebrate the victory. By the tens of thousands, they passed in disciplined columns under the triumphal arch of the Brandenburg Gate and down the Wilhelmstrasse, their bands blaring old martial airs to the thunderous beating of the drums, their jack boots pounding a mighty rhythm on the pavement, their torches held high and forming a ribbon of flame that illuminated the night and kindled the hurrahs of the onlookers massed on the sidewalks.

Previous page: Hitler reviews a parade of Party faithful at Nazi rally in Nuremberg, 1927. To his right, Rudolf Hess and Pfeffer von Salomon, first head of the S.S.

Left: Hitler broadcasts to the German people as Reich Chancellor on January 31, 1933.

Top right: "Day of the Seizure of Power." Massed ranks of S.A. and S.S. men march through the Brandenburg Gate in Berlin, January 30, 1933.

Right: Hitler, Goering and other members of the Nazi leadership greet an enthusiastic crowd from the balcony of the Reich Chancellery, January 30, 1933.

On the Wilhelmstrasse Adolf Hitler stood at an open window of the Chancellery, beside himself with excitement and joy, dancing up and down, jerking his arm up continually in the Nazi salute.

Tired but happy, Goebbels arrived home that night at three. Scribbling in his diary before retiring, he wrote: "It is almost like a dream. The new Reich has been born. Fourteen years of work have been crowned with victory. The German revolution has begun!"

The Third Reich, which was born on January 30, 1933, Hitler boasted would endure for a thousand years. It lasted 12 years and four months, but in that flicker of time, as history goes, it caused an eruption on this earth more violent and shattering than any previously experienced, making the German people the masters of Europe from the Atlantic to the Volga, from the North Cape to the Mediterranean. Then at the end it plunged them to the depths of a world war which their nation had cold-bloodedly provoked and during which it instituted a reign of terror and butchery outdoing all the savage oppressions of previous ages.

The man who led the Third Reich to such dizzy heights and to such a sorry end was a person of undoubted, if evil, genius. It is true that he found in the German people a natural instrument which he was able to shape to his own sinister ends. But without Adolf Hitler, who was possessed of a demonic personality, uncanny instincts, a cold ruthlessness, a soaring imagination and – until toward the end, when he overreached himself – an amazing capacity to size up people and situations, there almost certainly would never have been a Third Reich.

To some Germans and to most foreigners it appeared that a charlatan had come to power. But the majority of Germans were to follow him blindly, as if he had divine judgment, for the next 12 tempestuous years.

Hitler's Early Years

Considering his origins and his early life, it would be difficult to imagine a more unlikely figure to succeed to the mantle of Bismarck, the Hohenzollern emperors and President Hindenburg than this singular Austrian of peasant stock who was born at half past six on the evening of April 20, 1889, in the Gasthof zum Pommer, a modest inn in the town of Braunau am Inn, across the border from Bavaria.

The place of birth on the Austro-German frontier was to prove significant, for early in his life, as a mere youth, Hitler became obsessed with the idea that there should be no border between these two German-speaking peoples and that they both belonged in the same Reich. So strong and enduring were his feelings that at thirty-five, when he sat in a German prison dictating the book that would become the blueprint for the Third Reich, his very first lines were concerned with the symbolic significance of his birthplace. *Mein Kampf* begins with these words:

"Today is seems to me providential that fate should have chosen Braunau am Inn as my birthplace. For this little town lies on the boundary between two German states which we of the younger generation at least have made it our lifework to reunite by every means at our disposal. . . . This little city on the border seems to me the symbol of a great mission."

Adolf Hitler was the third son of the third marriage of a minor Austrian customs official who had been born an illegitimate child and who for the first thirty-nine years of his life bore his mother's name, Schicklgruber. The name Hitler appears in the maternal as well as the paternal line. Both Hitler's grandmother on his mother's side and his grandfather on his father's side were named Hitler, or rather variants of it, for the family name was variously written as Hiedler, Huetler, Huettler and Hitler. Adolf's mother was his father's second cousin, and an episcopal dispensation had to be obtained for the marriage.

The forebears of the future German Fuehrer, on

Below: Mass columns of S.A. celebrate the Nazi "Seizure of Power," January 30, 1933.

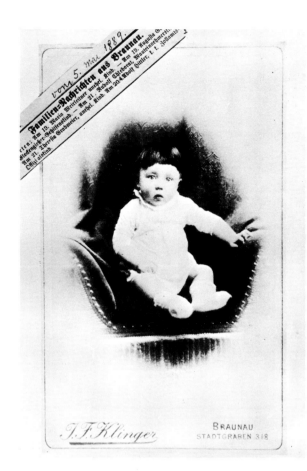

both sides, dwelt for generations in the Wald-viertel, a district in Lower Austria between the Danube and the borders of Bohemia and Moravia. In my own Vienna days I sometimes passed through it on my way to Prague or to Germany. It is a hilly, wooded country of peasant villages and small farms, and though only some fifty miles from Vienna it has a somewhat remote and impov-erished air, as if the main currents of Austrian life had passed it by. The inhabitants tend to be dour, like the Czech peasants just to the north of them. Intermarriage is common, as in the case of Hitler's parents, and illegitimacy is frequent.

On the mother's side there was a certain stability. For four generations Klara Poelzl's fam-ily remained on peasant holding Number 37 in the village of Spital. The story of Hitler's paternal ancestors is quite different. The spelling of the family name, as we have seen, changes; the place of residence also. There is a spirit of restlessness among the Hitlers, an urge to move from one vil-lage to the next, from one job to another, to avoid firm human ties and to follow a certain bohemian life in relations with women.

Johann Georg Hiedler, Adolf's grandfather, was a wandering miller, plying his trade in one vil-lage after another in Lower Austria. Five months after his first marriage, in 1824, a son was born, but the child and the mother did not survive. Eighteen years later, while working in Duerenthal, he mar-ried a forty-seven-year-old peasant woman from the village of Strones, Maria Anna Schicklgruber. Five years before the marriage, on June 7, 1837, Maria had had an illegitimate son whom she named Alois and who became Adolf Hitler's father. It is most probable that the father of Alois was Johann Hiedler, though conclusive evidence is lacking. At any rate Johann eventually married the woman, but contrary to the usual custom in such cases he did not trouble himself with legit-

imizing the son after the marriage. The child grew up as Alois Schicklgruber.

Anna died in 1847, whereupon Johann Hiedler vanished for thirty years, only to reappear at the age of eighty-four in the town of Weitra in the Waldviertel, the spelling of his name now changed to Hitler, to testify before a notary in the presence of three witnesses that he was the father of Alois Schicklgruber. Why the old man waited so long to take this step, or why he finally took it, is not known from the available records. According to Heiden, Alois later confided to a friend that it was done to help him obtain a share of an inher-itance from an uncle, a brother of the miller, who had raised the youth in his own household. At any rate, this tardy recognition was made on June 6, 1876, and on November 23 the parish priest at

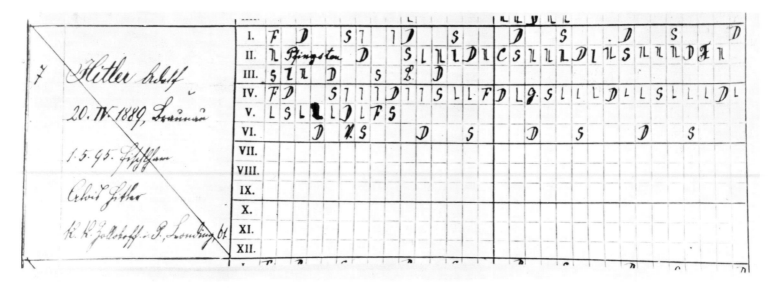

Above: Hitler's school report card from Lambach.

Below: Hitler seen in a school photograph when he was ten years old.

Doellersheim, to whose office the notarized statement had been forwarded, scratched out the name of Alois Schicklgruber in the baptismal registry and wrote in its place that of Alois Hitler.

From that time on Adolf's father was legally known as Alois Hitler, and the name passed on naturally to his son. It was only during the 1930s that enterprising journalists in Vienna, delving into the parish archives, discovered the facts about Hitler's ancestry and, disregarding old Johann Georg Hiedler's belated attempt to do right by a bastard son, tried to fasten on the Nazi leader the name of Adolf Schicklgruber.

There are many weird twists of fate in the strange life of Adolf Hitler, but none more odd than this one which took place thirteen years before his birth. Had the eighty-four-year-old wandering miller not made his unexpected reappearance to recognize the paternity of his thirty-nine-year-old son nearly thirty years after the death of the mother, Adolf Hitler would have been born Adolf Schicklgruber. There may not be much or anything in a name, but I have heard Germans speculate whether Hitler could have become the master of Germany had he been known to the world as Schicklgruber. It has a slightly comic sound as it rolls off the tongue of a South German. Can one imagine the frenzied German masses acclaiming a Schicklgruber with their thunderous "Heils"? "Heil Schicklgruber!"? Not only was "Heil Hitler!" used as a Wagnerian, paganlike chant by the multitude in the mystic pageantry of the massive Nazi rallies, but it became the obligatory form of greeting between Germans during the Third Reich, even on the telephone, where it replaced the conventional "Hello." "Heil Schicklgruber!"? It is a little difficult to imagine.

Since the parents of Alois apparently never lived together, even after they were married, the future father of Adolf Hitler grew up with his uncle, who though a brother to Johann Georg Hiedler spelled his name differently, being known as Johann von Nepomuk Huetler. In view of the undying hatred which the Nazi Fuehrer would develop from youth on for the Czechs, whose nation he ultimately destroyed, the Christian name is worthy of passing mention. Johann von Nepomuk was the national saint of the Czech people and some historians have seen in a Hitler being given this name an indication of Czech blood in the family.

Alois Schicklgruber first learned the trade of shoemaker in the village of Spital, but being restless, like his father, he soon set out to make his fortune in Vienna. At eighteen he joined the border police in the Austrian customs service near Salzburg, and on being promoted to the customs service itself nine years later he married Anna Glasl-Hoerer, the adopted daughter of a customs official. She brought him a small dowry and increased social status, as such things went in the old Austro-Hungarian petty bureaucracy. But the marriage was not a happy one. She was fourteen years older than he, of failing health, and she remained childless. After sixteen years they were separated and three years later, in 1883, she died.

Before the separation Alois, now legally known as Hitler, had taken up with a young hotel cook, Franziska Matzelsberger, who bore him a son, named Alois, in 1882. One month after the death of his wife he married the cook and three months later she gave birth to a daughter, Angela. The second marriage did not last long. Within a year Franziska was dead of tuberculosis. Six months later Alois Hitler married for the third and last time.

The new bride, Klara Poelzl, who would shortly become the mother of Adolf Hitler, was twenty-five, her husband forty-eight, and they had long known each other. Klara came from Spital, the ancestral village of the Hitlers. Her grandfather had been Johann von Nepomuk Huetler, with whom his nephew, Alois Schicklgruber-Hitler, had grown up. Thus Alois and Klara were second cousins and they found it necessary to apply for episcopal dispensation to permit the marriage.

It was a union which the customs official had first contemplated years before when he had taken Klara into his childless home as a foster daughter during his first marriage. The child had lived for years with the Schicklgrubers in Braunau, and as the first wife ailed Alois seems to have given thought to marrying Klara as soon as his wife died. His legitimation and his coming into an inheritance from the uncle who was Klara's grandfather occurred when the young girl was sixteen, just old enough to legally marry. But, as we have seen, the wife lingered on after the separation, and, perhaps because Alois in the meantime took up with the cook Franziska Matzelsberger, Klara, at the age of twenty, left the household and went to Vienna, where she obtained employment as a household servant.

She returned four years later to keep house for her cousin; Franziska too, in the last months of her life, had moved out of her husband's home. Alois Hitler and Klara Poelzl were married on January 7, 1885, and some four months and ten days later their first child, Gustav, was born. He died in infancy, as did the second child, Ida, born in 1886. Adolf was the third child of this third marriage. A younger brother, Edmund, born in 1894, lived only six years. The fifth and last child, Paula, born in 1896, lived to survive her famous brother.

Adolf's half-brother, Alois, and his half-sister, Angela, the children of Franziska Matzelsberger, also lived to grow up. Angela, a handsome young woman, married a revenue official named Raubal and after his death worked in Vienna as a housekeeper for a time, if Heiden's information is correct, as a cook in a Jewish charity kitchen. In 1928 Hitler brought her to Berchtesgaden as his housekeeper, and thereafter one heard a great deal in Nazi circles of the wondrous Viennese pastries and desserts she baked for him and for which he had such a ravenous appetite. She left him in 1936 to marry a professor of architecture in Dresden, and Hitler, by then Chancellor and dictator, was resentful of her departure and declined to send a wedding present. She was the only person in the family with whom, in his later years, he seems to have been close – with one exception. Angela had a daughter, Geli Raubal, an attractive young blond woman with whom, as we shall see, Hitler had the only truly deep love affair of his life.

In his early years, Hitler appears to have had little of the carefree spirit of youth. The world's problems weighed down on him. "He saw everywhere only obstacles and hostility," a boyhood friend remembered. "He was always up against something and at odds with the world. I never saw him take anything lightly."

Hitler was determined to be an artist, but his hopes were dashed: in 1907 he failed the entrance examinations to the Vienna Academy of Fine Arts. An even worse shock befell him the following year: on December 21, 1908, Hitler's mother died.

Above: The schoolroom where Hitler sat.

Below: Group photograph taken at Linz. Hitler back row, far right.

Above: Berliners read about the war crisis, August 1, 1914.

Below: Kaiser Wilhelm II awards Iron Crosses during World War I.

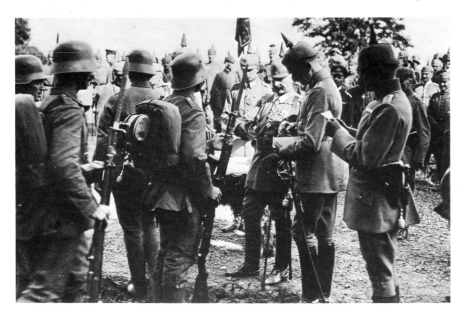

To the 19-year-old youth it was a dreadful blow: "I had honored my father, but my mother I had loved. Her death put a sudden end to all my plans. I was faced with the problem of somehow making my own living."

Somehow! He had no trade. He had always disdained manual labor. He had never tried to earn a cent. Indeed, the idea of earning his own living by any kind of regular employment was repulsive to him and would remain so throughout his life. But he was undaunted. Bidding his relatives farewell, he set out from his home in Linz for Vienna, declaring that he would not return until he had made good.

The next four years were a time of utter misery and destitution for Hitler. He lived by taking odd jobs: shoveling snow, beating carpets, carrying bags outside the West Railroad Station, occasionally working as a building laborer. He lived in flophouses or in the almost equally miserable quarters of a men's hostel, staving off hunger by frequenting the charity soup kitchens of the city.

But, unlike some of his ship-wrecked companions, he had none of the vices of youth. He neither smoked nor drank. He had nothing to do with women – not, so far as can be learned, because of any abnormality but simply because of an ingrained shyness.

Although Hitler says he eked out at least part of a living as "a small painter," he gives no details of this work in his autobiography except to remark that in the years 1909 and 1910 he had so far improved his position that he no longer had to work as a common laborer.

"By this time," he says, "I was working independently as a small draftsman and painter of water colors."

This is somewhat misleading, as is so much else of a biographical nature in *Mein Kampf*. Though the evidence of those who knew him at the time appears to be scarcely more trustworthy, enough of it has been pieced together to give a picture that is probably more accurate and certainly more complete.

That Adolf Hitler was never a house painter, as his political opponents taunted him with having been, is fairly certain. At least there is no evidence that he ever followed such a trade. What he did was draw or paint crude little pictures of Vienna, usually of some well-known landmark such as St. Stephen's Cathedral, the opera house, the Burgtheater. the Palace of Schoenbrunn or the Roman ruins in Schoenbrunn Park. According to his acquaintances he copied them from older works; apparently he could not draw from nature. They are rather stilted and lifeless, like a beginning architect's rough and careless sketches, and the human figures he sometimes added are so bad as to remind one of a comic strip. I find a note of my own made once after going through a portfolio of Hitler's original sketches: "Few faces. Crude. One almost ghoulish face." To Heiden, "they stand like tiny stuffed sacks outside the high, solemn palaces."

Probably hundreds of these pitiful pieces were sold by Hitler to the petty traders to ornament a wall, to dealers who used them to fill empty picture frames on display and to furniture makers who sometimes tacked them to the backs of cheap sofas and chairs after a fashion in Vienna in those days. Hitler could also be more commercial. He often drew posters for shopkeepers advertising such products as Teddy's Perspiration Powder, and there was one, perhaps turned out to make a little money at Christmas time, depicting Santa Claus selling brightly colored candles, and another showing St. Stephen's Gothic spire, which Hitler never tired of copying, rising out of a mountain of soap cakes.

This was the extent of Hitler's "artistic" achievement, yet to the end of his life he considered himself an "artist."

Bohemian he certainly looked in those vagabond years in Vienna. Those who knew him then remembered later his long black shabby overcoat, which hung down to his ankles and resembled a caftan and which had been given him by a Hungarian Jewish old-clothes dealer, a fellow inmate of the dreary men's hostel who had befriended him. They remembered his greasy black derby, which he wore the year round; his matted hair, brushed down over his forehead as in later years and, in the back, hanging disheveled over his soiled collar, for he rarely appeared to have had a haircut or a shave and the sides of his face and his chin were usually covered with the black stubble of an incipient beard. If one can believe Hanisch, who later become something of an artist, Hitler resembled "an apparition such as rarely occurs among Christians."

Left: Hitler cheering the outbreak of war among the patriotic crowd in front of the Feldherrnhalle, Munich, August 2, 1914.

His contemporaries of those days remembered, as had his teachers, the strong, staring eyes that dominated the face. And they recalled that the young man, for all his laziness when it came to physical labor, was a voracious reader, spendng much of his time devouring books. What did he learn in the school of hard knocks at Vienna? What were the ideas which he acquired there from his reading and his experience and which, as he says in *Mein Kampf*, would remain essentially unaltered to the end? They were mostly shallow and shabby, often grotesque and preposterous, and poisoned by outlandish prejudices. But they were important to the world, for they were to form part of the foundations for the Third Reich, which this bookish vagrant was soon to build.

Though he took no part in politics, Hitler followed avidly the activities of the major Austrian political parties. There now began to sprout in the mind of this unkempt frequenter of soup kitchens a political shrewdness which enabled him to see with amazing clarity the weaknesses and strengths of contemporary political movements and which, as it matured, would make him the master politician of Germany.

At first contact he developed a furious hatred for the working-class party of the Social Democrats. Yet he was intelligent enough to quench his feelings of rage in order to examine carefully the reasons for its popular success. He concluded that there were several, and years later he was to

remember and utilize them in building up the National Socialist Party: the party leaders knew, first, how to create a mass movement, without which any political party was useless; they had learned the art of propaganda among the masses; and, finally, they knew the value of using what he called "spiritual and physical terror."

Below: Mobile soup kitchens on the Home Front.

The Seeds of Nazism

This third lesson, though it was surely based on faulty observation and compounded of his own immense prejudices, intrigued the young Hitler.

"I understood the infamous spiritual terror which this movement exerts, particularly on the bourgeoisie; at a given sign it unleashes a barrage of lies and slanders against whatever adversary seems most dangerous, until the nerves of the attacked persons break down. This is a tactic based on precise calculation of all human weaknesses, and its result will lead to success with almost mathematical certainty."

No more precise analysis of Nazi tactics, as Hitler was to develop them, was ever written.

Hitler had been vaguely anti-Semitic before he came to the Austrian capital, but now he buried himself in anti-Semitic literature, which had a large sale in Vienna at the time. The Jews were largely responsible, he says he found, for prostitution, and the white-slave traffic. "When for the first time," he relates, "I recognized the Jew as the cold-hearted, shameless and calculating director of this revolting vice traffic in the scum of the big city, a cold shiver ran down my back."

There is a great deal of morbid sexuality in Hitler's ravings about the Jews. *Mein Kampf* is sprinkled with lurid allusions to uncouth Jews seducing innocent Christian girls and thus adulterating their blood. Hitler could write of the "nightmare vision of the seduction of hundreds of thousands of girls by repulsive, crooked-legged Jew bastards." One of the roots of Hitler's anti-Semitism may have been his tortured sexual envy. Though he was in his early 20's, so far as is known he had no relations of any kind with women during his sojourn in Vienna.

"Gradually," Hitler relates, "I began to hate the Jews. For me this was the time of the greatest spiritual upheaval I have ever had to go through. I had ceased to be a weak-kneed cosmopolitan and become an anti-Semite."

He was to remain a blind and fanatical one to the bitter end; his last testament, written a few hours before his death, would contain a final blast against the Jews, as responsible for the war which he had started and which was now finishing him and the Third Reich. This hatred would lead to a massacre so horrible and on such a scale as to leave a scar on civilization that will last as long as man is on earth.

In the spring of 1913, Hitler left Vienna and went to live in Germany, where his heart, he wrote, had always been. He was 24, and to everyone except himself he must have seemed a total failure. He had not become a painter, nor (as had been his other ambition) an architect. He had become nothing, so far as any one could see, but an eccentric vagabond. He had no friends, no family, no job, no home. He had, however, one thing: an unquenchable confidence in himself and a deep, burning sense of mission.

Nevertheless, in Munich, as in Vienna, he remained penniless, friendless and without a regular job. And then in the summer of 1914 the war came. On August 3 he volunteered for service in a Bavarian regiment. Now not only could the young vagabond satisfy his passion to serve his beloved adopted country, but he could escape from the failures and frustrations of his past. The war, which would bring death to so many millions, brought for him, at 25, a new start in life.

Right: Hitler recovering from a wound in a field hospital, standing second from right, back row.

The "Stab in the Back" Legend

Hitler was a courageous soldier. Later he would be accused of having been a coward, but there is no evidence for such a charge. During the war he was wounded twice, and he was twice decorated for bravery. Yet he was a peculiar soldier, as more than one of his comrades remarked. He never grumbled about the filth, the lice, the mud, the stench. "We all cursed this white crow among us," one of the men in his company later recalled. "He didn't go along with us when we damned the war to hell."

War he could endure. Defeat was to prove to be another matter.

On the dark autumn Sunday of November 10, 1918, Adolf Hitler experienced what out of the depths of his hatred and frustrations he called the greatest villainy of the century. The Kaiser had abdicated and fled. The war had been lost. On the morrow, an armistice would be signed at Compiègne in France.

"Everything went black before my eyes," Hitler says in recounting his reaction. "So all the sacrifices and privations had been in vain; in vain the hours in which, with mortal fear clutching at our hearts, we nevertheless did our duty. Did all this happen only so that a gang of wretched criminals could lay hands on the Fatherland?"

For the first time since he had stood at his mother's grave, he says, he broke down and wept. Like millions of his fellow countrymen then and forever after, he could not accept the blunt and shattering fact that Germany had lost the war, and he nurtured a fanatical belief in the legend of the "stab in the back." More than anything else, this myth that the German army had been not defeated in the field, but stabbed in the back by traitors at home, was to undermine the Weimar Republic and pave the way for Hitler's triumph.

The legend was fraudulent. General Erich Ludendorff, the leader of the high command, had insisted on September 28, 1918, on an armistice "at once," and his nominal superior, Field Marshal von Hindenburg, had supported him. In a letter written on October 2, Hindenburg flatly stated that the military situation made it imperative to stop the fighting. No mention was made of any stab in the back. In point of fact, the civilian government held out for several weeks against the army's demand for an armistice.

One had to live in Germany between the wars to realize how widespread was the acceptance of this incredible legend by the German people. The facts which exposed its deceit lay all around. The Germans of the Right would not face them. The culprits, they never ceased to bellow, were the "November criminals" – an expression which Hitler hammered into the consciousness of the people. It mattered not at all that the German Army, shrewdly and cowardly, had maneuvered the republican government into signing the armistice which the military leaders had insisted upon, and that it thereafter had advised the government to accept the Peace Treaty of Versailles. Nor did it seem to count that the Social Democratic Party had accepted power in 1918 only reluctantly and only to preserve the nation from utter chaos which threatened to lead to Bolshevism. It was not responsible for the German collapse. The blame for that rested on the old order, which had held the power. But millions of Germans refused to concede this. They had to find scapegoats for the defeat and for their humiliation and misery. They easily convinced themselves that they had found them in the "November criminals" who had signed the surrender and established democratic government in the place of the old autocracy. The gullibility of the Germans is a subject which Hitler often harps on in *Mein Kampf*. He was shortly to take full advantage of it.

"In these nights," Hitler said, "hatred grew in me, hatred for those responsible for this deed. Miserable and degenerate criminals! The more I tried to achieve clarity on the monstrous event in this hour, the more the shame of indignation and disgrace burned my brow." And then, he continued: "My own fate became known to me. I decided to go into politics."

Below: Corporal Adolf Hitler, 16th Bavarian Infantry Regiment.

Bottom: A French infantry attack on German trenches, France 1917.

The Birth of the Nazi Party

The prospects for a political career in Germany for this 30-year-old Austrian, without friends, funds or experience in politics, were less than promising. He returned to Munich in November 1918 to find his adopted city scarcely recognizable. Revolution had broken out here, and soon the Bavarian capital became a magnet for all those forces in Germany determined to overthrow the Republic and set up an authoritarian regime. It was in this fertile field that Adolf Hitler got his start.

Still assigned to the army, Hitler received orders one day in September 1919 from its political department to have a look at a tiny group in Munich which called itself the German Workers' Party. At first Hitler did not sense any importance in the party. After sitting through what he thought was a dull session of some 25 persons gathered in a beer cellar, he was not impressed. It was "a new organization like so many others. This was a time," he says, "in which anyone who was not satisfied with developments felt called upon to found a new party. Everywhere these organizations spring out of the ground, only to vanish silently after a time. I judged the German Workers' Party no differently."

But the next day he was astonished to receive a postcard saying that he had been accepted in the German Workers' Party. "I didn't know whether to be angry or to laugh," he remembered later. "I had no intention of joining a ready-made party, but wanted to found one of my own. What they asked of me was presumptuous and out of the question." He was about to say so in a letter when "curiosity won out" and he decided to go to a committee meeting to which he had been invited and explain in person his reasons for not joining "this absurd little organization."

"The tavern in which the meeting was to take place," he wrote, "was very run-down. In the dim light of a gas lamp four people sat at a table. Really, I was somewhat taken aback. The minutes of the last meeting were read, and the secretary was given a vote of confidence. Next came the treasury report – the association possessed seven marks and 50 pfennigs – terrible, terrible! This was club life of the worst sort. Was I to join this organization?"

Yet something about these shabby men in the ill-lit back room attracted him. That evening he returned to the barracks to "face the hardest question of my life: Should I join?" Reason, he admits, told him to decline. And yet the very unimportance of the organization would give him an opportunity "for real personal activity. After two days of agonized pondering and reflection, I finally came to the conviction that I had to take this step. It was the most decisive resolve of my life. From here, there could be no turning back."

Adolf Hitler was enrolled as the seventh member of the committee of the German Workers' Party.

It was a weird assortment of misfits who founded National Socialism. Among them were the confused locksmith Anton Drexler, who may be said to be the actual founder of the party; a drunken poet; an economic crank; a homosexual army officer. But it was now the former tramp, Adolf Hitler, not quite 31 and utterly unknown, who took the lead in building up what had been no more than a back-room debating society into what would soon be a formidable political party.

All the ideas which had been bubbling in his mind since the lonesome days in Vienna now found an outlet, and an inner energy which had not been observable in his makeup burst forth. He prodded his timid committee into organizing bigger meetings. He personally typed out and distributed invitations.

Later he recalled how once, after he had distributed 80 of these, "we sat waiting for the masses who were expected to appear. An hour late, the 'chairman' had to open the 'meeting.' We were again seven, the old seven."

Above: Revolutionary soldiers and sailors in Berlin, November 9, 1918.

Below: German delegates at the Peace Conference at Versailles, 1919.

Forging a Program

But he was not to be discouraged. At the start of 1920, Hitler took over the party's propaganda. He drew up a 25-point program, a hodgepodge for the workers, the lower middle class and the peasants, most of it forgotten by the time the party came to power. Yet, as in the case of *Mein Kampf*, the most important points were carried out.

The very first point in the program demanded the union of all Germans in a Greater Germany. Was this not exactly what Chancellor Hitler would insist on and get when he annexed Austria and its six million Germans, when he took the Sudetenland with its three million Germans? And was it not his demand for the return of German Danzig and the other areas in Poland inhabited predominantly by Germans which led to the German attack on Poland and brought on World War II? And cannot it be added that it was one of the world's misfortunes that so many in the interwar years either ignored or laughed off the Nazi aims which Hitler had taken the pains to put down in writing? Surely the anti-Semitic points of the program promulgated in the Munich beer hall on the evening of February 24, 1920, constituted a dire warning. The Jews were to be denied office and even citizenship in Germany and excluded from the press. All who had entered the Reich after August 2, 1914, were to be expelled.

A good many paragraphs of the party program were obviously merely a demagogic appeal to the mood of the lower classes at a time when they were in bad straits and were sympathetic to radical and even socialist slogans. Point 11, for example, demanded abolition of incomes unearned by work; Point 12, the nationalization of trusts; Point 13, the sharing with the state of profits from large industry; Point 14, the abolishing of land rents and speculation in land. Point 18 demanded the death penalty for traitors, usurers and profiteers, and Point 16, calling for the maintenance of "a sound middle class," insisted on the communalization of department stores and their lease at cheap rates to small traders. These were the ideas which Hitler was to find embarrassing when the big industrialists and landlords began to pour money into the party coffers, and of course nothing was ever done about them.

There were, finally, two points of the program which Hitler would carry out as soon as he became

Below: Revolutionaries with armored cars in Berlin, 1918.

Chancellor. Point 2 demanded the abrogation of the treaties of Versailles and St. Germain. The last point, number 25, insisted on "the creation of a strong central power of the State." This, like Points 1 and 2 demanding the union of all Germans in the Reich and the abolition of the peace treaties, was put into the program at Hitler's insistence and it showed how even then, when his party was hardly known outside Munich, he was casting his eyes on further horizons even at the risk of losing popular support in his own bailiwick.

Separatism was very strong in Bavaria at the time and the Bavarians, constantly at odds with the central government in Berlin, were demanding less, not more, centralization, so that Bavaria could rule itself. In fact, this was what it was doing at the moment; Berlin's writ had very little authority in the states. Hitler was looking ahead for power not only in Bavaria but eventually in the Reich, and to hold and exercise that power a dictatorial regime such as he already envisaged needed to constitute itself as a strong centralized authority, doing away with the semiautonomous states which under the Weimer Republic, as under the Hohenzollern Empire, enjoyed their own parliaments and governments. One of his first acts after January 30, 1933, was to swiftly carry out this final point in the party's program which so few had noticed or taken seriously. No one could say he had not given ample warning, in writing, from the very beginning.

Inflammatory oratory and a radical, catchall program, important as they were for a fledgling party, were not enough, and Hitler now turned his attention to providing more. What the masses needed, he thought, were not only ideas – a few simple ideas that he could ceaselessly hammer through their skulls – but symbols that would win their faith, pageantry and color that would arouse them, and acts of violence and terror that would attract adherents.

By the summer of 1920 the party's ranks had

swelled considerably, and Hitler now organized a bunch of roughneck war veterans into "strongarm" squads, later officially named the S.A. Outfitted in brown uniforms, these rowdies kept order at Nazi meetings and broke up those of the other parties. Once in 1921 Hitler personally led his storm troopers in an attack on a rival meeting, for which he was sentenced to three months in jail. He emerged something of a martyr and more popular than ever. "We got what we wanted," Hitler boasted to the police. "The National Socialist movement will ruthlessly prevent – if necessary by force – all meetings or lectures that are likely to distract the minds of our fellow countrymen."

Above: Philipp Scheidemann, member of the Council of People's Ministers, and General von Lequis, reviewing troops in Berlin, December 1918.

Left: Communist demonstrators in Munich, January 1919, carrying placards showing Karl Liebknecht and Rosa Luxemburg, leftist leaders murdered by Freikorps soldiers.

The Swastika

In the summer of 1920 Hitler, the frustrated artist but now becoming the master propagandist, came up with an inspiration which can only be described as a stroke of genius. What the party lacked, he saw, was an emblem, a flag, a symbol, which would express what the new organization stood for and appeal to the imagination of the masses, who, as Hitler reasoned, must have some striking banner to follow and to fight under. After much thought and innumerable attempts at various designs he hit upon a flag with a red background and in the middle a white disk on which was imprinted a black swastika. The hooked cross – the hakenkreuz – of the swastika, borrowed though it was from more ancient times, was to become a mighty and frightening symbol of the Nazi Party and ultimately of Nazi Germany. Whence Hitler got the idea of using it for both the flag and the insignia of the party he does not say in a lengthy note on the subject in *Mein Kampf*.

The hakenkreuz is as old, almost, as man on the planet. It has been found in the ruins of Troy and of Egypt and China. I myself have seen it in ancient Hindu and Buddhist relics in India. In more recent times it showed up as an official emblem in such Baltic states as Estonia and Finland, where the men of the German free corps saw it during the fighting of 1918-19. The Ehrhardt Brigade had it painted on their steel helmets when they entered Berlin during the Kapp putsch in 1920. Hitler had undoubtedly seen it in Austria in the emblems of one or the other anti-Semitic parties and perhaps he was struck by it when the Ehrhardt Brigade came to Munich. He says that numerous designs suggested to him by party members invariably included a swastika and that a "dentist from Sternberg" actually delivered a design for a flag that "was not bad at all and quite close to my own."

For the colors Hitler had of course rejected the black, red and gold of the hated Weimar Republic. He declined to adopt the old imperial flag of red, white and black, but he liked its colors not only because, he says, they form "the most brilliant harmony in existence," but because they were the colors of a Germany for which he had fought. But they had to be given a new form, and so a swastika was added.

Hitler reveled in his unique creation. *"A symbol it really is!"* he exlaims in *Mein Kampf*. *"In red* we see the social idea of the movement, in *white* the nationalist idea, in the *swastika* the mission of the struggle for the victory of the Aryan man."

Soon the swastika armband was devised for the uniforms of the storm troopers and the party members, and two years later Hitler designed the Nazi standards which would be carried in the massive parades and would adorn the stages of the mass meetings. Taken from old Roman designs, they consisted of a black metal swastika on top with a silver wreath surmounted by an eagle, and, below, the initials NSDAP on a metal rectangle from which hung cords with fringe and tassels, a square swastika flag with *"Deutschland Erwache!* (Germany Awake!)" emblazoned on it.

This may not have been "art," but it was propaganda of the highest order. The Nazis now had a symbol which no other party could match. The hooked cross seemed to possess some mystic power of its own, to beckon to action in a new direction the insecure lower middle classes which had been floundering in the uncertainty of the first chaotic postwar years. They began to flock under its banner.

Above left: The Munich beer hall room where Hitler first joined the Nazi Party.

Left: Revolutionary Soldiers' Council field gun in Berlin, 1918.

Advent of the "Fuehrer"

In 1921 the rising young agitator took over the undisputed leadership of the party. In doing so, he gave his fellow workers a first taste of the ruthlessness with which he was to gain so much success later on. When some of the other party members challenged his dictatorial tactics, Hitler offered to resign.

This was more than the party could afford. If he left, the budding Nazi Party would surely go to pieces. The committee refused to accept his resignation. Hitler now forced a complete capitulation on the other leaders. He demanded, and got, dictatorial powers for himself as the party's sole leader. Then and there, in July 1921, was established the "leadership principle" which was to be the law first of the Nazi Party and then of the Third Reich. The "Fuehrer" had arrived on the German scene.

Most of the men who were to become Hitler's closest subordinates were now in the party or would shortly enter it. Rudolf Hess joined in 1920. Son of a German wholesale merchant domiciled in Egypt, Hess had spent the first fourteen years of his life in that country and had then come to the Rhineland for his education. During the war he served for a time in the List Regiment with Hitler –

though they did not become acquainted then – and after being twice wounded became a flyer. He enrolled in the University of Munich after the war as a student of economics but seems to have spent much of his time distributing anti-Semitic pamphlets and fighting with the various armed bands then at loose in Bavaria. He was in the thick of the firing when the soviet regime in Munich was overthrown on May 1, 1919, and was wounded in the leg. One evening a year later he went to hear Hitler speak, was carried away by his eloquence and joined the party, and soon he became a close friend, a devoted follower and secretary of the leader. It was he who introduced Hitler to the geopolitical ideas of General Karl Haushofer, then a professor of geopolitics at the university.

Hess had stirred Hitler with a prize-winning essay which he wrote for a thesis, entitled "How Must the Man Be Constituted Who Will Lead Germany Back to Her Old Heights?" "Where all authority has vanished, only a man of the people can establish authority . . . The deeper the dictator was originally rooted in the broad masses, the better he understands how to treat them psychologically, the less the workers will distrust him, the more supporters he will win among these most energetic ranks of the people. He himself has nothing in common with the mass; like every great man he is all personality . . . When necessity commands, he does not shrink before bloodshed. Great questions are always decided by blood and iron . . . In order to reach his goal, he is prepared to trample on his closest friends . . . The lawgiver proceeds with terrible hardness . . . As the need arises, he can trample them [the people] with

Below: A group of Nazi supporters in Bavaria in 1920. Alfred Rosenberg stands in the middle row, third from left.

the boots of a grenadier.'' No wonder Hitler took to the young man. This was a portrait perhaps not of the leader as he was at the moment but of the leader he wanted to become – and did. For all his solemnity and studiousness, Hess remained a man of limited intelligence, always receptive to crackpot ideas, which he could adopt with great fanaticism. Until nearly the end, he would be one of Hitler's most loyal and trusted followers and one of the few who was not bitten by consuming personal ambition.

Alfred Rosenberg, although he was often hailed as the ''intellectual leader'' of the Nazi Party and indeed its ''philosopher,'' was also a man of mediocre intelligence. Rosenberg may with some truth be put down as a Russian. Like a good many Russian ''intellectuals,'' he was of Baltic German stock. The son of a shoemaker, he was born January 12, 1893, at Reval (now Tallinn) in Estonia, which had been a part of the Czarist Empire since 1721. He chose to study not in Germany but in Russia and received a diploma in architecture from the University of Moscow in 1917. He lived in Moscow through the days of the Bolshevik revolution and it may be that, as some of his enemies in the Nazi Party later said, he flirted with the idea of becoming a young Bolshevik revolutionary. In February 1918, however, he returned to Reval, volunteered for service in the German Army when it reached the city, was turned down as a ''Russian'' and finally, at the end of 1918, made his way to Munich, where he first became active in White Russian émigré circles.

Rosenberg then met Hitler's mentor the poet Dietrich Eckart and through him Hitler, and joined the party at the end of 1919. It was inevitable that a man who had actually received a diploma in architecture would impress the man who had failed even to get into a school of architecture. Hitler was also impressed by Rosenberg's ''learning'' and he liked the young Balt's hatred of the Jews and the Bolsheviks . . . Hitler made Rosenberg editor of the *Voelkischer Beobachter* [the party

Left: An idealised photograph of Hitler as he appeared in 1921.

Left: Hitler's membership card of the German Workers' Party, 1 January 1920. In the summer of that year the party name was changed to National Socialist German Workers Party (Nationalsozialistiche Deutsche Arbeiterpartei – NSDAP).

Below: Nazi supporters in Bavaria, 1920. Hitler standing second from left.

Above: Freikorps troops supporting the Kapp Putsch in Berlin, March 1920.

last commander of the famed Richthofen Fighter Squadron, holder of the Pour le Mérite, the highest war decoration in Germany, he found it even more difficult than most war veterans to return to the humdrum existence of peacetime civilian life. He became a transport pilot in Denmark for a time and later in Sweden. One day he flew Count Eric von Rosen to the latter's estate some distance from Stockholm and while stopping over as a guest fell in love with Countess Rosen's sister, Carin von Kantzow, née Baroness Fock, one of Sweden's beauties. Some difficulties arose. Carin von Kantzow was epileptic and was married and the mother of an eight-year-old son. But she was able to have the marriage dissolved and marry the gallant young flyer. Possessed of considerable means, she went with her new husband to Munich, where they lived in some splendor and he dabbled in studies at the university.

But not for long. He met Hitler in 1921, joined the party, contributed generously to its treasury (and to Hitler personally), threw his restless energy into helping Roehm organize the storm troopers and a year later, in 1922, was made commander of the S.A.

A swarm of lesser-known and, for the most part, more unsavory individuals joined the circle around the party dictator. Max Amann, Hitler's first sergeant in the List Regiment, a tough, uncouth character but an able organizer, was named business manager of the party and the *Voelkischer Beobachter* and quickly brought order into the finances of both. As his personal bodyguard Hitler chose Ulrich Graf, an amateur wrestler, a butcher's apprentice and a renowned brawler. As his "court photographer," the only man who for years was permitted to photograph him, Hitler had the lame Heinrich Hoffmann, whose loyalty was doglike and profitable, making him in the end a millionaire. Another favorite brawler was Christian Weber, a horse dealer, a former

newspaper] and for many years he continued to prop up this utterly muddled man, this confused and shallow "philosopher," as the intellectual mentor of the Nazi movement and as one of its chief authorities on foreign policy.

Like Rudolf Hess, Hermann Goering had also come to Munich some time after the war ostensibly to study economics at the university, and he too had come under the personal spell of Adolf Hitler. One of the nation's great war heroes, the

Right: Hitler speaking at a mass rally in Munich in the early days of the Nazi Party.

bouncer in a Munich dive and a lusty beer drinker. Close to Hitler in these days was Hermann Esser, whose oratory rivaled the leader's and whose Jew-baiting articles in the *Voelkischer Beobachter* were a leading feature of the party newspaper. He made no secret that for a time he lived well off the generosity of some of his mistresses. A notorious black-mailer, resorting to threats to "expose" even his own party comrades who crossed him, Esser became so repulsive to some of the older and more decent men in the movement that they demanded his expulsion. "I know Esser is a scoundrel," Hitler retorted in public, "but I shall hold on to him as long as he can be of use to me." This was to be his attitude toward almost all of his close collaborators, no matter how murky their past – or indeed their present. Murderers, pimps, homosexual perverts, drug addicts or just plain rowdies were all the same if they served his purposes.

He stood Julius Streicher, for example, almost to the end. This depraved sadist, who started life as an elementary-school teacher, was one of the most disreputable men around Hitler from 1922 until 1939, when his star finally faded. A famous fornicator, as he boasted, who blackmailed even the husbands of women who were his mistresses, he made his fame and fortune as a blindly fanatical anti-Semite. His notorious weekly, *Der Stuermer*, thrived on lurid tales of Jewish sexual crimes and Jewish "ritual murders"; its obscenity was nauseating, even to many Nazis. Streicher was also a noted pornographist. He became known as the "uncrowned King of Franconia" with the center of his power in Nuremberg, where his word was law and where no one who crossed him or displeased him was safe from prison and torture. Until I faced him slumped in the dock at Nuremberg, on trial for his life as a war criminal, I never saw him without a whip in his hand or in his belt, and he laughingly boasted of the countless lashings he had meted out.

Such were the men whom Hitler gathered around him in the early years for his drive to become dictator of a nation which had given the world a Luther, a Kant, a Goethe and a Schiller, a Bach, a Beethoven and a Brahms.

Below: "Red Army" supporters preparing for armed resistance in the Ruhr, Spring 1920.

The Trauma of Versailles

In the stormy years between 1921 and 1923, there was a dizzy succession of events for a politician to watch, and to take advantage of. In April 1921 the Allies presented Germany the bill for reparations: 33 billion dollars, which the Germans howled they could not pay. The mark, normally valued at four to the dollar, had begun to fall; by the summer of 1921 it had dropped to 72, a year later to 400, to the dollar. Political assassinations multiplied. The fledgling democratic Weimar Republic was in deep trouble, its very existence constantly threatened from both the extreme Right and the extreme Left.

At the end of the war the army leaders, Ludendorff and Hindenburg, had pushed political power into the hands of the reluctant Social Democrats. In doing so they managed also to place on the shoulders of these democratic leaders apparent responsibility for signing the surrender and ultimately the peace treaty, thus laying on them the blame for Germany's defeat. This was a shabby trick, one which the merest child would be expected to see through, but in Germany it worked. It doomed the Republic from the start.

Perhaps it need not have. In November 1918 the Social Democrats, holding absolute power, might have quickly laid the foundation for a lasting democratic republic. But to have done so they would have had to suppress permanently the feudal *Junker* landlords and other upper castes, the magnates who ruled over the great industrial cartels, the ranking officials of the civil service and, above all, the military caste and the general staff. This they could not bring themselves to do. Instead, they began by abdicating their authority to the force which had always been dominant in modern Germany: the army. The consequences of this failure were to be grave.

The new constitution which Germany adopted after the war was, on paper, the most liberal and democratic document of its kind the 20th century had seen, mechanically well-nigh perfect, full of ingenious and admirable devices which seemed to guarantee the working of an almost flawless democracy. The idea of cabinet government was borrowed from England and France, of a strong popular president from the United States, of the referendum from Switzerland. An elaborate system of proportional representation was established to give small minorities a right to be represented in parliament. No man in the world would be more free than a German, no government more democratic and liberal than his. On paper, at least.

But before the drafting of the constitution was finished, an event occurred which cast a spell of doom over it trand the Republic which it was to establish. This was the drawing up of the Treaty of Versailles, a document which came as a staggering blow to the Germans.

German memories did not appear to stretch back as far as one year, to March 3, 1918, when the then victorious German Supreme Command had

Above left: The new European boundaries imposed by the Treaty of Versailles.

Above: German housewives wait hopefully to buy meat, 1923. Such scenes and the problems they represented helped gain support for the Nazis' nationalist ideas.

imposed on a defeated Russia at Brest Litovsk a peace treaty which to a British historian, writing two decades after the passions of war had cooled, was a "humiliation without precedent or equal in modern history." It deprived Russia of a territory nearly as large as Austria-Hungary and Turkey combined, with 56,000,000 inhabitants, or 32 per cent of her whole population; 73 per cent of her total iron ore; 89 per cent of her total coal production; and more than 5,000 factories and industrial plants. Moreover, Russia was obliged to pay Germany an indemnity of six billion marks.

The day of reckoning arrived for the Germans in the late spring of 1919. The terms of the Versailles Treaty, laid down by the Allies without negotiation with Germany, were published in Berlin on May 7. They came as a staggering blow to a people who had insisted on deluding themselves to the last moment. Angry mass meetings were organized throughout the country to protest against the treaty and to demand that Germany refuse to sign it. Philip Scheidemann, who had become Chancellor during the Weimar Assembly, cried, "May the hand wither that signs this

Right: Berlin newspaper headline, July 28, 1923, announcing the inflated exchange rate of 1 million marks to the US dollar. The mark continued to fall until November when the rate was 130,000 million to the dollar.

Left: Hitler attending a rally of nationalist parties in Nuremberg, September 2, 1923.

defeating them in war. It gave back to the Poles the
lands, some of them only after a plebiscite, which
the Germans had taken during the partition of Pol-
and. This was one of the stipulations which infuriated the Germans the most, not only because
they resented separating East Prussia from the
Fatherland by a corridor which gave Poland access
to the sea, but because they despised the Poles.
Scarcely less infuriating to the Germans was that
the treaty forced them to accept responsibility for
starting the war and demanded that they turn
over to the Allies Kaiser Wilhelm II and some eight
hundred other "war criminals."

Reparations were to be fixed later, but a first
payment of five billion dollars in gold marks was
to be paid between 1919 and 1921, and certain
deliveries in kind – coal, ships, lumber, cattle, etc.
– were to be made in lieu of cash reparations.

But what hurt most was that Versailles virtually
disarmed Germany and thus, for the time being
anyway, barred the way to German hegemony in
Europe. And yet the hated Treaty of Versailles,
unlike that which Germany had imposed on
Russia, left the Reich geographically and econom-
ically largely intact and preserved her political
unity and her potential strength as a great nation.

The provisional government at Weimar was
strongly against accepting the "Versailles *Diktat*,"
as it was soon called. Only because the army
informed the government that German military
resistance would be futile – a fact that was soon
forgotten in Germany – did the national assembly
approve the signing of the peace treaty. From that
day on Germany became a house divided.

treaty!'' On May 8 Friedrich Ebert, who had
become Provisional President, and the government publicly branded the terms as "unrealizable
and unbearable." The next day the German delegation at Versailles wrote the unbending Clem-
enceau that such a treaty was "intolerable for any
nation." What was so intolerable about it? It restored Alsace-Lorraine to France, a parcel of territory to Belgium, a similar parcel in Schleswig to
Denmark – after a plebiscite – which Bismarck had
taken from the Danes in the previous century after

Suicide of an Economy

The conservatives would accept neither the treaty of peace nor the Republic which had ratified it. Nor, in the long run, would the army.

The conservatives still held the economic power. They owned the industries, the large estates and most of the country's capital. Their wealth could be used, and was, to subsidize political parties and a political press that would strive from then on to undermine the Republic.

The army began to circumvent the military restrictions of the peace treaty before the ink was dry. The officer corps managed not only to maintain the army in its old Prussian traditions, but to become the real center of political power in the new Germany. It became a state within a state, exerting an increasing influence on the nation's foreign and domestic policies. Under the Weimar Constitution the army could have been subordinated to the cabinet and parliament, as the military establishments of the other Western democracies were. But it was not. And so the Republic tottered from its birth.

Down in Bavaria the young firebrand Adolf Hitler grasped the strength of the nationalist, antidemocratic and antirepublican tide. He began to ride it.

He was greatly aided by the course of events, two in particular: the fall of the mark and the French occupation of the Ruhr. By the beginning of 1923 the mark had fallen to 7,000 to the dollar. Then, when Germany defaulted in deliveries of timber reparations to France, French troops occupied the Ruhr, the industrial heart of Germany.

This paralyzing blow to Germany's economy united the people momentarily as they had not

Above: French officers and their families entering an Officers Club in the Ruhr, 1923.

Left: Customs post between the French-occupied Ruhr and the rest of Germany, 1923.

Above: Women and children scavenging on a tip for coal, in 1923 at the height of the Great Inflation.

been united since 1914. The workers of the Ruhr declared a general strike and, with the help of the army, sabotage and guerrilla warfare were organized. The French countered with arrests, deportations and even death sentences. But not a wheel in the Ruhr turned.

The strangulation of Germany's economy hastened the final plunge of the mark. On the occupation of the Ruhr, it fell to 18,000 to the dollar; by July 1, 1923, it had dropped to 160,000; by August to a million. By November, when Hitler thought his hour had struck, it took four billion marks to buy a dollar, and thereafter the figures became trillions. German currency had become utterly worthless.

The life savings of the middle and working classes were wiped out. But something even more important was destroyed: the faith of the people in the economic structure of German society. What good were the standards and practices of such a society, which encouraged savings and investment and solemnly promised a safe return from them and then defaulted? Was this not a fraud upon the people?

And was not the democratic Republic, which had surrendered to the enemy and accepted the burden of reparations, to blame for the disaster? Unfortunately for its survival, the Republic did bear a responsibility. The inflation could have been halted by merely balancing the budget – a difficult but not impossible feat. Yet, goaded by the big industrialists and landlords, who stood to gain though the masses of the people were financially ruined, the government deliberately let the mark tumble in order to free the state of its public debts, to escape from paying reparations and to sabotage the French in the Ruhr.

The destruction of the currency enabled German heavy industry to wipe out its indebtedness by refunding its obligations in worthless marks. It also wiped out the war debts and thus left Germany financially unencumbered for a new war – a fact which was noted by the general staff.

The masses of the people, however, did not realize how much the industrial tycoons, the army and the state were benefiting from the ruin of the currency. All they knew was that a large bank account could not buy a straggly bunch of carrots, a half peck of potatoes, a pound of flour. They knew they were bankrupt, and they knew hunger. In their misery and hopelessness they made the Republic the scapegoat for all that happened.

Such times were heaven-sent for Adolf Hitler.

"The government calmly goes on printing these scraps of paper because, if it stopped, that would be the end of the government," he cried. "Because once the printing presses stopped – and that is the prerequisite for the stabilization of the mark – the swindle would at once be brought to light . . . Believe me, our misery will increase. The scoundrel will get by. The reason: because the State itself has become the biggest swindler and crook. A robbers' state! . . . If the horrified people notice that they can starve on billions, they must arrive at this conclusion: we will no longer submit to a State which is built on the swindling idea of the majority. We want a dictatorship . . ."

No doubt the hardships and uncertainties of the wanton inflation were driving millions of Germans toward that conclusion and Hitler was ready to lead them on. In fact, he had begun to believe that the chaotic conditions of 1923 had created an opportunity to overthrow the Republic which might not recur. But certain difficulties lay in his way if he were himself to lead the counterrevolution, and he was not much interested in it unless he was.

In the first place, the Nazi Party, though it was growing daily in numbers, was far from being even the most important political movement in Bavaria, and outside that state it was unknown. How could such a small party overthrow the Republic? Hitler, who was not easily discouraged by odds against him, thought he saw a way. He might unite under his leadership all the antirepublican, nationalist forces in Bavaria. Then with the support of the Bavarian government, the armed leagues and the Reichswehr stationed in Bavaria, he might lead a march on Berlin – as Mussolini had marched on Rome the year before – and bring the Weimar Republic down. Obviously Mussolini's easy success had given him food for thought.

The French occupation of the Ruhr, though it brought a renewal of German hatred for the traditional enemy and thus revived the spirit of nationalism, complicated Hitler's task. It began to unify the German people behind the republican government in Berlin which had chosen to defy France. This was the last thing Hitler wanted. His aim was to do away with the Republic. France could be taken care of after Germany had had its nationalist revolution and established a dictatorship. Against a strong current of public opinion Hitler dared to take an unpopular line: "No – not down with France, but down with the traitors of the Fatherland, down with the November criminals! That must be our slogan."

All through the first months of 1923 Hitler dedicated himself to making the slogan effective. In February, due largely to the organizational talents of Roehm, four of the armed "patriotic leagues" of Bavaria joined with the Nazis to form the so-called *Arbeitsgemeinschaft der Vaterlaendischen Kampfverbaende* (Working Union of the Fatherland Fighting Leagues) under the political leadership of Hitler. In September an even stronger group was established under the name of the *Deutscher Kampfbund* (German Fighting Union), with Hitler one of the triumvirate of leaders. This organization sprang from a great mass meeting held at Nuremberg on September 2 to celebrate the anniversary of the German defeat of France at Sedan in 1870. Most of the fascist-minded groups in southern Germany were represented and Hitler received something of an ovation after a violent speech against the national government. The objectives of the new *Kampfbund* were openly stated: the overthrow of the Republic and the tearing up of the Treaty of Versailles.

Above: Old tramp in Berlin, 1923.

Left: A crippled ex-officer begging in Berlin, 1923. Scenes like these were eagerly exploited by Hitler and his cohorts.

The Beer-Hall Putsch

In the fall of 1923 the German Republic and the state of Bavaria reached a point of crisis. Gustav Stresemann, the chancellor, announced the end of passive resistance in the Ruhr and the resumption of German reparation payments. Bavaria was in no mood to accept such a solution. The Bavarian cabinet proclaimed its own state of emergency and named the right-wing monarchist Gustav von Kahr as state commissioner with dictatorial powers. General Otto von Lossow, commander of the Reichswehr in Bavaria, and Colonel Hans von Seisser, the head of the state police, rounded out the triumvirate of provincial leadership. In Berlin it was feared that Bavaria might secede from the Reich and perhaps form a South German Union with Austria.

As tension mounted, a state of emergency was proclaimed in Germany, but Kahr refused to recognize that it had any application in Bavaria, and declined to carry out any orders from Berlin. When the national government demanded the suppression of Hitler's newspaper, the *Voelkischer Beobachter*, because of its vitriolic attacks on the Republic, Kahr contemptuously refused. Then, defying the constitution, Kahr forced the officers and men of the army to take a special oath of allegiance to the Bavarian government.

Above right: Hitler in Munich, 1923. On the left, Alfred Rosenberg, on the right, Julius Weber.

Right: S.A. column marching into Munich in 1923, before the Putsch.

This, to Berlin, was not only political but military rebellion, and the commander of the army, General von Seeckt, was now determined to put down both.

He issued a warning to the Bavarian triumvirate and to Hitler that any rebellion on their part would be opposed by force. But Hitler had begun to believe that the chaotic conditions of 1923 had created an opportunity to overthrow the Republic which might not recur. It was too late to draw back. His rabid followers were demanding action. One of his S.A. commanders urged him to strike at once. "The day is coming," he warned, "when I won't be able to hold the men back. If nothing happens now, they'll run away from us."

Hitler realized too that if the government gained much more time and began to succeed in restoring tranquility in the country, his own opportunity would be lost. Somehow he would have to put Kahr, Lossow and Seisser in a position where they would have to act with him and from which there would be no turning back. He decided to kidnap the triumvirate and force them to use their power at his bidding.

At this point a brief notice appeared in the press that Kahr would address a meeting of business organizations at Munich's Buergerbraukeller, a large beer hall on the outskirts of the city. The date was November 8. General von Lossow, Colonel von Seisser and other notables would be present. The Buergerbraukeller meeting provided the opportunity to rope in all three members of the triumvirate and at pistol point force them to join the Nazis in carrying out the revolution. Hitler decided to act at once. The storm troopers were hastily alerted for duty at the big beer hall.

About a quarter to nine on the evening of the meeting, after Kahr had been speaking for half an hour to some 3,000 beer-quaffing burghers, S.A. troops surrounded the Buergerbraukeller and Hitler pushed forward into the hall. While some of his men mounted a machine gun in the entrance, Hitler jumped up on a table and to attract attention fired a revolver shot toward the ceiling. Kahr paused in his discourse. The audience turned around to see the cause of the distrubance. Hitler made his way to the platform. A police major tried to stop him, but Hitler pointed the pistol at him and pushed on. Kahr, according to one eyewitness, had now become "pale and confused." He stepped back, and Hitler took his place.

"The national revolution has begun!" Hitler shouted. "This building is occupied by 600 heavily armed men. No one may leave the hall. Unless there is immediate quiet I shall have a machine gun posted in the gallery. The Bavarian and Reich governments have been removed and a provisional national government has been formed. The army and the police are marching on the city under the swastika banner."

This last was pure bluff. But in the confusion no one knew for sure. Hitler's revolver was real. It had gone off. The storm troopers with their rifles and machine guns were real. Hitler now ordered Kahr, Lossow and Seisser to follow him to a private room offstage. Prodded by storm troopers, the three highest officials of Bavaria did Hitler's bidding while the crowd looked on in amazement, and with increasing resentment. They began to grow so sullen that Goering felt it necessary to step to the rostrum and quiet them.

"There is nothing to fear," he cried. "You've no cause to grumble. You've got your beer!" And he informed them that in the next room a new government was being formed. It was, at the point of Adolf Hitler's revolver.

Once Hitler had herded his prisoners into the adjoining room, he told them, "No one leaves this room alive without my permission." He then informed them they would all have key jobs either in the Bavarian government or in the Reich government which he was forming with Ludendorff. With Ludendorff? Earlier in the evening Hitler had dispatched a crony to fetch the renowned general to the beer-house at once. For although the great war hero knew nothing of this Nazi conspiring, he had consistently lent his prestige to Rightist revolutionary movements, and Hitler had been cultivating him as a potential ally for some time.

The three prisoners at first refused even to speak to Hitler. He continued to harangue them. They did not answer.

Below: Munich Beer Hall Putsch, November 9, 1923. Himmler carrying a flag at a Nazi barricade.

Their continued silence unnerved Hitler. Finally he waved his gun at them. "I have four shots in my pistol! Three for my collaborators, if they abandon me. The last bullet for myself!" Pointing the weapon to his forehead, he cried, "If I am not victorious by tomorrow afternoon, I shall be a dead man!"

But he was getting nowhere with his talk. Not one of the three men who held the power of the Bavarian state agreed to join him, even at pistol point. The putsch wasn't going according to plan. Then Hitler acted on a sudden impulse. Without a further word, he dashed back into the hall. Mounting the tribune, he faced the sullen crowd and announced that the members of the triumvirate in the next room had joined him in forming a new national government.

"I propose that the direction of policy be taken over by me," he shouted. "Ludendorff will take over the leadership of the German national army. Tomorrow will find either a national government in Germany or us dead!"

Not for the first time and certainly not for the last, Hitler had told a masterful lie, and it worked. When the gathering heard that Kahr, General von Lossow and Police Chief von Seisser had joined Hitler, its mood abruptly changed. There were loud cheers. The sound of them impressed the three men still locked up in the little side room.

General Ludendorff now appeared as if out of a hat. The war hero was furious with Hitler for pulling such a complete surprise on him. He spoke scarcely a word to the brash young man. But Hitler did not mind, so long as Ludendorff lent his famous name to the undertaking and won over the three Bavarian leaders.

This Ludendorff proceeded to do; it is now a question of a great national cause, he said, and he advised the gentlemen to cooperate. Awed by the attention of the generalissimo, the trio appeared to give in. Ludendorff's timely arrival had saved Hitler. Overjoyed at his lucky break, Hitler led the others back to the platform, where each made a brief speech and swore loyalty to each other and to the new regime. The crowd leaped on chairs and tables in a delirium of enthusiasm, and Hitler beamed with joy. The meeting began to break up. Then news came of a clash between storm troopers and regular troops at the army engineers' barracks. Hitler decided to drive to the scene and settle the matter personally, leaving Ludendorff in charge of the beer hall.

Right: S.A. machine gun post in Munich, 1923.

The Storm Troopers March

This turned out to be a fatal error. Lossow, Kahr and Seisser slipped away. Soon news of the coup went out to Berlin, and orders came back to the army in Bavaria to suppress the putsch. Kahr ordered placards posted throughout Munich proclaiming: "The declarations extorted from myself, General von Lossow and Colonel von Seisser at the point of a revolver are null and void."

The triumph which earlier in the evening had seemed to Hitler so near and so easily won was rapidly fading. Hitler had planned a putsch, not a civil war. Despite his feverish excitement he realized that he lacked the strength to overcome the police and the army. He had wanted to make a revolution *with* the armed forces, not *against* them. But Ludendorff now proposed a plan that might still bring victory and avoid bloodshed.

German soldiers, even German police – who were mostly ex-soldiers – would never dare, he was sure, to fire on the legendary commander who had led them to great victories on both the Eastern and the Western fronts. He and Hitler would march with their followers to the center of the city and take it over. Not only would the police and the army not dare to oppose him; he was certain they would join him and fight under his orders.

Hitler agreed. There seemed no other way out.

Toward 11 o'clock on the following morning Hitler and Ludendorff led a column of some 3,000 storm troopers out of the gardens of the Buergerbraukeller toward the center of Munich. It was not

a very formidable armed force, but Ludendorff, who had commanded millions of Germany's finest troops, apparently thought it sufficient for his purposes.

On a bridge a few hundred yards north of the beer cellar the rebels met their first obstacle, a detachment of armed police barring the route. Goering sprang forward and threatened, if the police fired on his men, to shoot a number of hostages he said he had in the rear of his column. Whether Goering was bluffing or not, the police commander apparently believed he was not, and let the column cross the bridge. Shortly after noon

Above: Tenth anniversary parade of the Munich Beer Hall Putsch. Julius Streicher is in front, with Hitler and members of the "Old Guard" behind.

Below: Truck loads of S.A. men in a Munich square during the Putsch.

the marchers neared their objective, the War Ministry, where Roehm and his storm troopers were surrounded by soldiers of the Reichswehr. Neither side had fired a shot. Roehm and his men were all ex-soldiers, and they had many wartime comrades on the other side of the barbed wire. Neither side had any heart for killing.

To reach the War Ministry and free Roehm, Hitler and Ludendorff now led their column through the narrow Residenzstrasse. At the end of the gully-like street a detachment of police about 100 strong, armed with carbines, blocked the way. They were in a strategic spot, and this time they did not give way.

Which side fired first was never established. At any rate a shot was fired, and in the next instant a volley of shots rang out from both sides, spelling in that instant the doom of Hitler's hopes. Goering went down with a wound in his thigh. Within 60 seconds the firing stopped, but the street was already littered with bodies – 16 Nazis and three police dead or dying, many more wounded and the rest, including Hitler, clutching the pavement to save their lives. There was one exception and, had his example been followed, the day might have had a different ending. Ludendorff did not fling himself to the ground. Standing erect and proud in the best soldierly tradition, he marched calmly on between the muzzles of the police guns. He must have seemed a lonely and bizarre figure. Not one Nazi followed him. Not even Hitler.

In fact, according to the testimony of one of his own Nazi followers, which was supported by several other witnesses, Hitler "was the first to get up and turn back," leaving his dead and wounded comrades lying in the street. He was hustled into a waiting motorcar and spirited off to a country home, where, two days later, he was arrested.

Hitler on Trial

Within a few days all the rebel leaders except Goering and Hess were rounded up and jailed. The Nazi putsch had ended in a fiasco. The party was dissolved. National Socialism, to all appearances, was dead. Its dictatorial leader, who had run away at the first hail of bullets, seemed utterly discredited, his meteoric political career at an end.

But as it turned out, that career was merely interrupted, and not for long. Hitler was shrewd enough to see that his trial, far from finishing him, would provide a new platform from which he could not only discredit the authorities who had arrested him but – and this was more important – make his name known far beyond the confines of Bavaria and indeed of Germany itself.

Hitler was well aware that correspondents of the world press as well as of the leading German newspapers were flocking to Munich to cover the trial, which began on February 26, 1924. By the time it had ended 24 days later Hitler had transformed defeat into triumph, made Kahr, Lossow and Seisser share his guilt in the public mind – to their ruin – impressed the German people with his eloquence and the fervor of his nationalism, and emblazoned his name on the front pages of the world.

Although Ludendorff was easily the most famous of the ten prisoners in the dock, Hitler at once grabbed the limelight. From beginning to end he dominated the courtroom. (The Bavarian minister of justice, an old friend and protector of the Nazi leader, had seen to it that the judiciary would be lenient.) Hitler was allowed to interrupt as often as he pleased, to cross-examine witnesses at will and speak on his own behalf at any time and at any length. His opening statement consumed four hours, but it was only the first of many long harangues.

Though he might be in the dock facing a long prison sentence for high treason against his country, his confidence in himself, in the call to "govern a people," was undiminished. While in prison awaiting trial, he had already analyzed the reasons for the failure of the putsch and had vowed that he would not commit the same mistakes in the future. Recalling his thoughts thirteen years later after he had achieved his goal, he told his old followers, assembled at the Buergerbraukeller to celebrate the anniversary of the putsch, "I can calmly say that it was the rashest decision of my life. When I think back on it today, I grow dizzy . . . If today you saw one of our squads from the year 1923 marching by, you would ask, 'What workhouse have they escaped from?' . . . But fate meant well with us. It did not permit an action to succeed which, if it had succeeded, would in the end have inevitably crashed as a result of the movement's inner immaturity in those days and its deficient organizational and intellectual foundation . . . We recognized that it is not enough to overthrow the old State, but that the new State must previously have been built up and be ready to one's hand . . . In 1933 it was no longer a question of over-throwing a State by an act of violence; meanwhile the new State had been built up and all that remained to do was to destroy the last remnants of the old State – and that took but a few hours."

Before representatives of the world press Hitler proclaimed, "I alone bear the responsibility. But I am not a criminal because of that. There is no such thing as high treason against the traitors of 1918." And in a peroration that held the audience spellbound Hitler spoke the final words of his defense:

The army we have formed is growing from day to day. The hour will come when these rough companies will grow to battalions, the battalions to regiments, the regiments to divisions, that the old cockade will be taken from the mud, that the old flags will wave again, that there will be a reconciliation at the last great divine judgment which we are prepared to face.

Far left: Hitler as a prisoner at Landsberg, 1924.

Bottom, far left: The Munich Beer Hall Putsch conspirators before their trial in 1924. Left to right – Pernet, Weber, Frick, Kriebel, Ludendorff, Hitler, Brueckner, Roehm, Wagner.

Below: The garden at Landsberg where Hitler was imprisoned.

Mein Kampf

Above: Hitler leaving
Landsberg following his
early release in December
1924.

Facing page, top: Nazi
supporters distributing
propaganda in Berlin,
1924.

Facing page, below:
Communist Party
demonstration in Berlin,
1924.

Hitler wanted to call his book *Four and a Half Years of Struggle Against Lies, Stupidity and Cowardice*, but the hardheaded manager of the Nazi publishing business rebelled against such a ponderous, unsaleable title and shortened it to *Mein Kampf (My Struggle)*. During the Nazi regime, few Germans felt secure without a copy in the house.

Not every German who bought *Mein Kampf* necessarily read it. I have heard many a Nazi stalwart complain that it was hard going and not a few admit – in private – that they were never able to get through to the end of its 782 turgid pages. However, it might be argued that had more non-Nazi Germans read it before 1933, and had the foreign statesmen of the world perused it carefully while there was still time, both Germany and the world might have been saved from catastrophe. For whatever other accusations can be made against Hitler, no one can accuse him of not putting down in writing exactly the kind of Germany he intended to make if he came to power. The blueprint of the Third Reich and of the barbaric New Order which Hitler inflicted on conquered Europe, is spelled out in repellent detail.

Hitler's basic ideas were formed in his early 20s and we have his own word for it that he afterward altered nothing in his thinking. He was full of a burning passion for German nationalism, a hatred for democracy, Marxism and the Jews, and a certainty that Providence had chosen the "Aryans," especially the Germans, to be the master race.

In *Mein Kampf* he expanded his views and applied them to the problem of not only restoring Germany to a place in the sun but making a new kind of state, based on race, in which would be established the absolute dictatorship of the Leader – himself. The book contains, first, an outline of the future German state; and, second, a point of view, or, to use Hitler's favorite word, a *Weltanschauung*. That this view of life would strike a normal mind of the 20th century as a grotesque hodgepodge concocted by a half-baked, uneducated neurotic goes without saying. Yet it was embraced fanatically by millions of Germans.

Considerable editorial advice and pruning by three helpers could not prevent Hitler from meandering from one subject to another in *Mein Kampf*. He insisted on airing his thoughts at random on almost every conceivable subject, including culture, education, the theater, movies, comics, art, literature, history, sex, marriage, prostitution and syphilis. The problem of syphilis must be attacked, he states, by facilitating earlier marriages, and he gives a foretaste of the eugenics of the Third Reich by insisting that "marriage cannot be an end in itself, but must serve a higher goal: the preservation of the race. This alone is its task."

Here in *Mein Kampf* we come to the kernel of the Nazi idea of race superiority, of the conception of the master race, on which the Third Reich and Hitler's New Order in Europe were based. Hitler saw the world as a jungle where the fittest sur-

He turned his burning eyes directly on the judges.

For it is not you, gentlemen, who pass judgment on us. That judgment is spoken by the eternal court of history. You may pronounce us guilty a thousand times over, but the goddess of the eternal court of history will smile and tear to tatters the brief of the state prosecutor and the sentence of this court. For she acquits us.

In the end, Ludendorff was acquitted; Hitler and the other accused were found guilty. Hitler was sentenced to five years' imprisonment but was assured by the presiding judge that he would be eligible for parole after he had served six months. A little less than nine months later, Hitler was released from prison, free to resume his fight to overthrow the democratic state.

The putsch, though a fiasco, made Hitler a national figure and, in the eyes of many, a patriot and a hero.

That summer of 1924, serving his term in the old fortress-prison at Landsberg, Adolf Hitler, who was treated as an honored guest, with a room of his own and a splendid view, cleared out the visitors who flocked to pay him homage and began to dictate, to Rudolf Hess, chapter after chapter of the book that was to become the bible of Nazism.

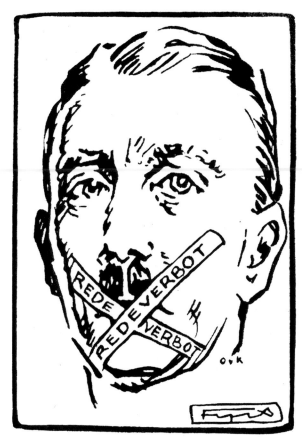

before Christmas 1924, he found a situation that would have led almost any other man to retire from public life. The Nazi Party and its press were banned; the former leaders were feuding and falling away. He himself was forbidden to speak in public. Many of his old comrades agreed that Hitler was finished, that he would now fade into oblivion as had so many other provincial politicians who had enjoyed brief notoriety during the years when the Republic was tottering.

But the Republic had weathered the storms – and was beginning to thrive. A financial wizard by the name of Hjalmar Schacht had stabilized the currency, and the ruinous inflation was over. The economy was rapidly recovering. For the first time since the defeat, the German people were beginning to have a normal life. Two weeks before Hitler was released, the Social Democrats had increased their vote by 30 percent in an election in which they championed the Republic. The Nazis had seen their vote fall from nearly two million in May 1924 to less than a million in December. Nazism appeared to be a dying cause. It had mushroomed on the country's misfortunes; now it was withering away. Or so most Germans and foreign observers believed. But not Adolf Hitler. He was not easily discouraged.

Behind the prison gates he had had time to ponder his past and its triumphs and mistakes. And there was born in him anew a burning sense of mission – for himself and for Germany – from which all doubts were excluded. In this exalted spirit he finished dictating volume one of *Mein Kampf* and went on immediately to volume two of his blueprint for the future. The blueprint may have seemed preposterous to most people, even in Germany. But it held forth a vision. It pointed the way toward a glorious German destiny.

vived and the strongest ruled – a "world where one creature feeds on the other and where the death of the weaker implies the life of the stronger." Such ideas were set down in all their appalling crudeness as he sat in Landsberg prison dictating and dreaming of the Third Reich he would build on these shoddy foundations.

When Hitler emerged from Landsberg five days

Rebuilding the Party

The prosperous years from 1925 until the coming of the Depression in 1929 were lean times for Hitler and the Nazi movement.

One scarcely heard of Hitler or the party except as butts of jokes – usually in connection with the Beer-Hall Putsch, as it came to be known. In the elections of May 20, 1928, the Nazi Party polled only 810,000 votes out of a total of 31 million cast, and the total membership of the National Socialist Party that year was only 108,000. The prime minister of Bavaria had lifted the ban on the Nazi Party and its newspaper. "The wild beast is checked," he told his minister of justice. "We can afford to loosen the chain." The Bavarian premier was one of the first, but by no means the last, of Germany's politicians to fall into this fatal error of judgment. For Hitler never lost hope. He was shrewd enough to realize that prosperous times were not propitious for him. But he was confident they would not last.

Hitler had now made up his mind to re-establish the Nazi Party as a political organization that would seek power exclusively through constitutional means. He explained the new tactics to a henchman. "Instead of working to achieve power by armed coup, we shall have to hold our noses and enter the Reichstag against the opposition deputies. If outvoting them takes longer than outshooting them, at least the result will be guaranteed by their own constitution. Sooner or later we shall have a majority, and after that – Germany."

On his release from Landsberg, he assured the Bavarian premier that the Nazi Party would act within the framework of the constitution. But in a speech on February 27, 1925, he allowed himself to be carried away by the enthusiasm of the crowd. His threats against the state were scarcely veiled, and the government again forbade him to speak in public – a ban that was to last two years. This was a heavy blow; a silenced Hitler was a defeated Hitler – so most people thought.

But again they were wrong. They forgot that Hitler was an organizer as well as a spellbinder. Now he set to work with furious intent to rebuild the National Socialist German Workers' Party on an unprecedentedly ambitious scale. Often working with the most shady lieutenants, he always remembered that the first job was to attract dues-paying members. By the end of 1925 they numbered just 27,000, but each year some progress was made: 49,000 members in 1926; 72,000 in 1927; 108,000 in 1928; 178,000 in 1929.

These politically lean years were, as Hitler later said, the best years of his personal life. Intent on plotting the future of the Nazi Party and of himself, he spent most of his time at a haven for rest and relaxation in the Bavarian Alps, above the village of Berchtesgaden, "I spent there the finest hours of my life," he said. "All my great projects were conceived and ripened there."

"At this period," he reminisced later, "I knew a lot of women. Several of them became attached to me. Why, then, didn't I marry? To leave a wife behind me? At the slightest imprudence, I ran the risk of going back to prison. So there could be no question of marriage for me." Contrary to the general opinion, Hitler liked the company of women, especially if they were beautiful. He returned to the subject time and again in his table talk at Supreme Headquarters during the war. "What lovely women there are in the world!" he exclaimed to his cronies one night, and he gave several examples in his personal experience. But so far as is known, it was with his niece that Adolf Hitler had the only deep love affair of his life.

Above: Hitler posing as the virile leader.

Left: First meeting of the Nazi Party in February 1925 following Hitler's release from prison. Left to right, Rosenberg, Buch, Schwarz, Hitler, Gregor Strasser and Himmler.

46

Hitler's Great Love

In the summer of 1928 Hitler rented a villa above Berchtesgaden and induced his widowed half-sister, Angela Raubal, to come keep house for him. Frau Raubal brought along her two daughters, Geli and Friedl. Geli was 20, with flowing blond hair, handsome features, a pleasant voice and a sunny disposition which made her attractive to men.

Hitler soon fell in love with her. He took her everywhere, to meetings and conferences, on long walks in the mountains and to the cafés and theaters in Munich. When in 1929 he rented a luxurious nine-room apartment in Munich, Geli was given her own room in it. Gossip about the party leader and his beautiful blond niece was inevitable, and some of the more prim – or envious – leaders suggested that Hitler cease showing off his sweetheart in public, or that he marry her. Hitler was furious at such talk.

Yet it is probable that Hitler intended to marry his niece. Early party comrades who were close to him at that time subsequently told me that a marriage seemed inevitable. That Hitler was deeply in love with her they had no doubt. Her own feelings are a matter of conjecture. She was clearly flattered by the attentions of a man now becoming famous, and indeed enjoyed them, but whether she reciprocated her uncle's love is not known.

In the end she certainly did not. Some deep rift, whose origins have never been fully ascertained, grew between them. Each was apparently jealous of the other. She resented his attentions to other women; he suspected that she had had a clandestine affair with his ex-bodyguard. She objected to her uncle's tyranny over her. He did not want her to be seen in the company of any man but himself. He forbade her to go to Vienna to continue her singing lessons; he wanted her for himself alone.

There are dark hints, too, that she was repelled by the masochistic inclinations of her lover, that this brutal tyrant in politics yearned to be enslaved by the woman he loved – a not uncommon urge in such men, according to sexologists.

Whatever it was that darkened their love, the quarrels became more violent, and at the end of the summer of 1931 Geli announced that she was returning to Vienna to resume her voice studies.

Below: Nazi Party rally, Nuremberg, 1927. Left to right, Himmler, Hess, Gregor Strasser, Hitler, Pfeffer von Salomon.

Left: Hitler travelling by plane electioneering, 1930. Left to right, Schreck, Schaub, Hanfstaengl, Dietrich, Brueckner.

Below: Hitler's niece, Geli Raubal.

Hitler forbade her to go. There was a scene between the two, witnessed by neighbors, when Hitler left his apartment on September 17, 1931. The young girl was heard to cry to her uncle from the window as he was getting into his car, "Then you won't let me go to Vienna?" and he was heard to respond, "No!"

The next morning Geli Raubal was found shot dead in her room. The state's attorney, after a thorough investigation, found that it was a suicide. Yet for years afterward in Munich there was murky gossip that Geli Raubal had been murdered – by Hitler in a rage, by Heinrich Himmler to eliminate a situation that had become embarrassing to the party. No credible evidence ever turned up to substantiate such rumors.

Hitler himself was struck down by grief. One of his companions later recounted that he had had to remain for the following two days and nights at Hitler's side to prevent him from taking his own life. For months he was inconsolable. To some of his closest henchmen he declared forever afterward that Geli Raubal was the only woman he ever loved, and he always spoke of her with the deepest reverence – and often in tears. Servants said that her room in the villa on the Obersalzberg, even after it was rebuilt and enlarged in the days of Hitler's chancellorship, remained as she had left it.

For a brutal, cynical man who always seemed to be incapable of love of any other human being, this passion of Hitler's for the youthful Geli Raubal stands out as one of the mysteries of his strange life. It cannot be rationally explained; but thereafter, it is almost certain, Adolf Hitler never seriously contemplated marriage until the day before he took his own life 14 years later in the last days of the Third Reich.

Now he could devote his fierce energies and all his talents to the task of fulfilling his destiny. The time for his final drive for power, for the dictatorship of a great nation, had arrived.

The Nazi Tide Gathers Force

The depression that spread over the world like a great conflagration toward the end of 1929 gave Adolf Hitler his opportunity, and he made the most of it. Like most great revolutionaries he could thrive only in evil times – at first when the masses were unemployed, hungry and desperate, and later when they were intoxicated by war.

Yet in one respect Hitler was unique among history's revolutionaries: He intended to make his revolution *after* achieving political power – in short, by constitutional means. To get votes Hitler had only to take advantage of the times, which once more, as the '30s began, saw the German people plunged into despair.

On October 24, 1929, the stock market in Wall Street crashed. The results in Germany were soon felt, disastrously. The cornerstone of German prosperity had been loans from abroad, principally from the United States, and world trade. When the flow of loans dried up and payment on old ones came due, the German financial structure was unable to stand the strain.

German industry could not keep its plants going, and production fell by almost half from 1929 to 1932. Millions were thrown out of work, small businesses went under, banks collapsed. Hitler had predicted the catastrophe, but no more than any other politician did he understand what had brought it about; perhaps he had less understanding than most, since he was both ignorant of and uninterested in economics. But he well understood the opportunities the Depression gave him.

The misery of the German people, their lives still scarred by the disastrous experience of the collapse of the mark less than ten years before, did not arouse his compassion. The suffering of his fellow Germans was not something to sympathize with, but rather something to transform cold-bloodedly into political support for his own ambitions. This he proceeded to do in the late summer of 1930.

At a moment when the economic crisis made strong government imperative, new elections were called for on September 14, 1930. Hitler realized that his opportunity had come sooner than he expected. The hard-pressed people were demanding a way out of their sorry predicament. The millions of unemployed wanted jobs. The shopkeepers wanted help. Some four million youths who had come of voting age since the last election wanted some prospect of a future.

To the millions of discontented people Hitler in a whirlwind campaign offered what seemed to them some measure of hope. He would make Germany strong again, refuse to pay reparations, repudiate the Versailles Treaty, stamp out corruption, and see to it that every German had a job and bread. To hopeless, hungry men seeking not only relief but new faith and new gods, the appeal was not without effect.

Though his hopes were high, Hitler was surprised by the election returns. Two years before, his party had polled 810,000 votes. This time he had counted on quadrupling the Nazi vote, but now the vote of the N.S.D.A.P. rose to 6,409,600, propelling it from the ninth and smallest party in parliament to the second largest.

To consolidate his new strong position, Hitler turned his attention toward winning over two powerful groups: the army and the big industrialists and financiers.

"I have always held the view," he declared, "that any attempt to replace the army was madness. We will see to it, when we come to power, that out of the present Reichswehr a great army of the German people shall arise."

As Hitler's tactics took effect, some of the

Right: Nazi Poster "The New Germany," 1933, linking the soldier of the First World War and the S.A. man.

Far right: Hitler reviewing an S.A. parade.

Left: Hitler and a group of Nazi supporters in Munich, 1930.

Right: Working class tenements in Berlin, 1932, divided between Nazi and Communist supporters.

Vem Neuen Deutschland

Erst Essen — dann Miete.

generals began to ponder whether National Socialism might not be just what was needed to unify the people, restore the old Germany, make the army great once more and enable the nation to shake off the humiliating Treaty of Versailles. Until this time, the senior officers had believed Hitler was trying to undermine the army; now they were reassured. The political blindness of the German army officers, which was to prove so fatal to them in the end, had begun to show.

The political ineptitude of the magnates of industry and finance was no less than that of the generals. It led them to the mistaken belief that if they coughed up large enough sums for Hitler he would be beholden to them and, if he ever came to power, do their bidding. That the Austrian upstart, as many of them regarded him in the '20s, might well take over control of Germany began to dawn on the business leaders after the sensational Nazi gains in the September elections of 1930.

"In the summer of 1931,"Otto Dietrich, Hitler's press chief first for the party and later for the Reich, relates, "the Fuehrer suddenly decided to concentrate systematically on cultivating the influential industrial magnates."

What magnates were they?

Their identity was a secret which was kept from all but the inner circle around the Leader. The party had to play both sides of the tracks. It had . . . to beguile the masses with the cry that the National Socialists were truly "socialists" and against the money barons. On the other hand, money to keep the party going had to be wheedled out of those who had an ample supply of it. Throughout the latter half of 1931, says Dietrich, Hitler "traversed Germany from end to end, holding private interviews with prominent [business] personalities." So hush-hush were some of these meetings that they had to be held "in some lonely

Above: Cartoon of 1932 showing Hitler as the pawn of big business. In fact the reverse proved true.

a wretched memory by the time he arrived for trial at Nuremberg. It included Georg von Schnitzler, a leading director of I.G. Farben, the giant chemical cartel; August Rosterg and August Diehn of the potash industry. (Funk speaks of his industry's "positive attitude toward the Fuehrer"); Wilhelm Cuno of the Hamburg-Amerika line; the brown-coal industry of central Germany; the Conti rubber interests; Otto Wolf, the powerful Cologne industrialist; Baron Kurt von Schroeder, the Cologne banker, who was to play a pivotal role in the final maneuver which hoisted Hitler to power; several leading banks, among which were the Deutsche Bank, the Commerz und Privat Bank, the Dresdener Bank, the Deutsche Kredit Gessellschaft; and Germany's largest insurance concern, the Allianz.

Wilhelm Keppler, one of Hitler's economic advisers, brought in a number of South German industrialists and also formed a peculiar society of businessmen devoted to the S.S. chief, Himmler, called the circle of Friends of the Economy (Freundeskreis der Wirtschaft), which later became known as the Circle of Friends of the Reichsfuehrer S.S., who was Himmler, and which raised millions of marks for this particular gangster to pursue his "researches" into Aryan origins. From the very beginning of his political career Hitler had been helped financially – and socially – by Hugo Bruckman, the wealthy Munich publisher, and by Carl Bechstein, the piano manufacturer, both of whose wives developed a touching fondness for the rising young Nazi leader. It was in the Bechstein mansion in Berlin that Hitler first met many of the business and army leaders and it was there that some of the decisive secret meetings took place which helped him finally to win the chancellorship.

Not all German businessmen jumped on the Hitler bandwagon after the Nazi election showing in 1930. Funk mentions that the big electric corporations Siemens and A.E.G. stood aloof, as did the king of the munition makers, Krupp von Bohlen und Halbach. Fritz Thyssen in his confessions declares that Krupp was a "violent opponent" of Hitler and that as late as the day before Hindenburg appointed him Chancellor Krupp urgently warned the old Field Marshal against such a folly. However, Krupp soon saw the light and quickly became, in the words of the repentant Thyssen, "a super Nazi."

In his final drive for power Hitler had considerable financial backing from a fairly large chunk of the German business world. What they did not seem to realise – and it was something which Hitler had never made any secret of – was that if the party ever took over Germany it would stamp out every German's personal freedom, including that of the bankers and their business friends.

Hitler had now gathered around him in the party the little band of fanatic, ruthless men who would help him in his final drive to power and who, with one exception, would be at his side to help him sustain that power during the years of the Third Reich, though another of them, who was closest of all to him and perhaps the ablest and most brutish of the lot, would not survive, even with his life, the second year of Nazi government. There were five who stood above the other followers at this time. These were Gregor Strasser, Roehm, Goering, Goebbels and Wilhelm Frick.

Goering had returned to Germany at the end of

forest glade. Privacy," explains Dietrich, "was absolutely imperative; the press must have no chance of doing mischief. Success was the consequence." . . .

We know from the interrogations of the industrialist Walther Funk in the Nuremberg jail after the war who some, at least, of the "influential industrial magnates" whom Hitler sought out were. Emil Kirdorf, the union-hating coal baron who presided over a political slush fund known as the "Ruhr Treasury" which was raised by the West German mining interests, had been seduced by Hitler at the party congress in 1929. Fritz Thyssen, the head of the steel trust, who lived to regret his folly and to write about it in a book called *I Paid Hitler*, was an even earlier contributor. He had met the Nazi leader in Munich in 1923, been carried away by his eloquence and forthwith made, through Ludendorff, an initial gift of 100,000 gold marks ($25,000) to the then obscure Nazi Party. Joining Thyssen was Albert Voegler, also a power in the United Steel Works. In fact the coal and steel interests were the principal sources of the funds that came from the industrialists to help Hitler over his last hurdles to power in the period between 1930 and 1933.

But Funk named other industries and concerns whose directors did not want to be left out in the cold should Hitler make it in the end. The list is a long one, though far from complete, for Funk had

1927, following a general political amnesty which the Communists had helped the parties of the Right put through the Reichstag. In Sweden, where he had spent most of his exile since the 1923 putsch, he had been cured of addiction to narcotics at the Langbro Asylum and when he was well had earned his living with a Swedish aircraft company. The dashing, handsome World War ace had now grown corpulent but had lost none of his energy or his zest for life. He settled down in a small but luxurious bachelor's flat in the Badischestrasse in Berlin (his epileptic wife, whom he deeply loved, had contracted tuberculosis and remained, an invalid, in Sweden), earned his living as adviser to aircraft companies and the German airline, Lufthansa, and cultivated his social contacts. These contacts were considerable and ranged from the former Crown Prince and Prince Philip of Hesse, who had married Princess Mafalda, the daughter of the King of Italy, to Fritz Thyssen and other barons of the business world, as well as to a number of prominent officers of the Army.

These were the very connections which Hitler lacked but needed, and Goering soon became active in introducng the Nazi leader to his friends and in counteracting in upper-class circles the bad odor which some of the Brownshirt ruffians exuded. In 1928 Hitler chose Goering as one of the twelve Nazi deputies to represent the party in the Reichstag, of which he became President when the Nazis became the largest party in 1932. It was in the official residence of the Reichstag President that many of the meetings were held and intrigues hatched which led to the party's ultimate triumph, and it was here – to jump ahead in time a little – that a plan was connived that helped Hitler to stay in power after he became Chancellor: to set the Reichstag on fire.

Ernst Roehm had broken with Hitler in 1925 and

Above: Nazi Party rally, 1929. Hitler holds the Nazi "Blood Banner."

Left: Hitler with industrialists in Dusseldorf, 1932. Left, Dr. Voegler, right Dr. Fritz Thyssen and Dr. Borbet.

Right: A variety of election posters on display in Berlin, July 1932, including examples for the Nazi Party, the Center Party, the Social Democrats and the Communists.

not long afterward gone off to join the Bolivian Army as a lieutenant colonel. Toward the end of 1930 Hitler appealed to him to return and take over again the leadership of the S.A., which was getting out of hand. Its members, even its leaders, apparently believed in a coming Nazi revolution by violence, and with increasing frequency they were taking to the streets to molest and murder their political opponents. No election, national, provincial or municipal, took place without savage battles in the gutters.

Passing notice must here be taken of one of these encounters, for it provided National Socialism with its greatest martyr. One of the neighborhood leaders of the S.A. in Berlin was Horst Wessel, son of a Protestant chaplain, who had for-

Below: S.A. march past Hitler in Brunswick, 1931.

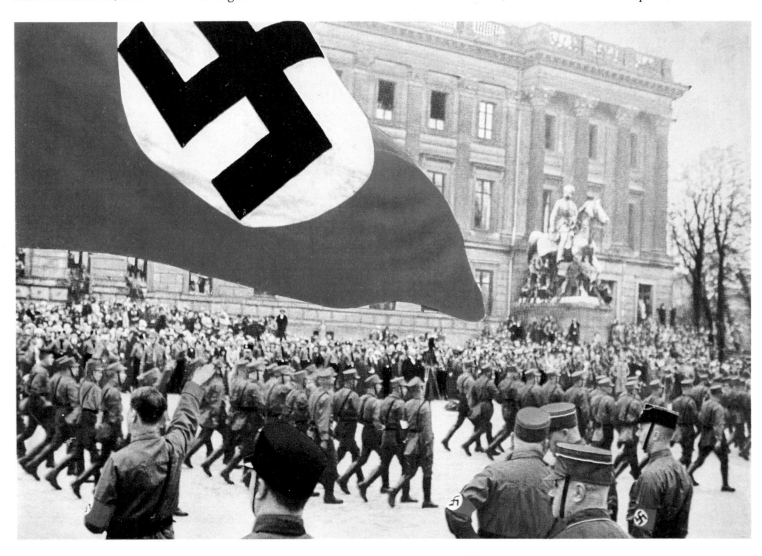

saken his family and his studies and gone to live in a slum with a former prostitute and devote his life to fighting for Nazism. Many anti-Nazis always held that the youth earned his living as a pimp, though this charge may have been exaggerated. Certainly he consorted with pimps and prostitutes. He was murdered by some Communists in February 1930 and would have passed into oblivion along with hundreds of other victims of both sides in the street wars had it not been for the fact that he left behind a song whose words and tune he had composed. This was the Horst Wessel song, which soon became the official song of the Nazi party and later the second official anthem – after "Deutschland ueber Alles" – of the Third Reich. Horst Wessel himself, thanks to Dr. Goebbels' skillful propaganda, became one of the great hero legends of the movement, hailed as a pure idealist who had given his life for the cause.

At the time Roehm took over the S.A., Gregor Strasser was undoubtedly the Number Two man in the Nazi Party. A forceful speaker and a brilliant organizer, he was the head of the party's most important office, the Political Organization, a post which gave him great influence among the provincial and local leaders whose labors he supervised. With his genial Bavarian nature, he was the most popular leader in the party next to Hitler, and, unlike the Fuehrer he enjoyed the personal trust and even liking of most of his political opponents. There were a good many at that time, within and without the party, who believed that Strasser might well supplant the moody, incalculable Austrian leader. This view was especially strong in the Reichswehr and in the President's Palace.

Otto, Gregor Strasser's brother, had fallen by the wayside. Unfortunately for him, he had taken seriously not only the word "socialist" but the word "workers" in the party's official name of National Socialist German Workers' Party. He had supported certain strikes of the socialist trade unions and demanded that the party come out for

Above: Hitler greeted by enthusiastic women supporters.

nationalization of industry. This of course was heresy to Hitler, who accused Otto Strasser of professing the cardinal sins of "democracy and liberalism." On May 21 and 22, 1930, the Fuehrer had a showdown with his rebellious subordinate and demanded complete submission. When Otto refused, he was booted out of the party. He tried to form a truly national "socialist" movement, the Union of Revolutionary National Socialists, which became known only as the Black Front, but in the September elections it failed to win any sizable number of Nazi votes away from Hitler.

Goebbels, the fourth member of the Big Five around Hitler, had remained an enemy and rival of Gregor Strasser ever since a falling out in 1926. Two years after that he had succeeded Strasser as propaganda chief of the party when the latter was moved up to head the Political Organization. He had remained as Gauleiter of Berlin, and his achievements in reorganizing the party there as well as his talents for propaganda had favorably

Left: The massed ranks at a Nazi Party rally listen attentively to the platform orators.

Right: Horst Wessel's grave in Berlin with a respectful Nazi guard in 1934.

Below: S.A. parade outside the Communist Party's headquarters in Berlin, January 1933.

impressed the Fuehrer. His glib but biting tongue and his nimble mind had not endeared him to Hitler's other chief lieutenants, who distrusted him. But the Nazi leader was quite content to see strife among his principal subordinates, if only because it was a safeguard against their conspiring together against his leadership. He never fully trusted Strasser, but in the loyalty of Goebbels he had complete confidence; moreover, the lame little fanatic was bubbling with ideas which were useful to him. Finally, Goebbels' talents as a rowdy journalist – he now had a Berlin newspaper of his own, *Der Angriff*, to spout off in – and as a rabble-rousing orator were invaluable.

Wilhelm Frick, the fifth and last member of the group, was the only colorless personality in it. He was a typical German civil servant. As a young police officer in Munich before 1923 he had served as one of Hitler's spies at police headquarters, and the Fuehrer always felt grateful to him. Often he had taken on the thankless tasks. On Hitler's instigation he had become the first Nazi to hold provincial office – in Thuringia – and later he became the leader of the Nazi Party in the Reichstag. He was doggedly loyal, efficient and, because of the façade of his retiring nature and suave manners, useful in contacts with wavering officials in the republican government.

Some of the lesser men in the party in the early Thirties would subsequently gain notoriety and frightening personal power in the Third Reich. Heinrich Himmler, the poultry farmer, who, with his pince-nez, might be mistaken for a mild, mediocre schoolmaster – he had a degree in agronomy from the Munich Technische Hochschule – was gradually building up Hitler's praetorian guard, the black-coated S.S. But he worked under the shadow of Roehm, who was commander of both the S.A. and the S.S., and he was little known, even in party circles, outside his native Bavaria. There was Dr. Robert Ley, a chemist by profession and a habitual drunkard, who was the Gauleiter of Cologne, and Hans Frank, the bright young lawyer and leader of the party's legal division. There was Walther Darré, born in 1895 in the Argentine, an able agronomist who was won over to National Socialism by Hess and whose book *The Peasantry as the Life Source of the Nordic Race* brought him to Hitler's attention and to a job as head of the Agricultural Department of the party. Rudolf Hess himself, personally unambitious and doggedly loyal to the Leader, held only the title of private secretary to the Fuehrer. The second private secretary was one Martin Bormann, a molelike man who preferred to burrow in the dark recesses of party life to further his intrigues and who once had served a year in prison for complicity in a political murder. The Reich Youth Leader was Baldur von Schirach, a romantically minded young man and an energetic organizer, whose mother was an American and whose great-grandfather, a Union officer, had lost a leg at Bull Run; he told his jailers at Nuremberg that he had become an anti-Semite at the age of seventeen after reading a book called *Eternal Jew*, by Henry Ford.

There was also Alfred Rosenberg, the ponderous, dim-witted Baltic pseudo philospher who, as we have seen, was one of Hitler's earliest mentors and who since the putsch of 1923 had poured out a stream of books and pamphlets of the most muddled content and style, culminating in a 700-page work entitled *The Myth of the Twentieth Century*. This was a ludicrous concoction of his half-baked ideas on Nordic supremacy palmed off as the fruit of what passed for erudition in Nazi circles – a book which Hitler often said jokingly he had tried unsuccessfully to read and which prompted Schirach, who fancied himself as a writer, to remark once that Rosenberg was "a man who sold more copies of a book no one ever read than any other author," for in the first ten years after its publication in 1930 it sold more than half a million copies. From the beginning to the end Hitler always had a warm spot in his heart for this dull, stupid, fumbling man, rewarding him with various party jobs such as editor of the *Voelkischer Beobachter* and other Nazi publications and naming him as one of the party's deputies in the Reichstag in 1930, where he represented the movement in the Foreign Affairs Committee.

Such was the conglomeration of men around the leader of the National Socialists. In a normal society they surely would have stood out as a grotesque assortment of misfits. But in the last chaotic days of the Republic they began to appear to millions of befuddled Germans as saviors. And they had two advantages over their opponents: They were led by a man who knew exactly what he wanted and they were ruthless enough, and opportunist enough, to go to any lengths to help him get it.

As the year of 1931 ran its uneasy course, with five million wage earners out of work, the middle classes facing ruin, the farmers unable to meet their mortgage payments, the Parliament paralyzed, the government floundering, the eighty-four-year-old President fast sinking into the befuddlement of senility, a confidence mounted in the breasts of the Nazi chieftains that they would not have long to wait. As Gregor Strasser publicly boasted, "All that serves to precipitate the catastrophe . . . is good, very good for us and our German revolution."

Below: Hitler at a meeting of Nazi members of the Reichstag in 1932.

Government by Decree

And catastrophe for the Republic was imminent. The weaknesses of the Weimar regime were obvious. There were too many political parties, and they were too much at cross-purposes. Too absorbed in looking after the special interests they represented, they were unable to form an enduring majority in the Reichstag that could back a stable government. Parliamentary government had become a matter of what the Germans called *Kuhhandel* – cattle trading – with the parties bargaining for special advantages for the groups which elected them, and the national interests be damned. It had become impossible to achieve a majority in the Reichstag for any policy – of the Left, the Center or the Right. Merely to carry on the business of government it was necessary to resort to Article 48 of the constitution, which in an emergency permitted the chancellor, if the president approved, to govern by decree.

Political power in Germany no longer resided, as it had since the birth of the Republic, in the people and in the body which expressed the people's will, the Reichstag. It was now concentrated in the hands of a senile president and in those of a few shallow, ambitious men around him who shaped his weary, wandering mind. Hitler saw this clearly, and it suited his purposes. It seemed most unlikely that he would ever win a clear majority in parliament. But the chaotic political situation offered him another opportunity of coming to power. Not at the moment, but soon.

Cabinet after cabinet toppled as the result of the paralysis, requiring an almost nonstop series of elections. Those of July 31, 1932, were the third held in Germany within five months. But far from being weary from so much electioneering, the Nazis threw themselves into the campaign with more fanaticism and force than ever before. From the size of the crowds that turned out to see Hitler it was evident that the Nazis were gaining ground, and the polling on July 31 brought a resounding victory for them. With 13,745,000 votes, the Nazis won 230 seats in the Reichstag, making them easily the largest party in parliament. In the four years since the 1928 elections, the Nazis had won some 13 million new votes. Yet the majority that would sweep the party into power still eluded Hitler. He had won only 37 percent of the total vote. The majority of Germans still opposed him.

The result was another impasse. As the strife-ridden year of 1932 approached its end, Berlin was full of cabals, and of cabals within cabals. There was one at the president's palace, where Hindenburg's son, Oskar, and his state secretary, Otto von Meissner, held sway behind the throne. There was one at the Kaiserhof hotel, where Hitler and the men around him were plotting not only for power but against one another.

Below: "We are for Adolf Hitler." Nazi election poster claiming workers' support.

Below right: General Kurt von Schleicher, last Chancellor of Germany before the Nazi takeover. Schleicher was later murdered during the "Night of the Long Knives" in 1934.

Left: Hitler addressing a rally in the Lustgarten, Berlin, 1933.

Below: "The Brown House," the Nazi Party headquarters in Munich.

Soon the webs of intrigue became so enmeshed that by New Year's 1933, none of the cabalists was sure who was double-crossing whom. Kurt v. Schleicher, the last chancellor of the Republic, once remarked to the French ambassador, "I stayed in power only 57 days, and on each and every one of them I was betrayed 57 times. Don't ever speak to me of 'German loyalty'!"

On January 15, the Nazis scored a local success in the elections of little Lippe. It was not much of an achievement. The total vote was only 90,000, of which the Nazis obtained 38,000, or 39 percent, an increase of some 17 percent over their previous poll. But, led by Goebbels, the Nazi leaders beat the drums over their "victory," and strangely enough it seems to have impressed a number of conservatives, including the men behind Hindenburg, principally State Secretary Meissner and the president's son, Oskar.

Hitler Becomes Chancellor

On the evening of January 22, these two gentlemen stole out of the presidential quarters, grabbed a taxi to avoid being noticed and drove to the suburban home of a hitherto unknown Nazi by the name of Joachim von Ribbentrop. According to Meissner, Oskar von Hindenburg had been opposed to any truck with the Nazis up to this fateful evening. Hitler now insisted on having a private talk with him. Hindenburg assented and withdrew with Hitler to another room, where they were closeted together for an hour.

What Hitler said to the president's son, who was not noted for a brilliant mind or a strong character, has never been revealed. It was generally believed in Nazi circles that Hitler made both offers and threats, the latter consisting of hints to disclose to the public tax evasion on the Hindenburg estate. One can only judge the offers by the fact that a few months later 5000 tax-free acres were added to the Hindenburg family property and that in August 1934 Oskar was jumped from colonel to major general in the army.

There is no doubt that Hitler made a strong

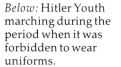

Below: Hitler Youth marching during the period when it was forbidden to wear uniforms.

impression on the president's son. "In the taxi on the way back," Meissner later recounted, "the only remark he made was that it could not be helped – the Nazis had to be taken into the government. My impression was that Hitler had succeeded in getting him under his spell."

It only remained for Hitler to cast his spell over the father. This admittedly was more difficult for, whatever the old field marshal's deficiencies of mind, age had not softened his granite character. More difficult, but not impossible. For here Hitler had an invaluable (if fairly untrustworthy) ally in the person of Franz von Papen, who had served briefly as chancellor during the summer of 1932.

Everyone laughed at his appointment, wrote the French ambassador in Berlin, because Papen "enjoyed the peculiarity of being taken seriously by neither his friends nor his enemies." He was reputed to be superficial, ambitious, vain, crafty, and an intriguer. Nevertheless, he had the confidence of the president, and he now set to work to employ his influence on Hitler's behalf. Finally, at noon on January 28, Papen was entrusted by the president to explore the possibilities of forming a government under Hitler "within the terms of the constitution."

On the wintry morning of January 30, 1933, the tragedy of the Weimar Republic, of the Germans' bungling attempt for 14 frustrating years to make democracy work, came to an end.

Papen later described it: "At about half-past ten the members of the proposed cabinet met in my

Second left: Reich President Field Marshal von Hindenburg and his son Oskar.

Left: Hitler greeting an enthusiastic crowd from the balcony of the Chancellery, January 30, 1933.

Bottom: "Not the most comfortable seat." A contemporary US cartoon underestimates the security of Hitler's position as Chancellor.

house and walked across the garden to the presidential palace, where we waited. At last we were shown to the president, and I made the necessary formal introductions. Hindenburg made a short speech about the necessity of full co-operation in the interests of the nation, and we were then sworn in. The Hitler cabinet had been formed."

In this way, by way of the back door, by means of a shabby political deal with the old-school reactionaries he privately detested, the former tramp from Vienna, the derelict of the First World War, the violent revolutionary, became chancellor of the great nation. To be sure, the National Socialists held only three of the eleven posts in the cabinet and except for the chancellorship these were not key positions. Papen was confident that with the help of the staunch old president, who was his friend and protector, and with the support of his conservative colleagues, he would dominate it. But this frivolous, conniving politician did not know Hitler.

In the former Austrian vagabond the conservative classes thought they had found a man who, while remaining their prisoner, would help them attain their goals. The destruction of the republic was only the first step. What the conservatives then wanted was an authoritarian Germany which at home would put an end to "democratic nonsense" and in foreign affairs tear off the shackles of Versailles, rebuild a great army and with its military power restore the country to its place in the sun.

These were Hitler's aims, too. And though he brought what the conservatives had lacked, a mass following, the Right was sure that he would remain in its pocket. Such a commanding position would allow the conservatives, they thought, to achieve their ends without the barbarism of unadulterated Nazism. Admittedly they were decent, God-fearing men according to their lights.

The Germans imposed the Nazi tyranny on themselves. Many of them, perhaps a majority, did not quite realize it at that noon hour on January 30, 1933, when President von Hindenburg, acting in a perfectly constitutional manner, entrusted the chancellorship to Adolf Hitler.

But they were soon to learn.

2. Hitler on the March
The Years of Triumph

The Years of Triumph

When Hitler became chancellor of the Third Reich in 1933, Germany's position could hardly have been worse. Virtually disarmed and nearly bankrupt, she was plagued by unemployment and torn by political dissension. She was by far the weakest big power in the West, and her neighbors, particularly Poland, France and the Soviet Union, were hostile, suspicious and well armed.

Yet in little more than seven years this vagabond from the gutters of Vienna transformed Germany into the mightiest state in Europe and, by a storm of conquests unprecedented in swiftness and scope, made her absolute master of half the Continent.

How did he do it?

Acting with the speed, brutality, and consummate trickery which were always the hallmark of his tactics, he first consolidated his authority inside Germany.

For the first time – in the last relatively free election Germany was to have, that scheduled for March 5, 1933 – the Nazi Party now could employ all the vast resources of the government to win votes. Goebbels was jubilant. "Now it will be easy," he wrote in his diary on February 3, "to carry on the fight, for we can call on all the resources of the State. Radio and press are at our disposal. We shall stage a masterpiece of propaganda. And this time, naturally, there is no lack of money."

By the beginning of February the Hitler government had banned all Communist meetings and shut down the Communist press. Social Democrat rallies were either forbidden or broken up by the S.A. rowdies, and the leading Socialist newspapers were continually suspended. Even the Catholic Center Party did not escape the Nazi terror. Stegerwald, the leader of the Catholic Trade Unions, was beaten by Brownshirts when he attempted to address a meeting, and Bruening was obliged to seek police protection at another rally after S.A. troopers had wounded a number of his followers. Altogether fifty-one anti-Nazis were listed as murdered during the electoral campaign, and the Nazis claimed that eighteen of their own had been done to death.

Goering's key position as Minister of the Interior of Prussia now began to be noticed. Ignoring the restraining hand of Papen, who as Premier of Prussia was supposedly above him, Goering removed hundreds of republican officials and replaced them with Nazis, mostly S.A. and S.S. officers. He ordered the police to avoid "at all costs" hostility to the S.A., the S.S. and the Stahlhelm, a conservative group, but on the other hand to show no mercy to those who were "hostile to the State." He urged the police "to make use of firearms" and warned that those who didn't would be punished. This was an outright call for the shooting down of all who opposed Hitler by the police of a state (Prussia) which controlled two

Previous page: "The New Germany." The launch ceremony for the aircraft carrier *Graf Zeppelin* in 1938. In the event the ship was never completed during the war.

Right: S.S. guard unit, Dachau concentration camp, May 1933. Dachau was the first of the concentration camps to be established, in March 1933.

Below right: "The Fuehrer orders, We follow." Hitler Youth propaganda in Berlin, 1934.

Below: Hitler speaks at the Potsdam Garrison Church to Germany's élite, 21 March 1933. President Hindenburg is seated in front of Hitler.

thirds of Germany. Just to make sure that the job would be ruthlessly done, Goering on February 22 established an auxiliary police force of 50,000 men, of whom 40,000 were drawn from the ranks of the S.A. and the S.S. and the rest from the Stahlhelm. Police power in Prussia was thus largely carried out by Nazi thugs. It was a rash German who appealed to such a "police" for protection against the Nazi terrorists.

And yet despite all the terror the "Bolshevik revolution" which Goebbels, Hitler and Goering were looking for failed to "burst into flames." If it could not be provoked, might it not have to be invented?

On February 24, Goering's police raided the Karl Liebknecht Haus, the Communist headquarters in Berlin. It had been abandoned some weeks before by the Communist leaders, a number of whom had already gone underground or quietly slipped off to Russia. But piles of propaganda pamphlets had been left in the cellar and these were enough to enable Goering to announce in an official communiqué that the seized "documents" proved that the Communists were about to launch the revolution. The reaction of the public and even of some of the conservatives in the government was one of skepticism. It was obvious that something more sensational must be found to stampede the public before the election on March 5.

The Reichstag Fire

On the evening of February 27, four of the most powerful men in Germany were gathered at two separate dinners in Berlin. In the exclusive Herrenklub in the Vosstrasse, Vice-Chancellor von Papen was entertaining President von Hindenburg. Out at Goebbels' home, Chancellor Hitler had arrived to dine *en famille*. According to Goebbels, they were relaxing, playing music on the gramophone and telling stories. "Suddenly," he recounted later in his diary, "a telephone call from Dr Ernst 'Putzi' Hanfstaengl: 'The Reichstag is on fire!' I am sure he is telling a tall tale and decline even to mention it to the Fuehrer."

But the diners at the Herrenklub were just around the corner from the Reichstag.

"Suddenly [Papen later wrote] we noticed a red glow through the windows and heard sounds of shouting in the street. One of the servants came hurrying up to me and whispered: "The Reichstag is on fire!" which I repeated to the President. He got up and from the window we could see the dome of the Reichstag looking as though it were illuminated by searchlights. Every now and again a burst of flame and a swirl of smoke blurred the outline."

The Vice-Chancellor packed the aged President home in his own car and hurried off to the burning building. In the meantime Goebbels, according to his account, had had second thoughts about Putzi Hanfstaengl's "tall tale," had made some telephone calls and learned that the Reichstag was in flames. Within a few seconds he and his Fuehrer were racing "at sixty miles an hour down the Charlottenburger Chaussee toward the scene of the crime."

Above: Police inspect the burned out Reichstag, 1934.

Above right: "Blood and Soil." A Nazi poster for a Farmers' and Peasants' rally, 1937.

Left: The S.S. text of the "Road to Freedom" at Dachau Concentration Camp.

Right: Nazi Party rally at Nuremberg.

That it was a crime, a Communist crime, they proclaimed at once on arrival at the fire. Goering, sweating and puffing and quite beside himself with excitement, was already there ahead of them declaiming to heaven, as Papen later recalled, that "this is a Communist crime against the new government." To the new Gestapo chief, Rudolf Diels, Goering shouted, "This is the beginning of the Communist revolution! We must not wait a minute. We will show no mercy. Every Communist official must be shot, where he is found. Every Communist deputy must this very night be strung up."

The whole truth about the Reichstag fire will probably never be known. Nearly all those who knew it are now dead, most of them slain by Hitler in the months that followed. Even at Nuremberg the mystery could not be entirely unraveled, though there is enough evidence to establish beyond a reasonable doubt that it was the Nazis who planned the arson and carried it out for their own political ends.

From Goering's Reichstag President's Palace an underground passage, built to carry the central heating system, ran to the Reichstag building. Through this tunnel Karl Ernst, a former hotel bellhop who had become the Berlin S.A. leader, led a small detachment of storm troopers on the night of February 27 to the Reichstag, where they scattered gasoline and self-igniting chemicals and then made their way quickly back to the palace the way they had come. At the same time a half-witted Dutch Communist with a passion for arson, Marinus van der Lubbe, had made his way into the huge, darkened and to him unfamiliar building and set some small fires of his own. This feeble-minded pyromaniac was a godsend to the Nazis. He had been picked up by the S.A. a few days before after having been overheard in a bar boasting that he had attempted to set fire to several public buildings and that he was going to try the Reichstag next.

The coincidence that the Nazis had found a demented Communist arsonist who was out to do exactly what they themselves had determined to do seems incredible but is nevertheless supported by the evidence. The idea for the fire almost certainly originated with Goebbels and Goering, Hans Gisevius, an official in the Prussian Ministry of the Interior at the time, testified at Nuremberg that "it was Goebbels who first thought of setting the Reichstag on fire," and Rudolf Diels, the Gestapo chief, added in an affidavit that "Goering knew exactly how the fire was to be started" and had ordered him "to prepare, prior to the fire, a list of people who were to be arrested immediately after it." General Franz Halder, Chief of the German General Staff during the early part of World War II, recalled at Nuremberg how on one occasion Goering had boasted of his deed . . .

Van der Lubbe, it seems clear, was a dupe of the Nazis. He was encouraged to try to set the Reichstag on fire. But the main job was to be done – without his knowledge, of course – by the storm troopers. Indeed, it was established at the subsequent trial at Leipzig that the Dutch half-wit did not possess the means to set so vast a building on fire so quickly. Two and a half minutes after he entered, the great central hall was fiercely burning. He had only his shirt for tinder. The main fires, according to the testimony of experts at the

Above: Money specially printed for use in Oranienburg concentration camp.

screamed at the Bulgarian, "Out with you, you scoundrel!" . . .

Torgler and the three Bulgarians were acquitted, though the German Communist leader was immediately taken into "protective custody," where he remained until his death during the second war. Van der Lubbe was found guilty and decapitated.

The trial, despite the subserviency of the court to the Nazi authorities, cast a great deal of suspicion on Goering and the Nazis, but it came too late to have any practical effect. For Hitler had lost no time in exploiting the Reichstag fire to the limit.

On the day following the fire, February 28, he prevailed on President Hindenburg to sign a decree "for the Protection of the People and the State" suspending the seven sections of the constitution which guaranteed individual and civil liberties. Described as a "defensive measure against Communist acts of violence endangering the state," the decree laid down that: "Restrictions on personal liberty: on the right of free expression of opinion, including freedom of the press; on the rights of assembly and association; and violations of the privacy of postal, telegraphic and telephonic communications; and warrants or house searchers, orders for confiscations as well as restrictions on property, are also permissible beyond the legal limits otherwise prescribed."

In addition, the decree authorized the Reich government to take over complete power in the federal states when necessary and imposed the death sentence for a number of crimes, including "serious disturbances of the peace" by armed persons.

Thus with one stroke Hitler was able not only to legally gag his opponents and arrest them at his will but, by making the trumped-up Communist threat "official," as it were, to throw millions of the middle class and the peasantry into a frenzy of fear that unless they voted for National Socialism at the elections a week hence, the Bolsheviks might take over. Some four thousand Communist officials and a great many Social Democrat and liberal leaders were arrested, including members of

trial, had been set with considerable quantities of chemicals and gasoline. It was obvious that one man could not have carried them into the building, nor would it have been possible for him to start so many fires in so many scattered places in so short a time.

Van der Lubbe was arrested on the spot and Goering, as he afterward told the court, wanted to hang him at once. The next day Ernst Torgler, parliamentary leader of the Communists, gave himself up to the police when he heard that Goering had implicated him, and a few days later Georgi Dimitroff, a Bulgarian Communist who later became Prime Minister of Bulgaria, and two other Bulgarian Communists, Popov and Tanev, were apprehended by the police. Their subsequent trial before the Supreme Court at Leipzig turned into something of a fiasco for the Nazis and especially for Goering, whom Dimitroff, acting as his own lawyer, easily provoked into making a fool of himself in a series of stinging cross-examinations. At one point, according to the court record, Goering

Right: Hitler, Goering and other leading Nazis at the Reichstag after the Fire.

Left: S.A. with Communist prisoners in Berlin, March 6, 1934, as the Nazis took advantage of the opportunity offered by the Reichstag Fire.

Below: Van der Lubbe (with bowed head), the man accused of being the arsonist, at the Reichstag Fire Trial.

the Reichstag, who, according to the law, were immune from arrest. This was the first experience Germans had had with Nazi terror backed up by the government. Truckloads of storm troopers roared through the streets all over Germany, breaking into homes, rounding up victims and carting them off to S.A. barracks, where they were tortured and beaten. The Communist press and political meetings were suppressed; the Social Democrat newspapers and many liberal journals were suspended and the meetings of the democratic parties either banned or broken up. Only the Nazis and their Nationalist allies were permitted to campaign unmolested.

With all the resources of the national and Prussian governments at their disposal and with plenty of money from big business in their coffers, the Nazis carried on an election propaganda such as Germany had never seen before. For the first time the State-run radio carried the voices of Hitler, Goering and Goebbels to every corner of the land. The streets, bedecked with swastika flags, echoed to the tramp of the storm troopers. There were mass rallies, torchlight parades, the din of loudspeakers in the squares. The billboards were plastered with flamboyant Nazi posters and at night bonfires lit up the hills. The electorate was in turn cajoled with promises of a German paradise, intimidated by the brown terror in the streets and frightened by "revelations" about the Communist "revolution."

On March 23, 1933, Hitler maneuvered the Reichstag into turning over its constitutional powers to him, supposedly on a temporary basis. By passing a so-called Enabling Act, which made it possible for Hitler to rule by decree with a show of legality, the legislature committed suicide and signaled the end of parliamentary democracy in the Third Reich. For, armed with such sweeping powers, which he had no intention of giving up, he soon banned all opposition political parties and enforced the ruling by means of concentration camps and systematic terror.

Hitler's Propaganda Machine

Adroit use of the press, radio, movies and other means of public information was one of the secrets of the Nazi successes. The control exerted by Goebbel's Propaganda Ministry was so absolute that even those with access to foreign newspapers could find themselves a little taken in by some of the dubious assertions of the German media.

Top, far left: A poster proclaims "We Remain Comrades," an example of Nazi Arbeitsfront (Labor Service) propaganda.

Left: Hitler proudly parades with Nazi banners. The careful and impressive orchestration of parades and demonstrations was an important part of Nazi technique intended to reinforce the image of might and triumph which the Nazis asserted.

Bottom left: Perhaps the most important element of all, Hitler's own skills at public speaking.

Right: Reich Propaganda Minister Dr. Josef Goebbels, in many respects the most able of Hitler's lieutenants.

Bottom right: "All Germany hears the Fuehrer." The radio broadcasts played a vital part.

Below: A German Youth Festival poster of 1934. Indoctrination proceeded apace in the schools and the Nazi youth organisations.

Deutsches Jugendfest
SONNABEND DEN 30. JUNI 1934
FÖRDERT DIE DEUTSCHE JUGEND DURCH DEN KAUF DES FESTABZEICHENS

Ganz Deutschland hört den Führer
mit dem Volksempfänger

The Blood Purge of June 30, 1934

Roehm, the chief of staff of the S.A., now swollen to two and a half million storm troopers, had not been put off by Hitler's gesture of appointing him to the cabinet nor by the Fuehrer's friendly personal letter of New Year's Day 1934. In February he presented to the cabinet a lengthy memorandum proposing that the S.A. should be made the foundation of a new People's Army and that the armed forces, the S.A. and S.S. and all veterans' groups should be placed under a single Ministry of Defense, over which – the implication was clear – he should preside. No more revolting idea could be imagined by the officer corps, and its senior members not only unanimously rejected the proposal but appealed to Hindenburg to support them. The whole tradition of the military caste would be destroyed if the roughneck Roehm and his brawling Brownshirts should get control of the Army. Moreover, the generals were shocked by the tales, now beginning to receive wide circulation, of the corruption and debauchery of the homosexual clique around the S.A. chief. As General von Brauchitsch would later testify, "rearmament was too serious and difficult a business to permit the participation of peculators, drunkards and homosexuals."

For the moment Hitler could not afford to offend the Army, and he gave no support to Roehm's proposal. Indeed, on February 21 he secretly told Anthony Eden, who had come to Berlin to discuss the disarmament impasse, that he was prepared to reduce the S.A. by two thirds and to agree to a system of inspection to make sure that the remainder received neither military training nor arms – an offer which, when it leaked out, further inflamed the bitterness of Roehm and the S.A. As the summer of 1934 approached, the relations between the S.A. chief of staff and the Army High Command continued to deteriorate. There were stormy scenes in the cabinet between Roehm and General von Blomberg, and in March the Minister of Defense protested to Hitler that the S.A. was secretly arming a large force of special staff guards with heavy machines guns – which was not only a threat against the Army but, General von Blomberg added, an act done so publicly that it threatened Germany's clandestine rearmament under the auspices of the Reichswehr.

It is plain that at this juncture Hitler, unlike the headstrong Roehm and his cronies, was thinking ahead to the day when the ailing Hindenburg would breathe his last. He knew that the aged President as well as the Army and other conservative forces in Germany were in favor of a restoration of the Hohenzollern monarchy as soon as the Field Marshal had passed away. He himself had other plans, and when early in April the news was secretly but authoritatively conveyed to him and Blomberg from Neudeck that the President's days were numbered, he realized that a bold stroke must soon be made. To ensure its success

Below: S.A. raiding a trades union building in Leipzig.

he would need the backing of the officer corps; to obtain that support he was prepared to go to almost any length.

The occasion for confidential parleys with the Army soon presented itself. On April 11 the Chancellor, accompanied by General von Blomberg and the commanders in chief of the Army and the Navy, General Freiherr von Fritsch and Admiral Raeder, set out on the cruiser *Deutschland* from Kiel for Koenigsberg to attend the spring maneuvers in East Prussia. The Army and Navy commanders were told of Hindenburg's worsening condition and Hitler, backed by the compliant Blomberg, bluntly proposed that he himself, with the Reichswehr's blessing, be the President's successor. In return for the support of the military, Hitler offered to suppress Roehm's ambitions, drastically reduce the S.A. and guarantee the Army and Navy that they would continue to be the sole bearers of arms in the Third Reich. It is believed that Hitler also held out to Fritsch and Raeder the prospect of an immense expansion of the Army and Navy, if they were prepared to go along with him. With the fawning Raeder there was no question but that he would, but Fritsch, a tougher man, had first to consult his senior generals. This consultation took place at Bad Nauheim on May 16, and after the "Pact of the *Deutschland*" had been explained to them, the highest officers of the German Army unanimously endorsed Hitler as the successor to President Hindenburg. For the Army this *political* decision was to prove of historic significance. By voluntarily offering to put itself in the unrestrained hands of a megalomaniacal dictator it was sealing its own fate. As for Hitler, the deal would make his dictatorship supreme. With the stubborn Field Marshal out of the way, with the prospect of the restoration of the Hohenzollerns snuffed out, with himself as head of state as well as of government, he could go his way alone and unhindered. The price he paid for this elevation to supreme power was paltry: the sacrifice of the S.A. He did not need it, now that he had all the authority. It was a raucous rabble that only embarrassed him. Hitler's contempt for the narrow minds of the generals must have risen sharply that spring. They could be had, he must have thought, for surprisingly little. It was a judgment that he held, unaltered, except for one bad moment in June, to the end – his end and theirs.

Yet, as summer came, Hitler's troubles were far from over. An ominous tension began to grip Berlin. Cries for the "second revolution" multiplied, and not only Roehm and the storm troop leaders but Goebbels himself, in speeches and in the press which he controlled, gave vent to them. From the conservative Right, from the Junkers and big industrialists around Papen and Hindenburg, came demands that a halt be called to the revolution, that the arbitrary arrests, the persecution of the Jews, the attacks against the churches, the arrogant behavior of the storm troopers be curbed, and that the general terror organized by the Nazis come to an end.

Within the Nazi Party itself there was a new and ruthless struggle for power. Roehm's two most powerful enemies, Goering and Himmler, were uniting against him. On April 1 Himmler, chief of the black-coated S.S., which was still an arm of the S.A. and under Roehm's command, was named

Above: Religious support for the Nazis.

by Goering to be chief of the Prussian Gestapo, and he immediately began to build up a secret-police empire of his own. Goering, who had been made a *General der Infanterie* by Hindenburg the previous August (though he was Minister of Aviation), gladly shed his shabby brown S.A. uniform for the more showy one of his new office, and the change was symbolic: as a general and a member of a family from the military caste, he quickly sided with the Army in its fight against Roehm and the S.A. To protect himself in the jungle warfare which was now going on, Goering also recruited his own personal police force, the Landespolizeigruppe General Goering, several thousand men strong, which he concentrated in the former Cadet School at Lichterfelde, where he had first entered the Army and which was strategically located on the outskirts of Berlin.

At the beginning of June Hitler had a showdown with Roehm which, according to his own account given to the Reichstag later, lasted for nearly five hours and which "dragged on until midnight." It was, Hitler said, his "last attempt" to come to an understanding with his closest friend in the movement . . . According to Hitler, Roehm left him with the "assurance that he would do everything possible to put things right." Actually, Hitler later claimed Roehm began "preparations to eliminate me personally."

This was almost certainly untrue. Though the whole story of the purge, like that of the Reichstag fire, will probably never be known, all the evidence that has come to light indicates that the S.A. chief never plotted to put Hitler out of the way. Unfortunately the captured archives shed no more light on the purge than they do on the Reichstag fire; in both cases it is likely that all the incriminating documents were destroyed on the orders of Goering.

Whatever was the real nature of the long conversation between the two Nazi veterans, a day or two after it took place Hitler bade the S.A. go on leave for the entire month of July, during which the storm troopers were prohibited from wearing uniforms or engaging in parades or exercises. On June 7, Roehm announced that he himself was going on sick leave but at the same time he issued a warning: "If the enemies of S.A. hope that the S.A. will not be recalled, or will be recalled only in part after its leave, we may permit them to enjoy this brief hope. They will receive their answer at such time and in such form as appears necessary.

72

The S.A. is and remains the destiny of Germany.''

Before he left Berlin Roehm invited Hitler to confer with the S.A. leaders at the resort town of Wiessee, near Munich, on June 30. Hitler readily agreed and indeed kept the appointment, though not in a manner which Roehm could possibly have imagined. Perhaps not in a way, either, that Hitler himself at this moment could foresee. For, as he later admitted to the Reichstag, he hesitated "again and again before taking a final decision . . . I still cherished the secret hope that I might be able to spare the movement and my S.A. the shame of such a disagreement and that it might be possible to remove the mischief without severe conflicts."

"It must be confessed," he added, "that the last days of May continuously brought to light more and more disquieting facts." But did they? Later Hitler claimed that Roehm and his conspirators had made preparations to seize Berlin and take him into custody. But if this were so why did all the S.A. leaders depart from Berlin early in June, and – even more important – why did Hitler leave Germany at this moment and thus provide an opportunity for the S.A. chiefs to grab control of the State in his absence?

For on June 14 the Fuehrer flew to Venice to hold the first of many conversations with his fellow fascist dictator, Mussolini. The meeting, incidentally, did not go off well for the German leader, who, in his soiled raincoat and battered soft hat, seemed ill at ease in the presence of the more experienced Duce, resplendent in his glittering, bemedaled black Fascisti uniform and inclined to be condescending to his visitor. Hitler returned to Germany in a state of considerable irritation and called a meeting of his party leaders in the little town of Gera in Thuringia for Sunday, June 17, to report on his talks with Mussolini and to assess the worsening situation at home. As fate would have it, another meeting took place on that Sun-

day in the old university town of Marburg which attracted much more attention in Germany and indeed in the world, and which helped bring the critical situation to a climax.

The dilettante Papen, who had been rudely shoved to the sidelines by Hitler and Goering but who was still nominally Vice-Chancellor and still enjoyed the confidence of Hindenburg, summoned enough courage to speak out publicly against the excesses of the regime which he had done so much to foist on Germany. In May he had seen the ailing President off to Neudeck – it was the last time he was to see his protector alive – and the grizzly but enfeebled old Field Marshal had said to him: "Things are going badly, Papen. See what you can do to put them right."

Thus encouraged, Papen had accepted an invitation to make an address at the University of Marburg on June 17. The speech was largely written by one of his personal advisers, Edgar Jung, a brilliant Munich lawyer and writer and a Protestant, though certain ideas were furnished by one of the Vice-Chancellor's secretaries, Herbert von Bose, and by Erich Klausener, the leader of Catholic Action – a collaboration that soon cost all three of them their lives. It was a courageous utterance and, thanks to Jung, eloquent in style and dignified in tone. It called for an end of the revolution, for a termination of the Nazi terror, for the restoration of normal decencies and the return of some measure of freedom, especially of freedom of the press.

The speech, when it became known, was widely heralded in Germany, but it fell like a bombshell on the little group of Nazi leaders gathered at Gera, and Goebbels moved quickly to see that it became known as little as possible. He forbade the broadcast of a recording of the speech scheduled for the same evening as well as any reference to it in the press, and ordered the police to seize copies of the *Frankfurter Zeitung* which

Below: Launching the 'pocket battleship' *Admiral Scheer.* Cleverly designed to appear to keep within the limits laid down by the Versailles Treaty, the *Scheer* and her sister ships were the foundation of the new German Navy.

were on the streets with a partial text. But not even the absolute powers of the Propaganda Minister were sufficient to keep the German people and the outside world from learning the contents of the defiant address. The wily Papen had provided the foreign correspondents and diplomats in Berlin with advance texts, and several thousand copies were also very hastily run off on the presses of Papen's newspaper, *Germania*, and secretly distributed.

On learning of the Marburg speech, Hitler was stung to fury. In a speech the same afternoon at Gera he denounced the ''pygmy who imagines he can stop, with a few phrases, the gigantic renewal of a people's life.'' Papen was furious too, at the suppression of his speech. He rushed to Hitler on June 20 and told him he could not tolerate such a ban ''by a junior minister,'' insisted that he had spoken ''as a trustee for the President,'' and then and there submitted his resignation, adding a warning that he ''would advise Hindenburg of this immediately.''

This was a threat that obviously worried Hitler, for he was aware of reports that the President was so displeased with the situation that he was considering declaring martial law and handing over power to the Army. In order to size up the seriousness of this danger to the very continuance of the Nazi regime, he flew to Neudeck on the following day, June 21, to see Hindenburg. His reception could only have increased his fears. He was met by General von Blomberg and quickly saw that his Defense Minister's usual lackeylike attitude toward him had suddenly disappeared. Blomberg instead was now the stern Prussian general and he brusquely informed Hitler that he was authorized by the Field Marshal to tell him that unless the present state of tension in Germany was brought quickly to an end the President would declare martial law and turn over the control of the State to the Army. When Hitler was permitted to see Hindenburg for a few minutes in the presence of von Blomberg, the old President confirmed the ultimatum.

This was a disastrous turn of affairs for the Nazi Chancellor. Not only was his plan to succeed the President in jeopardy; if the Army took over, that

Above: Poster of the anti-Semitic Nazi propaganda film, ''The Eternal Jew.''

Left: Nazi Party flags at the Nuremberg rally, 1933.

Above: Goebbels casts his vote in the referendum of August 19, 1934. The vote overwhelmingly supported Hitler's seizure of supreme power after the death of President Hindenburg earlier that month.

would be the end of him and of Nazi government. Flying back to Berlin the same day he must have reflected that he had only one choice to make if he were to survive. He must honor his pact with the Army, suppress the S.A. and halt the continuance of the revolution for which the storm troop leaders were pressing. The Army, backed by the venerable President, it was obvious, would accept no less.

And yet, in that last crucial week of June, Hitler hesitated -- as least as to how drastic to be with the S.A. chiefs to whom he owed so much. But now Goering and Himmler helped him to make up his mind. They had already drawn up the scores they wanted to settle, long lists of present and past enemies they wished to liquidate. All they had to do was convince the Fuehrer of the enormity of the "plot" against him and of the necessity for swift and ruthless action. According to the testimony at Nuremberg of Wilhelm Frick, the Minister of the Interior and one of Hitler's most faithful followers, it was Himmler who finally succeeded in convincing Hitler that "Roehm wanted to start a putsch. The Fuehrer," Frick added, "ordered Himmler to suppress the putsch." Himmler, he explained, was instructed to put it down in Bavaria, and Goering in Berlin.

The Army prodded Hitler too and thereby incurred a responsibility for the barbarity which was soon to take place. On June 25 General von Fritsch, the Commander in Chief, put the Army in a state of alert, cancelling all leaves and confining the troops to barracks. On June 28 Roehm was expelled from the German Officers' League – a plain warning that the S.A. chief of staff was in for trouble. And just to make sure that no one, Roehm, above all, should have any illusions about where the Army stood, Blomberg took the unprecedented step of publishing a signed article on June 29 in the *Voelkischer Beobachter*, affirming that "the Army . . . stands behind Adolf Hitler . . . who remains one of ours."

The Army, then, was pressing for the purge, but it did not want to soil its own hands. That must be done by Hitler, Goering and Himmler, with their black-coated S.S. and Goering's special police. Hitler left Berlin on Thursday, June 28, for Essen to attend the wedding of a local Nazi gauleiter, Josef Terboven. The trip and its purpose hardly suggest that he felt a grave crisis to be imminent. On the same day Goering and Himmler ordered special detachments of the S.S. and the "Goering Police" to hold themselves in readiness. With Hitler out of town, they evidently felt free to act on their own. The next day, the twenty-ninth, the Fuehrer made a tour of Labor Service camps in Westphalia, returning in the afternoon to Godesberg on the Rhine, where he put up at a hotel on the riverbank run by an old war comrade, Dreesen. That evening Goebbels, who seems to have hesitated as to which camp to join – he had been secretly in touch with Roehm – arrived in Godesberg, his mind made up, and reported what Hitler later described as "threatening intelligence" from

Berlin. Karl Ernst, a former hotel bellhop and ex-bouncer in a café frequented by homosexuals, whom Roehm had made leader of the Berlin S.A., had alerted the storm troopers. Ernst, a handsome but not a bright young man, believed then and for the remaining twenty-four hours or so of his life that he was faced by a putsch from the Right, and he would die shouting proudly, "Heil Hitler!"

Hitler later claimed that up to this moment, June 29, he had decided merely to "deprive the chief of staff [Roehm] of his office and for the time being keep him in custody and arrest a number of S.A. leaders whose crimes were unquestioned . . . and in an earnest appeal to the others, I would recall them to their duty.

"However, [he told the Reichstag on July 13] . . . at one o'clock in the night I received from Berlin and Munich two urgent messages concerning alarm summonses: first, in Berlin an alarm muster had been ordered for four P.M. . . . and at five P.M. action was to begin with a surprise attack; the government buildings were to be occupied . . . Second, in Munich the alarm summons had already been given to the S.A.; they had been ordered to assemble at nine o'clock in the evening . . . That was mutiny!"

Hitler never revealed from whom the "urgent messages" came but the implication is that they were sent by Goering and Himmler. What is certain is that they were highly exaggerated. In Berlin, S.A. Leader Ernst thought of nothing more drastic than to drive to Bremen that Saturday with his bride to take ship for a honeymoon at Madeira. And in the south, where the S.A. "conspirators" were concentrated?

At the moment of 2 A.M. on June 30 when Hitler, with Goebbels at his side, was taking off for Munich from Hangelar Airfield near Bonn, cap-

Above: National leadership at the Berlin Opera. Left to right, Goering, von Blomberg, Hitler, von Hindenburg, von Papen, Raeder.

tain Roehm and his S.A. lieutenants were peacefully slumbering in their beds at the Hanslbauer Hotel at Wiessee on the shores of the Tegernsee. Edmund Heines, the S.A. Obergruppenfuehrer of Silesia, a convicted murderer, a notorious homosexual with a girlish face on the brawny body of a piano mover, was in bed with a young man. So far did the S.A. chiefs seem from staging a revolt that Roehm had left his staff guards in Munich. There appeared to be plenty of carousing among the S.A. leaders but no plotting.

Hitler and his small party (Otto Dietrich, his press chief, and Viktor Lutze, the colorless but loyal S.A. leader of Hanover, had joined it) landed in Munich at 4 A.M. on Saturday, June 30, and found that some action already had been taken.

Left: Himmler and Roehm inspect S.A. and S.S. units in 1933.

Above: Schoolchildren at a Nazi rally in Coburg, 1934.

Below: The Nazi anti-Semitic newspaper *Der Stuermer* displayed on a public notice board.

Fuehrer, according to Otto Dietrich's account, entered Roehm's room alone, gave him a dressing down and ordered him to be brought back to Munich and lodged in Stadelheim prison, where the S.A. chief had served time after his participation with Hitler in the Beer Hall Putsch in 1923. After fourteen stormy years the two friends, who more than any others were responsible for the launching of the Third Reich, for its terror and its degradation, who though they had often disagreed had stood together in the moments of crisis and defeats and disappointments, had come to a parting of the ways, and the scar-faced, brawling battler for Hitler and Nazism had come to the end of his violent life.

Hitler, in a final act of what he apparently thought was grace, gave orders that a pistol be left on the table of his old comrade. Roehm refused to make use of it. "If I am to be killed, let Adolf do it himself," he is reported to have said. Thereupon two S.S. officers, according to the testimony of an eyewitness, a police lieutenant, given twenty-three years later in a postwar trial at Munich in May 1957, entered the cell and fired their revolvers at Roehm point-blank. "Roehm wanted to say something," said this witness, "but the S.S. officer motioned him to shut up. Then Roehm stood at attention – he was stripped to the waist – with his face full of contempt." And so he died, violently as he had lived, contemptuous of the friend he had helped propel to the heights no other German had ever reached, and almost certainly, like hundreds of others who were slaughtered that day – like Schneidhuber, who was reported to have cried, "Gentlemen, I don't know what this is all about, but shoot straight" – without any clear idea of what was happening, or why, other than that it was an act of treachery which he, who had lived so long with treachery and committed it so often himself, had not expected from Adolf Hitler.

In Berlin, in the meantime, Goering and Himmler had been busy. Some 150 S.A. leaders were rounded up and stood against a wall of the Cadet School at Lichterfelde and shot by firing squads of Himmler's S.S. and Goering's special police.

Among them was Karl Ernst, whose honeymoon trip was interrupted by S.S. gunmen as his car neared Bremen. His bride and his chauffeur were wounded; he himself was knocked unconscious and flown back to Berlin for his execution . . . Gregor Strasser was seized at his home in Berlin at noon on Saturday and dispatched a few hours later in his cell in the Prinz Albrechtstrasse Gestapo jail on the personal orders of Goering.

Papen was luckier. He escaped with his life. But his office was ransacked by an S.S. squad, his principal secretary, Bose, shot down at his desk, his confidential collaborator, Edgar Jung, who had been arrested a few days earlier by the Gestapo, murdered in prison, another collaborator, Erich Klausener, leader of Catholic Action, slain in his office in the Ministry of Communications, and the rest of his staff, including his private secretary, Baroness Stotzingen, carted off to concentration camp. When Papen went to protest to Goering, the latter, who at that moment had no time for idle talk, "more or less," he later recalled, threw him out, placing him under house arrest at his villa, which was surrounded by heavily armed S.S. men and where his telephone was cut and he was for-

Major Walther Buch, head of USCHLA, the party court, and Adolf Wagner, Bavarian Minister of the Interior, aided by such early cronies of Hitler as Emil Maurice, the ex-convict and rival for Geli Raubal's love, and Christian Weber, the horse dealer and former cabaret bouncer, had arrested the Munich S.A. leaders, including Obergruppen-fuehrer Schneidhuber, who was also chief of police in Munich. Hitler, who was now working himself up to a fine state of hysteria, found the prisoners in the Ministry of the Interior. Striding up to Schneidhuber, a former Army colonel, he tore off his Nazi insignia and cursed him for his "treason."

Shortly after dawn Hitler and his party sped out of Munich toward Wiessee in a long column of cars. They found Roehm and his friends still fast asleep in the Hanslbauer Hotel. The awakening was rude. Heines and his young male companion were dragged out of bed, taken outside the hotel and summarily shot on the order of Hitler. The

bidden to have any contact with the outside world – an added humiliation which the Vice-Chancellor of Germany swallowed remarkably well. For within less than a month he defiled himself by accepting from the Nazi murderers a new assignment as German minister to Vienna, where the Nazis had just slain Chancellor Dollfuss.

How many were slain in the purge was never definitely established. In his Reichstag speech of July 13, Hitler announced that sixty-one persons were shot, including nineteen "higher S.A. leaders," that thirteen more died "resisting arrest" and that three "committed suicide" – a total of seventy-seven. *The White Book of the Purge*, published by émigrés in Paris, stated that 401 had been slain, but it identified only 116 of them. At the Munich trial in 1957, the figure of "more than 1,000" was given.

Hitler proceeded to regiment all Germany, taking over and nazifying its institutions one by one. He destroyed the power of labor by seizing the trade unions' funds and imprisoning their leaders, and thereafter forbade all strikes. He bound farmers to the land as in the days of serfdom, suppressed small businesses and forced the businessmen into the ranks of wage earners. Similarly he seized control of the churches, took over the schools, prostituted the courts, muzzled the press and made it a Nazi propaganda arm.

Some four and a half months after Hitler became Chancellor, there occurred in Berlin a scene which had not been witnessed in the Western world since the late Middle Ages. At about midnight a torchlight parade of thousands of students ended at a square on Unter den Linden opposite the University of Berlin. Torches were put to a huge pile of books that had been gathered there, and as the flames enveloped them more books were thrown on the fire until some twenty thousand had been consumed. The book burning had begun.

Many of the books tossed into the flames in Berlin that night by the joyous students under the approving eye of Dr. Goebbels had been written by authors of world reputation. They included,

Above: "Youth serve their Fuehrer: all ten-year-olds in the Hitler Youth."

Left: Nazi students and S.A. men joyfully burning books in Berlin.

among German writers, Thomas and Heinrich Mann, Lion Feuchtwanger, Jakob Wassermann, Arnold and Stefan Zweig, Erich Maria Remarque, Walther Rathenau, Albert Einstein, Alfred Kerr and Hugo Preuss, the last named being the scholar who had drafted the Weimar Constitution. But not only the works of dozens of German writers were burned. A good many foreign authors were also included: Jack London, Upton Sinclair, Helen Keller, Margaret Sanger, H. G. Wells, Havelock Ellis, Arthur Schnitzler, Freud, Gide, Zola, Proust. In the words of a student proclamation, any book was condemned to the flames "which acts subversively on our future or strikes at the root of German thought, the German home and the driving forces of our people."

Dr. Goebbels, the new Propaganda Minister, who from now on was to put German culture into a Nazi strait jacket, addressed the students as the burning books turned to ashes. "The soul of the German people can again express itself. These flames not only illuminate the final end of an old era; they also light up the new."

Hitler smashed all individual freedom and replaced it with a regimentation which was unparalleled even for the Germans. Yet he was rewarded with increasing public adulation. Why?

The foremost reason was that whereas six million wage earners had recently been out of work, the average man now had a job and the assurance that he would keep it. Beyond that, whatever his crimes against humanity, Hitler had unleashed a dynamic force of incalculable proportions which had long been pent up in the German people.

To what purpose he would direct this resurgence of energy Hitler had already made clear in *Mein Kampf* and in a hundred speeches. He would fulfill the two great passions of his life, the creation of a mighty military machine and the direction of Germany's foreign policy toward conquest.

Above: Nazi enforced boycott of Jewish shops in Berlin.

Left: Nazi Party rally Nuremberg 1934. Saluting the flag at front are, left to right, Himmler, Hitler, Lutze.

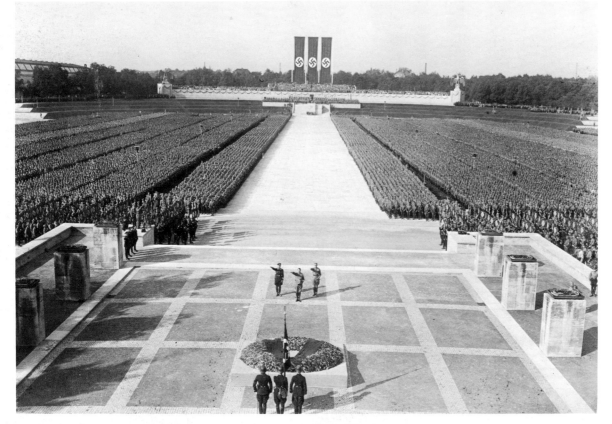

Right: Reichsarbeitsdienst (Labor Service) units march past Hitler in Nuremberg, 1934.

The Probe Across the Rhine

To talk peace, to prepare secretly for war and to proceed with enough caution to avoid preventive action by the Versailles powers – such were Hitler's tactics during his first two years in power.

He built up the armed services with unflagging energy. The army was ordered to treble its numerical strength, from 100,000 to 300,000 by October 1, 1934. Goebbels was admonished never to allow the words ''General Staff' to appear in the press, since Versailles forbade the very existence of this organization. The official rank list of the German army ceased to be published lest its swollen roster of officers give the game away to foreign intelligence.

Submarines, which Versailles prohibited were, under secret construction in Finland, Holland and Spain. As minister of aviation – supposedly *civil* aviation – Goering put manufacturers to work designing warplanes, and the training of military pilots began immediately under the camouflage of the League for Air Sports.

A visitor to the Ruhr and Rhineland industrial areas in those days might have been struck by the intense activity of the armament works, especially those of Krupp, chief German gunmakers for three quarters of a century, and I.G. Farben, the great chemical trust. Although Krupp had been forbidden by the Allies to continue in the armament business after 1919, the company had really not been idle. As Krupp would boast in 1942, when the German armies occupied most of Europe, ''the basic principle of armament and turret design for tanks had already been worked out in 1926 . . . Of the guns being used in 1939-41, the most important ones were already fully complete in 1933.'' Farben scientists had saved Germany from early disaster in the First World War by the invention of a process to make synthetic nitrates from air after the country's normal supply of nitrates from Chile was cut off by the British blockade. Now under Hitler the trust set out to make Germany self-sufficient in two materials without which modern war could not be fought: gasoline and rubber, both of which had had to be imported. The problem of making synthetic gasoline from coal had actually been solved by the company's scientists in the mid-Twenties. After 1933, the Nazi government gave I.G. Farben the go-ahead with orders to raise its synthetic oil production to 300,000 tons a year by 1937. By that time the company had also discovered how to make synthetic rubber from coal and other products of which Germany had a sufficiency, and the first of four plants was set up at Schkopau for large-scale production of *buna*, as the artificial rubber became known. By the beginning of 1934, plans were approved by the Working Committee of the Reich Defense Council for the mobilization of some 240,000 plants for war orders. By the end of that year rearmament, in all its phases, had become so massive it was obvious that it could no longer be concealed from the suspicious and uneasy powers of Versailles.

On Saturday, March 16, 1935, the chancellor decreed a law establishing universal military service and providing for a peacetime army of 36 divisions – roughly half a million men. That was the end of the military restrictions of the Treaty of Versailles – unless France and Britain took action. As Hitler had expected, they protested but did not act. Hitler had gotten away with his gamble.

Still, it would not do to rest on his laurels. He was now determined to occupy the demilitarized zone of the Rhineland. ''Hitler's sole hesitancy,''

Right: S.A. bicycle units in Nuremberg.

Above: Mussolini greets Hitler in Italy, 1934.

Left: Nazi flags in the Saar, January 1935. In a referendum in that month the people of the Saar voted to be re-united with the rest of Germany and Hitler announced he had no further claims on French territory.

observed French Ambassador André François-Poncet, probably the best-informed ambassador in Berlin, "is now concerned with the appropriate moment to act."

All through the winter of 1935-36 Hitler bided his time. France and Britain, he could not help but note, were preoccupied with stopping Italy's aggression in Abyssinia, but Mussolini seemed to be getting by with it. Despite its much-publicized sanctions, the League of Nations was proving itself impotent to halt a determined aggressor.

On March 1, Hitler reached his decision, somewhat to the consternation of his generals. Most of them were convinced that the French would make mincemeat of the small German forces gathered for the move into the Rhineland. Nevertheless, on

Left: Hitler Jungvolk in Berlin, 1939. The Jungvolk section of the Hitler Youth was for boys aged between 10 and 14. Entry into the Jungvolk was accompanied by an oath of loyalty to Hitler.

Above: German troops march into the Rhineland, 1936.

March 2, 1936, in obedience to his master's instructions, General Blomberg, minister of war and commander in chief of the armed forces, issued orders for the occupation of the Rhineland. It was, he told the senior commanders, to be a "surprise move." Blomberg expected it to be a "peaceful operation." If it turned out that it was not – that the French would fight – Blomberg had already planned his countermeasure, which was to be a hasty retreat back over the Rhine!

But the French, paralyzed by internal strife and sinking into defeatism, did not know this when a token force of three German battalions paraded across the Rhine bridges at dawn on March 7. Just a few hours later the Fuehrer was standing in the Reichstag before a delirious audience, expounding on his desire for peace and his latest ideas of how to maintain it. That evening I noted in my diary the scene that follows:

" 'Men of the German Reichstag!' Hitler said in a deep, resonant voice. 'In this historic hour, when, in the Reich's western provinces, German troops are marching into their future peacetime garrisons, we all unite in two sacred vows. . . . .'

"He could go no further. It was news to this parliamentary mob that German soldiers were already on the move into the Rhineland. All the militarism in their German blood surged to their heads. They sprang, yelling and crying, to their feet, their hands raised in slavish salute. The new messiah played his role superbly. His head lowered, as if in all humbleness, he waited patiently for silence. Then, his voice choking with emotion, he uttered the two vows:

" 'First, we swear to yield to no force whatever in restoration of the honor of our people. Secondly, we pledge that we have no territorial demands to make in Europe! Germany will never break the peace!'

"It was a long time before the cheering stopped. A few generals made their way out. Behind their smiles, however, I could not help detecting a nervousness. I ran into General von Blomberg. His face was white, his cheeks twitching."

And with reason. The minister of defense, who five days before had issued in his own handwriting the order to march, was losing his nerve. But the French never made the slightest move to oppose the Germans. The most General Gamelin, chief of the French general staff, would do was to concentrate 13 divisions near the German frontier, to reinforce the Maginot Line.

Even this was enough to throw a scare into the German high command. Blomberg, backed by most of the officers at the top, wanted to pull back the battalions that had crossed the Rhine. As one of them testified at Nuremberg, "Considering the situation we were in, the French army could have blown us to pieces."

It could have – and, had it, that almost certainly would have been the end of Hitler, after which history might have taken quite a different turn, for the dictator could never have survived such a fiasco. Hitler himself admitted as much. "A retreat on our part," he conceded later, "would have spelled collapse."

It was Hitler's iron nerve alone, which now, as during many crises that lay ahead, saved the situation and, confounding the reluctant generals, brought success. Confident that the French would not march, he bluntly turned down all suggestions by the wavering high command for pulling back.

"What would have happened," he exclaimed in a bull session with his cronies at headquarters on March 27, 1942, in recalling the Rhineland coup, "if anybody other than myself had been at the head of the Reich? Anyone you care to mention would have lost his nerve. What saved us was my unshakable obstinacy and my amazing aplomb."

In retrospect, it is easy to see that Hitler's successful gamble in the Rhineland brought him a victory more staggering and more fatal in its immense consequences than could be comprehended at the time. At home it fortified his popularity and his power, raising them to heights which no German ruler of the past had ever enjoyed. It assured his ascendancy over his generals, who had hesitated and weakened at a moment of crisis when he had held firm. It taught them that in foreign politics and even in military affairs his judgment was superior to theirs. They had feared that the French would fight; he knew better. And finally, and above all, the Rhineland occupation, small as it was as a military operation, opened the way, as only Hitler (and Churchill, alone, in England) seemed to realize, to vast new opportunities in a Europe which was not only shaken but whose strategic situation was irrevocably changed by the parading of three German battalions across the Rhine bridges.

Conversely, it is equally easy to see, in retrospect, that France's failure to repel the Wehrmacht battalions and Britain's failure to back her in what would have been nothing more than a police action was a disaster for the West from which sprang all the later ones of even greater magni-

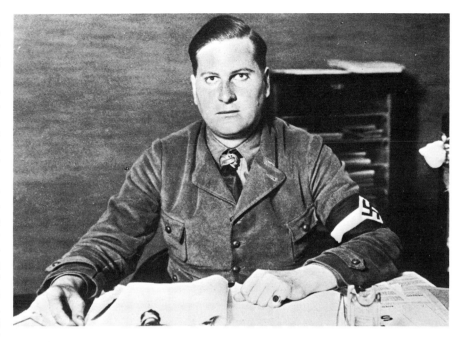

tude. In March 1936 the two Western democracies were given their last chance to halt, without the risk of a serious war, the rise of a militarized, aggressive, totalitarian Germany and, in fact – as we have seen Hitler admitting – bring the Nazi dictator and his regime tumbling down. They let the chance slip by.

For France, it was the beginning of the end. Her allies in the East, Russia, Poland, Czechoslovakia, Rumania and Yugoslavia, suddenly were faced with the fact that France would not fight against German aggression to preserve the security system which the French government itself had taken the lead in so laboriously building up. But more than that. These Eastern allies began to realize that even if France were not so supine, she

Above: Reich Youth Leader Baldur von Schirach. By 1939 the Hitler Youth had over 7.7 million members, two thirds of the possible maximum, but in 1939 a law established conscription for all on the same basis as adult military service.

Left: Himmler with the famous film director Leni Riefenstahl at Nuremberg, 1934. Riefenstahl directed the famous pro-Nazi movie *Triumph of the Will.*

Right: German cavalry enter the Rhineland, 1936.

Below: German parade in Berlin during the Olympic Games, August 1936. Hitler hoped that the Games would demonstrate the supposed racial superiority of Aryan German athletes. In fact the black American Jesse Owens was the outstanding performer.

would soon not be able to lend them much assistance because of Germany's feverish construction of a West Wall behind the Franco-German border. The erection of this fortress line, they saw, would quickly change the strategic map of Europe, to their detriment. They could scarcely expect a France which did not dare, with her one hundred divisions, to repel three German battalions, to bleed her young manhood against impregnable German fortifications while the Wehrmacht attacked in the East. But even if the unexpected took place, it would be futile. Henceforth the French could tie down in the West only a small part of the growing German Army. The rest would be free for operations against Germany's Eastern neighbors.

As the German foreign minister openly explained to the American ambassador in the spring of 1936, "As soon as our fortifications are constructed and the countries of Central Europe realize that France cannot enter German territory at will, all those countries will begin to feel very differently about their foreign policies, and a new constellation will develop."

As Dr. Kurt von Schuschnigg, chancellor of Austria, related in his memoirs, "I knew that in order to save Austrian independence I had to embark on a course of appeasement. Everything had to be avoided which could give Germany a pretext for intervention, and everything had to be done to secure in some way Hitler's toleration of the status quo." "Everything," as it turned out, was not enough.

Austria's Death Warrant

But there was to be a breathing space. In his address to the Reichstag on January 30, 1937, Hitler proclaimed, "The time of so-called surprises has ended." And, in truth, there were no spectacular surprises during 1937. The year for Germany was one of consolidation and further preparation for the objectives which, that November, the Fuehrer would lay down to a handful of his highest officers. It was a year devoted to forging armaments, training troops, trying out the new air force in the Spanish Civil War, developing ersatz gasoline and rubber, cementing the Rome-Berlin Axis and watching for weak spots in Paris, London and Vienna.

But even in this "peaceful" year, Austrian Nazis, financed and egged on by Berlin, maintained a campaign of terror in that country. Bombings took place nearly every day in some part of the nation, and in the mountain provinces there were massive and often violent Nazi demonstrations. Plans were uncovered disclosing that Nazi thugs were preparing to kill Schuschnigg.

Finally, in February 1938 Schuschnigg was summoned to Hitler's mountain retreat at Obersalzberg for a "conference." A man of impeccable Old World Austrian manners, Schuschnigg began the conversation with a graceful tidbit about the magnificent view and the fine weather that day. Hitler cut him short: "We did not gather here to speak of the fine view or of the weather." Then the storm broke. "You have done everything to avoid a friendly policy," Hitler fumed. The whole history of Austria is just one uninterrupted act of high treason."

Shocked at Hitler's outburst, the quiet-mannered Austrian chancellor tried to remain conciliatory and yet stand his ground. After an hour of argument, he asked his antagonist to enumerate his complaints, but the Fuehrer simply launched into another tirade against Austria. He then gave Schuschnigg until that afternoon to "come to terms" – without specifying what the terms were.

That afternoon, after cooling his heels for two hours in an anteroom, Schuschnigg was ushered into the presence of Joachim von Ribbentrop, the new German foreign minister. Ribbentrop presented a two-page "agreement" which, he announced, must be signed forthwith. The Fuehrer would permit no discussion.

Schuschnigg felt relieved to have at least something definite from Hitler. But as he perused the document his relief evaporated. For here was a German ultimatum calling on him to turn the Austrian government over to the Nazis within one week.

But what could he do? He was summoned again to Hitler. He found the Fuehrer pacing excitedly up and down in his study.

Hitler: "Herr Schuschnigg, here is the draft of the document. There is nothing to be discussed. I will not change one single iota. You will either sign it as it is and fulfill my demands within three days, or I will order the march into Austria."

Schuschnigg capitulated. He told Hitler he was willing to sign. But he reminded him that under the Austrian constitution only the president of the republic had the legal power to accept such an agreement. At this answer, Schuschnigg later recounted, Hitler seemed to lose his self-control. He ran to the doors, opened them and shouted, "General Keitel!" Then, turning back to Schuschnigg, he said, "I shall have you called later!"

This was pure bluff, but the harassed Austrian chancellor, who had been made aware of the presence of high-ranking German generals all day, perhaps did not know it. Keitel later told how Hitler greeted him with a broad grin when he

Below: Local Nazi Party officials at work.

Right: Nazi youths demonstrate in Graz, Austria, 1938.

Below: Enthusiastic Viennese demonstrate in favor of the Anschluss on the Heldenplatz, March 12, 1938.

rushed in and asked for orders. "There are no orders," Hitler chuckled. "I just wanted to have you here." Thirty minutes later, Schuschnigg signed Hitler's document. It was Austria's death warrant.

Hitler had given Schuschnigg four days – until Tuesday, February 15 – to send him a "binding reply" that he would carry out the ultimatum, and an additional three days – until February 18 – to fulfill its specific terms. Schuschnigg returned to Vienna on the morning of February 12 and immediately sought out President Miklas. Wilhelm Miklas was a plodding, mediocre man of whom the Viennese said that his chief accomplishment in life had been to father a large brood of children. But there was in him a certain peasant solidity, and in this crisis at the end of fifty-two years as a state official he was to display more courage than any other Austrian. He was willing to make certain concessions to Hitler such as amnestying the Austrian Nazis, but he balked at putting the Viennese Nazi sympathizer Arthur Seyss-Inquart in charge of the police and the Army. Papen duly reported this to Berlin on the evening of February 14. He said Schuschnigg hoped "to overcome the resistance of the President by tomorrow."

At 7:30 that same evening Hitler approved orders drawn up by General Keitel to put military pressure on Austria: "Spread false, but quite credible news, which may lead to the conclusion of military preparations against Austria."

Before the threat of armed invasion President Miklas gave in and on the last day of grace, February 15, Schuschnigg formally advised Ambassador von Papen that the Berchtesgaden agreement would be carried out before February 18. On February 16 the Austrian government announced a general amnesty for Nazis, including those convicted in the murder of Dollfuss, and made public the reorganized cabinet, in which Arthur Seyss-Inquart was named Minister of Security. The next day this Nazi Minister hurried off to Berlin to see Hitler and receive his orders.

Seyss-Inquart, the first of the quislings, was a

Left: Nazis force Jews to scrub the pavements in Vienna.

Below: Hitler greets Seyss-Inquart in Vienna.

pleasant-mannered, intelligent young Viennese lawyer who since 1918 had been possessed with a burning desire to see Austria joined with Germany. This was a popular notion in the first years after the war. Indeed, on November 12, 1918, the day after the armistice, the Provisional National Assembly in Vienna, which had just overthrown the Hapsburg monarchy and proclaimed the Austrian Republic, had tried to effect an Anschluss by affirming that "German Austria is a component part of the German Republic." The victorious Allies had not allowed it and by the time Hitler came to power in 1933 there was no doubt that the majority of Austrians were against their little country's joining with Nazi Germany. But to Seyss-Inquart, as he said at his trial in Nuremberg, the Nazis stood unflinchingly for the Anschluss and for this reason he gave them his support. He did not join the party and took no part in its rowdy excesses. He played the role, rather, of a respectable front for the Austrian Nazis and after a July 1936 agreement by which he was appointed State Councilor, he concentrated his efforts, aided by Papen and other German officials and agents, in burrowing from within. Strangely, both Schuschnigg and Miklas seem to have trusted him almost to the end. Later Miklas, a devout Catholic as was Schuschnigg, confessed that he was favorably impressed by the fact that Seyss was "a diligent churchgoer." The man's Catholicism and also the circumstance that he, like Schuschnigg, had served in a Tyrolean *Kaiserjaeger* regiment during the First World War, in which he was severely wounded, seems to have been the basis of the trust which the Austrian Chancellor had for him. Schuschnigg, unfortunately, had a fatal inability to judge a man on more substantial grounds. Perhaps he thought he could keep his new Nazi Minister in line by simple bribes. He himself tells in his book of the magic effect of $500 on Seyss-Inquart a year before when he threatened to resign as State Councilor. But Hitler had bigger prizes with which to dazzle the ambitious young lawyer, as Schuschnigg was soon to learn.

Above: German Jews trying to emigrate, 1939.

On February 20 Hitler made his long-expected speech to the Reichstag . . . Though he spoke warmly of Schuschnigg's "understanding" and of his "warmhearted willingness" to bring about a closer understanding between Austria and Germany – a piece of humbug which impressed Prime Minister Neville Chamberlain – the Fuehrer issued a warning which, however much lost on London, did not fall upon deaf ears in Vienna – and in Prague. "Over ten million Germans live in two of the states adjoining our frontiers . . . There must be no doubt about one thing. Political separation from the Reich may not lead to deprivation of rights – that is, the general rights of self-determination. It is unbearable for a world power to know there are racial comrades at its side who are constantly being afflicted with the severest suffering for their sympathy or unity with the whole nation, its destiny and its *Weltanschauung*. To the interests of the German Reich belong the protection of those German peoples who are not in a position to secure along our frontiers their political and spiritual freedom by their own efforts." That was blunt, public notice that henceforth Hitler regarded the future of the seven million Austrians and the three million Sudeten Germans as the affair of the Third Reich.

Within four weeks, by a combination of ruthless military pressure, propaganda and subversion, the Nazis succeeded in taking complete control of Austria. In order to "legalize" this act of naked aggression, Hitler announced that a plebiscite on the so-called Anschluss would be held on April 10.

In a fair and honest election the plebiscite might have been close. As it was, it took a very brave Austrian to vote no. In the polling station I visited in Vienna that Sunday afternoon, wide slits in the polling booths gave the Nazi election committee a good view of how one voted. In the country districts few bothered – or dared – to cast their ballots in the secrecy of the booth; they voted openly for all to see. I happened to broadcast at 7:30 that evening, a half hour after the polls had closed, when few votes had yet been counted. A Nazi official assured me before the broadcast that the Austrians were voting 99 percent *Ja*. That was the figure officially given later – 99.08 percent in Greater Germany, 99.75 in Austria. And so, for the moment, Austria passed out of history.

For the first weeks the behavior of the Vienna Nazis was worse than anything I had seen in Germany. There was an orgy of sadism. Day after day large numbers of Jewish men and women could be seen scrubbing Schuschnigg signs off the sidewalk and cleaning the gutters. While they worked on their hands and knees with jeering storm stroopers standing over them, crowds gathered to taunt them. Hundreds of Jews, men and women, were picked off the streets and put to work cleaning public latrines and the toilets of the barracks where the S.A. and the S.S. were quartered. Tens of thousands more were jailed. Their worldly possessions were confiscated or stolen. I myself, from our apartment in the Plosslgasse, watched squads of S.A. men carting off silver, tapestries, paintings and other loot from the Rothschild palace next door. Baron Louis de Rothschild himself was later able to buy his way out of Vienna by turning over his steel mills to the German Goering Works. Perhaps half of the city's 180,000 Jews managed, by the time the war started, to purchase their freedom to emigrate by handing over what they owned to the Nazis.

This lucrative trade in human freedom was handled by a special organization set up under the S.S. by Reinhard Heydrich, the "Office for Jewish Emigration," which became the sole Nazi agency authorized to issue permits to Jews to leave the country. Administered from the beginning to the end by an Austrian Nazi, a native of Hitler's home town of Linz by the name of Karl Adolf Eichmann, it was to become eventually an agency not of emigration but of extermination and to organize the slaughter of more than four million persons, mostly Jews. Himmler and Heydrich also took advantage of their stay in Austria during the first weeks of the Anschluss to set up a huge concentration camp at Mauthausen, on the north bank of the Danube near Enns. It was too much trouble to continue to transport thousands of Austrians to the concentration camps of Germany. Austria, Himmler decided, needed one of its own. Before the Third Reich tumbled to its fall the non-Austrian prisoners were to outnumber the local inmates and Mauthausen was to achieve the dubious record as the German concentration camp (the *extermination* camps in the East were something else) with the largest number of officially listed executions – 35,318 in the six and a half years of its existence.

Despite the Gestapo (*Geheime Staatspolizei*, Secret State Police), terror led by Himmler and Heydrich after the Anschluss Germans flocked by the hundreds of thousands to Austria, where they could pay with their marks for sumptuous meals not available in Germany for years and for bargain-priced vacations amid Austria's matchless mountains and lakes. German businessmen and bankers poured in to buy up the concerns of dispossessed Jews and anti-Nazis at a fraction of their value.

Without firing a shot and without interference from Great Britain, France and Russia, whose military forces could have overwhelmed him, Hitler had added seven million subjects to the Reich and gained a strategic position of immense value to his future plans. He now possessed in Vienna the nerve center of Central Europe and the gateway to Southeast Europe. Moreover, with his armies flanking Czechoslovakia on three sides, he had rendered that country militarily indefensible.

No time was to be lost in taking advantage of this situation.

Hitler Swallows His Pride

"Case Green" was the code name of Hitler's plan for a surprise attack on Czechoslovakia, first drawn up in June 1937. Now, the easy conquest of Austria made Case Green a matter of some urgency; the plan must be brought up to date and prepared for.

The Republic of Czechoslovakia, which Hitler was determined to destroy, was the creation of the peace treaties, so hateful to the Germans, after World War I. It was the most democratic, enlightened and prosperous state in Central Europe. But it was gripped by a domestic problem which in over 20 years it had not been able entirely to solve; the question of its minorities, including the three and a quarter million Sudeten Germans who lived within its borders.

The Sudeten Germans fared tolerably well in the Czechoslovak state – certainly better than any other minority in the country. But their plight was for Hitler a pretext (as Danzig was to be a year later in regard to Poland) for cooking up a stew in a land he coveted, confusing and misleading its friends

Left: Reichsleiter Martin Bormann, national organizer of the Nazi Party in the years before the war.

Below: S.S. Leibstandarte parade in Berlin on Hitler's birthday, April 20, 1938.

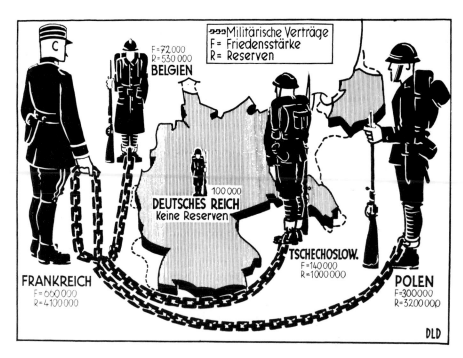

Militärische Verträge
F = Friedensstärke
R = Reserven

F = 72.000
R = 530.000
BELGIEN

100.000
DEUTSCHES REICH
Keine Reserven

TSCHECHOSLOW.
F = 140.000
R = 1.000.000

FRANKREICH
F = 660.000
R = 4.100.000

POLEN
F = 300.000
R = 3.200.000

DLD

Above: Nazi propaganda map showing Germany, with her army limited by the Versailles Treaty, surrounded by France and her "chained Allies."

Below: Lord Halifax, British Foreign Secretary, and Goering, on a visit to Goering's country estate, November 1937.

and concealing his real purpose. Now he issued instructions to the Nazi-dominated Sudeten German Party that "demands should be made which are unacceptable to the Czech government."

The stew began to simmer, and by the weekend which began on Friday, May 20, 1938, it was believed in Prague and London that Hitler was about to launch aggression against Czechoslovakia. The Czechs began to mobilize. Now Britain, France and Russia displayed a firmness and unity in the face of the German threat which they were not to show again until a new world war had almost destroyed them.

The Czech mobilization sent Hitler into a fit of fury, and his feelings were not assuaged by dispatches telling of continual calls by the British and French ambassadors warning Germany that aggression against Czechoslovakia meant a European war – even though the furthest the British would go was to warn that "in the event of a European conflict it was impossible to foresee whether Britain would not be drawn into it."

The Fuehrer, brooding in his mountain retreat above Berchtesgaden, felt deeply humiliated by the Czechs and by the support given them in London and Paris. Nothing could have put him in a blacker, uglier mood. His fury was all the more intense because he was accused, prematurely, of being on the point of committing an aggression which he indeed intended to commit. That very weekend, in fact, he had gone over a new plan for "Green." But now it could not be carried out. Swallowing his pride, he ordered the Foreign Office to inform the Czech envoy on Monday, May 23, that Germany had no aggressive intentions toward Czechoslovakia.

In Prague, London, Paris and Moscow, government leaders breathed a sigh of relief. The crisis had been mastered. Hitler had been given a lesson. He must now know he could not get away with aggression as easily as he had in Austria.

Little did they know the Nazi dictator.

After sulking at Obersalzberg a few more days, during which there grew within him a burning rage to get even with Czechoslovakia, he convoked the ranking officers of the Wehrmacht to hear a momentous decision: "Czechoslovakia shall be wiped off the map!" he thundered. Case Green was again brought out and revised. The first sentence of the new directive read; "It is my unalterable decision to smash Czechoslovakia by military action in the near future."

What "the near future" meant was explained in a covering letter. "Green's execution must be assured by October 1, 1938, at the latest."

It was a date which Hitler would adhere to through thick and thin, through crisis after crisis and at the brink of war, without flinching.

A Step Toward Surrender

The first crisis arose within the German ranks – a rift between Hitler and some of the highest-ranking generals of the army. The opposition to the Fuehrer's grandiose plans for aggression was led by General Ludwig Beck, chief of the Army General Staff, who henceforth would assume the leadership of such resistance as there was to Hitler in the Third Reich. Beck now began to perceive that Hitler's policy of deliberately risking war with Britain, France and Russia – against the advice of the top generals – would, if carried out, be the ruin of Germany. On May 5 he wrote the first of a series of memoranda strenuously opposing any such action. They are brilliant papers, blunt as to unpleasant facts and full of solid reasoning and logic. Although Beck overestimated the strength of will of Britain and France, and the power of the French army, his long-range predictions turned out, so far as Germany was concerned, to be deadly accurate.

Beck was convinced, he wrote in his May 5 memorandum, that a German attack would provoke a European war in which Britain, France and Russia would oppose Germany and in which the United States would be the arsenal of the Western democracies. Germany simply could not win such a war. Its lack of raw materials alone made victory impossible.

Hitler, however, pressed forward with his plans for aggression, and Beck now maintained that the generals had reached the limits of their allegiance. If Hitler insisted on war, they should resign in a

Above: Generaloberst Ludwig Beck.

Left: Hitler inspecting an S.S. guard outside the Kroll Opera House, February 1938.

Above: "Man of the People," Julius Streicher, on the right, greets an old comrade. Streicher was editor of the anti-Semitic newspaper *Der Stuermer.*

by the spinelessness of his brother officers. On August 18 Beck resigned.

Ordinarily the resignation of a chief of the Army General Staff in the midst of a crisis, and especially of one so highly respected as was General Beck, would have caused a storm in military circles and even given rise to repercussions abroad. But here again Hitler showed his craftiness. Though he accepted Beck's resignation at once, and with great relief, he forbade any mention of it in the press or even in the official government and military gazettes and ordered the retired General and his fellow officers to keep it to themselves. It would not do to let the British and French governments get wind of dissension at the top of the German Army at this critical juncture and it is possible that Paris and London did not hear of the matter until the end of October, when it was officially announced in Berlin. Had they heard, one could speculate, history might have taken a different turning; the appeasement of the Fuehrer might not have been carried so far.

Beck himself, out of a sense of patriotism and loyalty to the Army, made no effort to bring the news of his quitting to the public's attention. He was disillusioned, though, that not a single general officer among those who had agreed with him and backed him in his opposition to war felt called upon to follow his example and resign. He did not try to persuade them. He was, as Hassell later said of him, "pure Clausewitz, without a spark of Bluecher or Yorck" – a man of principles and thought, but not of action. He felt that Brauchitsch, as Commander in Chief of the Army, had let him down at a decisive moment in German history, and this embittered him. Beck's biographer and friend noted years later the General's "deep bitterness" whenever he spoke of his old commander. On such occasions he would shake with emotion and mutter, "Brauchitsch left me in the lurch."

Beck's successor as Chief of the Army General

body. In that case, he argued, war was impossible, since there would be nobody to lead the armies.

Beck was now aroused as he had never been before in his lifetime. The whole folly of the Third Reich, its tyranny, its terror, its corruption, suddenly dawned on him. The German people must be freed from the Nazi thrall. A state ruled by law must be restored.

To further this purpose Beck arranged a secret meeting of the commanding generals. His arguments left a deep impression on most of them, but no decisive action was taken. The meeting of the top brass of the German army broke up without their having had the courage to call Hitler to account, and Beck saw that he had been defeated

Right: Hitler at an army war game 1937. Left, General Halder, right, General von Fritsch.

Staff – though his appointment was kept a secret by Hitler for several weeks, until the end of the crisis – was Franz Halder, fifty-four years old, who came from an old Bavarian military family and whose father had been a general. Himself trained as an artillery man, he had served as a young officer on the staff of Crown Prince Rupprecht in the First World War. Though a friend of Roehm in the first postwar Munich days, which might have made him somewhat suspect in Berlin, he had risen rapidly in the Army and for the past year had served as Beck's deputy. In fact, Beck recommended him to Brauchitsch as his successor, for he was certain that his deputy shared his views.

Halder became the first Bavarian and the first Catholic ever to become Chief of the German General Staff – a severe break with the old Protestant Prussian tradition of the officer corps. A man of wide intellectual interests, with a special bent for mathematics and botany (my own first impression of him was that he looked like a university professor of mathematics or science) and a devout Christian, there was no doubt that he had the mind and the spirit to be a true successor to Beck. The question was whether, like his departed chief, he lacked the knack of taking decisive action at the proper moment. And whether, if he did not lack it, at that moment he had the character to disregard his oath of allegiance to the Fuehrer and move resolutely against him. For Halder, like Beck, though not at first a member of a growing conspiracy against Hitler, knew about it and apparently, again like Beck, was willing to back it. As the new chief of the General Staff, he became the key figure in the first serious plot to overthrow the dictator of the Third Reich.

Above: Hitler returns from Italy, 1938.

Left: German panzers in Berlin, 1938.

Birth of a Conspiracy Against Hitler

After five and a half years of National Socialism it was evident to the few Germans who opposed Hitler that only the Army possessed the physical strength to overthrow him. The workers, the middle and upper classes, even if they had wanted to, had no means of doing it. They had no organization outside of the Nazi party groups and they were, of course, unarmed. Though much would later be written about the German "resistance" movement, it remained from the beginning to the end a small and feeble thing, led, to be sure, by a handful of courageous and decent men, but lacking followers.

The very maintenance of its bare existence was, admittedly, difficult in a police state dominated by terror and spying. Moreover, how could a tiny group – or even a large group, had there been one – rise up in revolt against the machine guns, the tanks, the flame throwers of the S.S.?

In the beginning, what opposition there was to Hitler sprang from among the civilians; the generals, as we have seen, were only too pleased with a system which had shattered the restrictions of the Versailles Treaty and given them the heady and traditional task of building up a great army once again. Ironically, the principal civilians who emerged to lead the opposition had served the Fuehrer in important posts, most of them with an initial enthusiasm for Nazism which dampened only when it began to dawn on them in 1937 that Hitler was leading Germany toward a war which it was almost sure to lose.

One of the earliest of these to see the light was Carl Goerdeler, the mayor of Leipzig, who, first appointed Price Controller by Bruening, had continued in that job for three years under Hitler. A conservative and a monarchist at heart, a devout Protestant, able, energetic and intelligent, but also indiscreet and headstrong, he broke with the Nazis in 1936 over their anti-Semitism and their franzied rearmament and, resigning both his posts, went to work with heart and soul in opposition to Hitler. One of his first acts was to journey to France, England and the United States in 1937 to discreetly warn of the peril of Nazi Germany.

The light came a little later to two other eventual conspirators, Johannes Popitz, Prussian Minister of Finance, and Dr. Hjalmar H. G. Schacht. Both had received the Nazi Party's highest decoration, the Golden Badge of Honor, for their services in shaping Germany's economy for war purposes. Both had begun to wake up to what Hitler's real goal was in 1938. Neither of them seems to have been fully trusted by the inner circle of the opposition because of their past and their character.

Right: German gains from 1935 to the outbreak of war.

Below: Men of the German Condor Legion in Spain 1939. Hitler and Mussolini sent support to Franco's right-wing Nationalists in the Spanish Civil War.

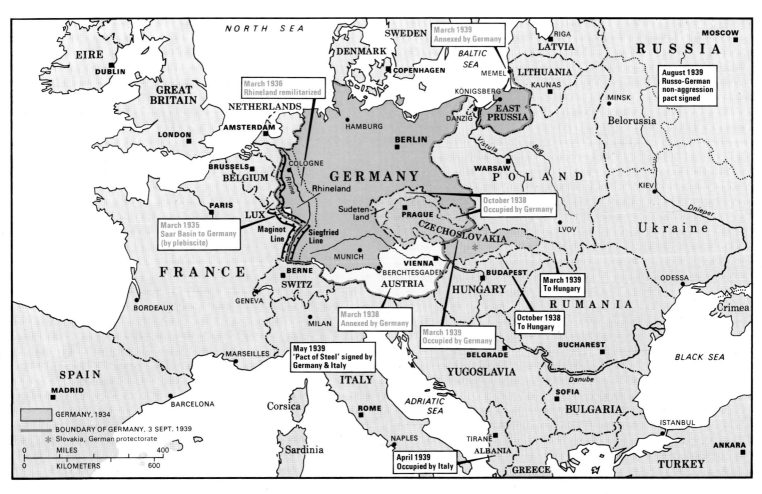

Map legend:

March 1939
Annexed by Germany

March 1936
Rhineland remilitarized

August 1939
Russo-German
non-aggression
pact signed

March 1935
Saar Basin to Germany
(by plebiscite)

October 1938
Occupied by Germany

March 1939
To Hungary

October 1938
To Hungary

March 1938
Annexed by Germany

March 1939
Occupied by Germany

May 1939
'Pact of Steel' signed by
Germany & Italy

April 1939
Occupied by Italy

GERMANY, 1934
BOUNDARY OF GERMANY, 3 SEPT. 1939
Slovakia, German protectorate

MILES 400
KILOMETERS 600

Schacht was too opportunist, and the diplomat Ulrich von Hassell remarked in his diary that the Reichsbank president had a capacity "for talking one way and acting another," an opinion, he says, that was shared by Generals Beck and von Fritsch. Popitz was brilliant but unstable. A fine Greek scholar as well as eminent economist, he, along with General Beck and Hassell, was a member of the Wednesday Club, a group of sixteen intellectuals who gathered once a week to discuss philosophy, history, art, science and literature and who as time went on – or ran out – formed one of the centers of the opposition.

Ulrich von Hassel became a sort of foreign-affairs adviser to the resistance leaders. His dispatches as ambassador in Rome during the war in Abyssinia and the Spanish Civil War had been full of advice to Berlin on how to keep Italy embroiled with France and Britain and therefore on the side of Germany. Later he came to fear that war with France and Britain would be fatal to Germany and that even a German alliance with Italy would be too. Far too cultivated to have anything but contempt for the vulgarism of National Socialism, he did not, however, voluntarily give up serving the regime. He was kicked out of the diplomatic service in the big military, political and Foreign Office shake-up which Hitler engineered on February 4, 1938. A member of an old Hanover noble family, married to the daughter of Grand Admiral von Tirpitz, the founder of the German Navy, and a gentleman of the old school to his finger tips, Hassell, like so many others of his class, seems to have needed the shock of being cast out by the Nazis before he became much interested in doing anything to bring them down. Once this had happened, this sensitive, intelligent, uneasy man devoted himself to that task and in the end,

Above: Production line for the "Kubelwagen," the German equivalent of the Jeep, at the Volkswagen works at Wolfsburg.

sacrificed his life to it, meeting a barbarous end following the July 1944 Bomb Plot.

There were others, lesser known and mostly younger, who had opposed the Nazis from the beginning and who gradually came together to form various resistance circles. One of the leading intellects of one group was Ewald von Kleist, a gentleman farmer and a descendant of the great poet. He worked closely with Ernst Niekisch, a former Social Democrat and editor of *Widerstand* (Resistance), and with Fabian von Schlabrendorff, a young lawyer, who was the great-grandson of Queen Victoria's private physician and confidential adviser, Baron von Stockmar. There were former trade-union leaders such as Julius Leber, Jakob Kaiser and Wilhelm Leuschner. Two Gestapo officials, Artur Nebe, the head of the criminal police, and Bernd Gisevius, a young career police officer, became valuable aides as the conspiracies developed. The latter became the darling of the American prosecution at Nuremberg and wrote a book which sheds much light on the anti-Hitler plots, though most historians take the book and the author with more than a grain of salt.

There were a number of sons of venerable families in Germany: Count Helmuth von Moltke, great-grandnephew of the famous Field Marshal, who later formed a resistance group of young idealists known as the Kreisau Circle; Count Albrecht Bernstorff, nephew of the German ambassador in Washington during the First World War; Freiherr Karl Ludwig von Guttenberg, editor of a fearless Catholic monthly; and Pastor Dietrich Bonhoeffer, a descendant of eminent Protestant clergymen on both sides of his family, who regarded Hitler as Antichrist and who believed it a Christian duty to "eliminate him."

Nearly all of these brave men would persevere until, after being caught and tortured, they were executed by rope or by axe or merely murdered by the S.S.

For a good long time this tiny nucleus of civilian resistance had little success in interesting the Army in its work. As Field Marshal von Blomberg testified at Nuremberg, "Before 1938-39 German generals did not oppose Hitler. There was no reason to oppose him, since he produced the results they desired." There was some contact between Goerdeler and General von Hammerstein, but the former commander in chief of the German Army had been in retirement since 1934 and had little influence among the active generals. Early in the regime Schlabrendorff had got in touch with Colonel Hans Oster, chief assistant to Admiral Canaris in the Abwehr, the Intelligence Bureau of OKW, and found him to be not only a staunch anti-Nazi but willing to try to bridge the gulf between the military and civilians. However, it was not until the winter of 1937-38, when the generals were subjected to the successive shocks engendered by Hitler's decision to go to war, his shake-up of the military command, which he himself took over, and his shabby treatment of General von Fritsch, that some of them became aware of the danger to Germany of the Nazi dictator. The resignation of General Beck toward the end of August 1938, as the Czech crisis grew more menacing, provided a further awakening, and though none of his fellow officers followed him into retirement as he had hoped, it immediately became evident that the fallen Chief of the General Staff was the one person around whom both the recalcitrant generals and the civilian resistance leaders could rally. Both groups respected and trusted him.

Another consideration became evident to both of them. To stop Hitler, force would now be necessary, and only the Army possessed it. But who in the Army could muster it? Not Hammerstein and not even Beck, since they were in retirement. What was needed, it was realized, was to bring in generals who at the moment had actual command of troops in and around Berlin and who thus could act effectively on short notice. General Halder, the new chief of the Army General Staff, had no actual forces under his command. General von Brauchitsch had the whole Army, but he was not fully trusted. His authority would be useful but he could be brought in only, the conspirators felt, at the last minute.

As it happened, certain key generals who were willing to help were quickly discovered and initiated into the budding conspiracy. Three of them held commands which were vital to the success of the venture: General Erwin von Witzleben, commander of the all-important Wehrkreis III, which comprised Berlin and the surrounding areas; General Count Erich von Brockdorff-Ahlefeld, commander of the Potsdam garrison, which was made up of the 23rd Infantry Division; and General Erich Hoepner, who commanded an armored division in Thuringia which would, if necessary, repulse any S.S. troops attempting to relieve Berlin from Munich.

The plan of the conspirators, as it developed toward the end of August, was to seize Hitler as soon as he had issued the final order to attack Czechoslovakia and hale him before one of his own People's Courts on the charge that he had tried recklessly to hurl Germany into a European

Left: "Germany Occupied by the Enemy." A propaganda book written by German political exiles on the "truth about the Third Reich."

Below: Hitler and Dr. Schacht, President of the Reichs Bank.

war and was therefore no longer competent to govern. In the meantime, for a short interim, there would be a military dictatorship followed by a provisional government presided over by some eminent civilian. In due course a conservative democratic government would be formed.

There were two considerations on which the success of the coup depended and which involved the two key conspirators, General Halder and General Beck. The first was timing. Halder had arranged with OKW that he personally be given forty-eight hours' notice of Hitler's final order to attack Czechoslovakia. This would give him the time to put the plot into execution before the troops could cross the Czech frontier. Thus he would be able not only to arrest Hitler but to prevent the fatal step that would lead to war.

The second factor was that Beck must be able to convince the generals beforehand and the German people later (during the proposed trial of Hitler) that an attack on Czechoslovakia would bring in Britain and France and thus precipitate a European war, for which Germany was not prepared and which it would certainly lose. This had been the burden of his memoranda all summer and it was the basis of all that he was now prepared to do: to preserve Germany from a European conflict which he believed would destroy her – by overthrowing Hitler.

Alas for Beck, and for the future of most of the world, it was Hitler and not the recently resigned Chief of the General Staff who proved to have the shrewder view of the possibilities of a big war. Beck, a cultivated European with a sense of history, could not conceive that Britain and France would willfully sacrifice their self-interest by not intervening in case of a German attack on Czechoslovakia. He had a sense of history but not of contemporary politics. Hitler had. For some time now

he had felt himself reinforced in his judgment that Prime Minister Chamberlain would sacrifice the Czechs rather than go to war and that, in such a case, France would not fulfill her treaty obligations to Prague.

The Wilhelmstrasse had not failed to notice dispatches published in the New York newspapers as far back as May 14 in which their London correspondents had reported an "off-the-record" luncheon talk with Chamberlain at Lady Astor's. The British Prime Minister, the journalists reported, had said that neither Britain nor France nor probably Russia would come to the aid of Czechoslovakia in the case of a German attack, that the Czech state could not exist in its present form and that Britain favored, in the interest of peace, turning over the Sudetenland to Germany. Despite angry questions in the House of Commons, the Germans noted, Chamberlain had not denied the veracity of the American dispatches.

On June 1, the Prime Minister had spoken, partly off the record, to British correspondents, and two days later *The Times* had published the first of its leaders which were to help undermine the Czech position; it had urged the Czech government to grant "self-determination" to the country's minorities "even if it should mean their secession from Czechoslovakia" and for the first time it had suggested plebiscites as a means of determining what the Sudetens and the others desired. A few days later the German Embassy in London informed Berlin that the *Times* editorial was based on Chamberlain's off-the-record remarks and that it reflected his views. On June 8 Ambassador von Dirksen told the Wilhelmstrasse that the Chamberlain government would be willing to see the Sudeten areas separated from Czechoslovakia providing it was done after a plebiscite and "not interrupted by forcible measures on the part of Germany."

All this must have been pleasing for Hitler to hear. The news from Moscow also was not bad. By the end of June Friedrich Werner Count von der Schulenburg, the German ambassador to Russia, was advising Berlin that the Soviet Union was "hardly likely to march in defense of a bourgeois state," i.e., Czechoslovakia. By August 3, Ribbentrop was informing the major German diplomatic missions abroad that there was little fear of intervention over Czechoslovakia by Britain, France or Russia.

It was on that day, August 3, that Chamberlain had packed off Lord Runciman to Czechoslovakia on a curious mission to act as a "mediator" in the Sudeten crisis. I happened to be in Prague that day of his arrival and after attending his press conference and talking with members of his party remarked in my diary that "Runciman's whole mission smells." Its very announcement in the House of Commons on July 26 had been accompanied by a piece of prevaricating by Chamberlain himself which must have been unique in the experience of the British Parliament. The Prime Minister had said that he was sending Runciman "in response to a request from the government of Czechoslovakia." The truth was that Runciman had been forced down the throat of the Czech government by Chamberlain. But there was an underlying and bigger falsehood. Everyone, including Chamberlain, knew that Runciman's mission to "mediate" between the Czech govern-

Right: Ernst Niekisch, a former Social Democrat, the editor of the anti-Nazi publication *Widerstand* (Resistance).

ment and the Sudeten leaders was impossible and absurd. They knew that Konrad Henlein, the Sudeten leader, was not a free agent and could not negotiate, and that the dispute now was between Prague and Berlin. My diary notes for the first evening and subsequent days make it clear that the Czechs knew perfectly well that Runciman had been sent by Chamberlain to pave the way for the handing over of the Sudetenland to Hitler. It was a shabby diplomatic trick.

And now the summer of 1938 was almost over. Runciman puttered about in the Sudetenland and in Prague, making ever more friendly gestures to the Sudeten Germans and increasing demands on the Czech government to grant them what they wanted. Hitler, his generals and his Foreign Minister were frantically busy. On August 23, the Fuehrer entertained aboard the liner *Patria* in Kiel Bay during naval maneuvers the Regent of Hungary, Admiral Horthy, and the members of the Hungarian government. If they wanted to get in on the Czech feast, Hitler told them, they must hurry. "He who wants to sit at the table," he put it, "must at least help in the kitchen." The Italian ambassador, Bernardo Attolico, was also a guest on the ship. But when he pressed Ribbentrop for the date of "the German move against Czechoslovakia" so that Mussolini could be prepared, the German Foreign Minister gave an evasive answer. The Germans, it was plain, did not quite trust the discretion of their Fascist ally. Of Poland they were now sure. All through the summer Ambassador von Moltke in Warsaw was reporting to Berlin that not only would Poland decline to help

Left: Pastor Dietrich Bonhoeffer, an eminent church leader, was an important member of the German resistance. He was killed by the Nazis following the 1944 Bomb Plot.

Below: Hitler attending a celebration of the life of Richard Wagner, his favorite composer. Left, Winifred Wagner, daughter-in-law of the composer, right, Carl Goerdeler. At the time of the photograph (1934), Goerdeler was mayor of Leipzig but later was prominent in the resistance.

Czechoslovakia by allowing Russia to send troops and planes through or over her territory, but Colonel Józef Beck, the Polish Foreign Minister, was casting covetous eyes on a slice of Czech territory, the Teschen area. Beck already was exhibiting that fatal shortsightedness, so widely shared in Europe that summer, which in the end would prove more disastrous than he could imagine.

At OKW (the High Command of the Armed Forces) and at OKH (the High Command of the Army) there was incessant activity. Final plans were being drawn up to have the armed forces ready for the push-off into Czechoslovakia by October 1. On August 24, Colonel Jodl at OKW wrote an urgent memorandum for Hitler stressing that "the fixing of the *exact* time for the 'incident' which will give Germany provocation for military intervention is most important." The timing of X Day, he explained, depended on it. "No advance measures may be taken before X minus 1 for which there is not an innocent explanation, as otherwise we shall appear to have manufactured the incident. . . ."

On September 12, Hitler delivered a brutal and bombastic speech, dripping with venom against the Czech state, to a delirious mass of Nazi fanatics gathered in the huge stadium at Nuremberg. The repercussions were immediate. The outburst inspired a revolt in the Sudetenland, which, after two days of savage fighting, the Czech government put down by rushing in troops and declaring martial law.

Next day the French cabinet sat all day, remaining hopelessly divided on whether it should honor its treaty obligations to defend Czechoslovakia in case of a German attack, which it believed imminent. That evening the British ambassador in Paris was summoned for an urgent conference with French Prime Minister Daladier. The latter appealed to Neville Chamberlain to try at once to make the best bargain he could with the German dictator. At 11 o'clock that same night the British prime minister got off an urgent message to Hitler:

"In view of the increasingly critical situation, I propose to come over at once to see you with a view to trying to find a peaceful solution. I propose to come across by air and am ready to start tomorrow."

The surrender that was to culminate in Munich had begun.

Below: Gestapo file photograph of Erich Honecker, Communist activist 1935. Honecker later became one of the leaders of East Germany.

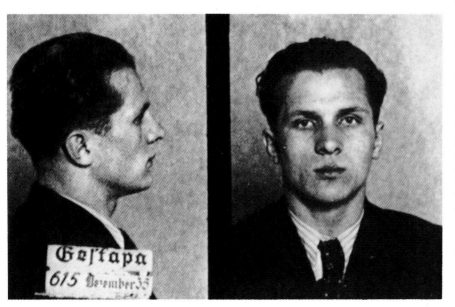

Hitler Pulls Back from the Brink

"Good heavens!" ("*Ich bin vom Himmel gefallen!*") Hitler exclaimed when he read Chamberlain's message. He was astounded but highly pleased that the man who presided over the destinies of the mighty British Empire should come pleading to him, and flattered that Chamberlain – who was 69 years old and had never traveled in an airplane before – should make the long seven-hour flight to Berchtesgaden at the farthest extremity of Germany. Hitler had not even the grace to suggest a meeting place on the Rhine, which would have shortened the trip by half.

Hitler began his conversation with Chamberlain, as he did his speeches, with a long harangue about all that he had done for the German people, for peace and for an Anglo-German *rapprochement*. There was now one problem he was determined to solve. The three million Germans in Czechoslovakia must "return" to the Reich. Then he sprang his proposal:

"Would Britain agree to a cession of the Sudeten region to Germany, or would she not?" Chamberlain expressed satisfaction that they "had now got down to the crux of the matter." He replied that he could not commit himself until he had consulted his cabinet and the French, but added that *"he could state personally that he recognized the principle of the detachment of the Sudeten areas. He wished to return to England to report to the government and secure their approval of his personal attitude."*

From this surrender at Berchtesgaden, all else ensued.

While the British leader was consulting with his cabinet and the French authorities, Hitler went ahead with his military and political plans for the invasion of Czechoslovakia. But as the negotiations progressed, a series of events occurred which made Hitler hesitate. In order to stir up war fever among the populace the Fuehrer ordered a parade of a motorized division through the German capital at dusk on September 27, an hour when hundreds of thousands of Berliners would be pouring out of their offices onto the streets. It turned out to be a terrible fiasco – at least for the Supreme Commander. The people of Berlin simply did not want to be reminded of war. In my diary that night I noted down the scene.

"I went out, expecting to see a tremendous demonstration. I pictured the scenes I had read of in 1914 when the cheering throngs tossed flowers at the marching soldiers, and the girls ran up and kissed them. But today people ducked into the subways, refused to look on, and the handful that did stood at the curb in utter silence. It has been the most striking demonstration against war I've ever seen.

"There weren't 200 people at the Wilhelmsplatz, where Hitler stood on a balcony reviewing the troops. He looked grim, then angry, and soon went inside, leaving his soldiers to parade by unreviewed."

Within the chancellery there was further bad

news. A dispatch from Budapest said that Yugoslavia and Rumania had informed the Hungarian government that they would move against Hungary militarily if she attacked Czechoslovakia. That would spread the war to the Balkans, something Hitler did not want.

The news from Paris was still graver. A telegram from the German military attaché warned that France's partial mobilization was so much like a total one "that I reckon with the completion of the deployment of the first 65 divisions on the German frontier by the sixth day of mobilization." Against such a force the Germans had, as Hitler knew, barely a dozen divisions.

Whether Hitler knew that the order was going out that evening for the mobilization of the British fleet cannot be established. But he did know that Prague was defiant, Paris rapidly mobilizing, London stiffening, his own people apathetic, his leading generals dead against him, and that his latest ultimatum on the Czech question expired at 2 P.M. the next day.

At 10:30 that night, Hitler telegraphed an urgent letter to Chamberlain in London. His letter was moderate in tone, beautifully calculated to appeal to Chamberlain. It was a straw which the prime minister eagerly grasped. He replied:

"After reading your letter, I feel certain that you can get all essentials without war, and without delay."

The next day, a few minutes before 2 P.M. on September 28, just as his ultimatum was to expire, Hitler made up his mind. Invitations were hastily issued to the heads of government of Great Britain, France and Italy to meet the Fuehrer at Munich at noon on the following day to settle the Czech question. The Czechs were not even asked to be present at their own death sentence.

When Chamberlain interrupted a speech in the House of Commons to report Hitler's 11th-hour invitation, the ancient chamber reacted with a mass hysteria unprecedented in its history. There was wild shouting and throwing of papers into the air;

many were in tears and one voice was heard above the tumult which seemed to express the deep sentiments of all: "Thank God for the prime minister!"

Jan Masaryk, the Czech minister, son of the founding father of the Czechoslovak Republic, looked on from the diplomatic gallery, unable to believe his eyes. Later he called on the prime minister and the foreign secretary in Downing Street to find out whether his country, which would have to make all the sacrifices, would be invited to Munich. They answered that it would not, that Hitler would not stand for it. Masaryk struggled to keep control of himself.

"If you have sacrificed my nation to preserve the peace of the world," he finally said, "I will be the first to applaud you. But if not, gentlemen, God help your souls!"

Above: Hitler with the famous automobile designer, Dr Ferdinand Porsche, and Reichsleiter Robert Ley.

Left: Gestapo and S.A. men check the identity papers of passers-by outside a Berlin cafe, possibly during a control on the movement of Jews.

The Shame of Munich

The talks at the Munich conference, which began at 12:45 P.M. on September 29, were anticlimactic; they constituted little more than a mere formality of rendering to Hitler exactly what he wanted when he wanted it. For despite their outward show of firmness, Hitler had by now sensed that both England and France would go to almost any length to avoid war. ("Our enemies are little worms," he told his generals later. "I saw them at Munich.") At every step, the more Chamberlain had conceded, the more Hitler had demanded – and got.

Shortly after 1 A.M. on September 30, Hitler, Chamberlain, Mussolini and Daladier affixed their signatures to the Munich Agreement, providing for the German Army to march into Czechoslovakia on October 1, 1938, as the Fuehrer had always said it would, and to complete the occupation of the Sudetenland by October 10. Hitler had got what he wanted.

Chamberlain returned to London in triumph. "My good friends," he announced to a cheering crowd, "this is the second time in our history that there has come back from Germany to Downing Street peace with honor. I believe it is peace in our time."

The *Times* declared that "no conqueror returning from a victory on the battlefield has come adorned with nobler laurels." There was a spontaneous movement to raise a "National Fund of Thanksgiving" in Chamberlain's honor, which he graciously turned down. Only Duff Cooper, the First Lord of the Admiralty, resigned from the cabinet, and when in the ensuing Commons debate Winston Churchill, still a voice in the wilderness, began to utter his memorable words, "We have sustained a total, unmitigated defeat," he was forced to pause, as he later recorded, until the storm of protest against such a remark had subsided.

The mood in Prague was naturally quite different. At 6:20 A.M. on September 30, the German chargé d'affaires had routed the Czech Foreign Minister, Dr. Kamil Krofta, out of bed and handed him the text of the Munich Agreement together with a request that Czechoslovakia send two representatives to the first meeting of the "International Commission," which was to supervise the execution of the accord, at 5 P.M. in Berlin.

For President Beneš, who conferred all morning at the Hradschin Palace with the political and military leaders, there was no alternative but to submit. Britain and France had not only deserted his country but would now back Hitler in the use of armed force should he turn down the terms of Munich. At ten minutes to one, Czechoslovakia surrendered, "under protest to the world," as the official statement put it. "We were abandoned. We stand alone," General Sirovy, the new Premier, explained bitterly in a broadcast to the Czechoslovak people at 5 P.M.

To the very last Britain and France maintained their pressure on the country they had seduced and betrayed. During the day the British, French and Italian ministers went to see Dr. Krofta to make sure that there was no last-minute revolt of the Czechs against the surrender. The German chargé, Dr. Hencke, in a dispatch to Berlin described the scene. "The French Minister's attempt to address words of condolence to Krofta was cut short by the Foreign Minister's remark: 'We have been forced into this situation; now everything is at an end; today it is our turn, tomorrow it will be the turn of others.' The British Minister succeeded with difficulty in saying that Chamberlain had done his utmost; he received the same answer as the French Minister. The Foreign Minister was a completely broken man and intimated only one wish: that the three Ministers should quickly leave the room."

President Beneš resigned on October 5 on the insistence of Berlin and, when it became evident that his life was in danger, flew to England and exile. He was replaced provisionally by General Sirovy. On November 30, Dr. Emil Hácha, the Chief Justice of the Supreme Court, a well-intentioned but weak and senile man of sixty-six, was selected by the National Assembly to be President of what remained of Czecho-Slovakia, which was now officially spelled with a hyphen.

What Chamberlain and Daladier at Munich had neglected to give Germany in Czechoslovakia the so-called "International Commission" proceeded to hand over. This hastily formed body consisted

Below: Hitler with, left to right, General von Fritsch and General von Blomberg.

Left: Hitler being briefed on the occupation of the Sudetenland, 1938.

Below: Bonnet, the French Foreign Minister, Daladier, the French Premier, and General Gamelin, the French C-in-C pictured in London in August 1938.

of the Italian, British and French ambassadors and the Czech minister in Berlin and Baron von Weizsaecker, the State Secretary in the German Foreign Office. Every dispute over additional territory for the Germans was settled in their favor, more than once under the threat from Hitler and OKW to resort to armed force. Finally, on October 13, the commission voted to dispense with the plebiscites which the Munich Agreement had called for in the disputed regions. There was no need for them.

The Poles and the Hungarians, after threatening military action against the helpless nation, now swept down, like vultures, to get a slice of Czechoslovak territory. Poland, at the insistence of Foreign Minister Józef Beck, took over some 650 square miles of territory around Teschen, comprising a population of 228,000 inhabitants, of whom 133,000 were Czechs. Hungary got a larger slice in the award meted out on November 2 by Ribbentrop and Italian Foreign Minister Ciano: 7,500 square miles, with a population of 500,000 Magyars and 272,000 Slovaks.

Moreover, the truncated and now defenseless

country was forced by Berlin to install a pro-German government of obvious fascist tendencies. It was clear that from now on the Czechoslovak nation existed at the mercy of the Leader of the Third Reich.

Under the terms of the agreement Czechoslovakia was forced to cede to Germany 11,000 square miles of territory, in which dwelt 2,800,000 Sudeten Germans and 800,000 Czechs. Within this area lay all the vast Czech fortifications which had formed the most formidable defensive line in Europe, with the possible exception of the French Maginot Line.

But that was not all. According to German figures, the dismembered country lost 66 percent of its coal, 86 percent of its chemicals, 70 percent of its iron and steel, 70 percent of its electric power. A prosperous industrial nation was split up and bankrupted overnight. And for what?

It has been argued that Munich gave the two Western democracies nearly a year to catch up with the Germans in rearmament. The facts belie such an argument. As Churchill, backed up by every serious Allied military historian, has written, "The year's breathing space said to be 'gained' by Munich left Britain and France in a much worse position compared to Hitler's Germany than they had been at the Munich crisis."

Germany was in no position to go to war against Czechoslovakia *and* France and Britain, not to mention Russia. Had she done so, she would have been quickly and easily defeated, and that would have been the end of the Third Reich.

For France, Munich was a disaster. Her military position in Europe was destroyed. After Munich, how could her remaining allies in Eastern Europe have any confidence in France's written word? What value now were alliances with France? The answer in Warsaw, Bucharest and Belgrade was, not much; and there was a scramble in these capitals to make the best deal possible, while there was still time, with the Nazi conqueror.

And yet, despite his staggering victory, Hitler was disappointed with the results of Munich. "That fellow," he exclaimed on his return to Berlin, "has spoiled my entry into Prague!" Chamberlain had forced the Czechs to submit to all his demands and thereby had deprived him of a *military* conquest of Czechoslovakia, which was what he had really wanted all along.

"It was clear to me from the first moment," he later confided to his generals, "that I could not be satisfied with the Sudeten German territory. That was only a partial solution."

A few days after Munich the German dictator set in motion plans to achieve a "total" solution.

Left: Prime Minister Daladier and German Foreign Minister Ribbentrop inspect an S.S. Guard of Honor in Munich during the Sudeten crisis.

Below left: The Munich Conference. Left to right, Mussolini, Hitler, Schmidt (interpreter) and Chamberlain.

Below: Chamberlain after returning from Munich with the signed agreement.

The Acme of Chicanery

Utterly disregarding his pledge to guarantee the frontiers of the rump Czech state, Hitler instituted a campaign of propaganda and internal subversion designed to force the nation to break up, which would afford him a pretext to march in and "restore order."

On March 14, 1939, with German armies poised along his country's frontiers, Dr. Emil Hácha, president of Czechoslovakia, who was suffering from a heart ailment, came to Berlin to plead with Hitler for his nation's life. The Fuehrer received him courteously enough but, when it became clear that he would accept nothing less than total surrender of the Czechs, Hácha and his foreign minister balked.

"The German ministers were pitiless," one diplomat reported. "They literally hounded Dr. Hácha and his foreign minister around the table on which the documents were lying, thrusting the papers continually before them, pushing pens into their hands, incessantly repeating that if they continued in their refusal half of Prague would lie in ruins from bombing within two hours."

At last, after having collapsed in a faint and been restored to consciousness by injections from a German doctor, Hácha was forced to sign. The official document said:

"The Czechoslovak president, in order to achieve pacification, placed the fate of the Czech people in the hands of the Fuehrer of the German Reich. The Fuehrer expressed his intention of taking the Czech people under the protection of the Reich, and of guaranteeing them autonomous development."

Hitler's chicanery had reached, perhaps, its summit. It did not occur to him – how could it? – that the end of Czechoslovakia might be the beginning of the end of Germany. From this dawn of March 15, 1939, the road to war, to defeat, to disaster, as we now know, stretched just ahead. It would be a short road and as straight as a line could be. And once hurtling down it, Hitler, like Napoleon before him, could not stop.

At 6 A.M. on March 15 German troops poured into Bohemia and Moravia. They met no resistance and by evening Hitler was able to make the triumphant entry into Prague which he felt Chamberlain had cheated him of at Munich. Before leaving Berlin he had issued a grandiose proclamation to the German people, repeating the tiresome lies about the "wild excesses" and "terror" of the

Below: Jubilant Sudeten Germans greet German troops crossing the frontier.

Czechs which he had been forced to bring an end to, and proudly proclaiming, "Czechoslovakia has ceased to exist!"

That night he slept in Hradschin Castle, the ancient seat of the kings of Bohemia high above the River Moldau where more recently the despised Masaryk and Beneš had lived and worked for the first democracy Central Europe had ever known. The Fuehrer's revenge was complete, and that it was sweet he showed in the series of proclamations which he issued. He had paid off all the burning resentments against the Czechs which had obsessed him as an Austrian in his vagabond days in Vienna three decades before and which had flamed anew when Beneš dared to oppose him, the all-powerful German dictator, over the previous year. A long night of German savagery now settled over Prague and the Czech lands.

But now, suddenly and unexpectedly, Neville Chamberlain experienced a great awakening. On March 17 he jettisoned a prepared speech on domestic policy and quickly jotted down notes for one of quite a different kind.

"We are told," he said, "that this seizure of territory has been necessitated by disturbances in Czechoslovakia. If there were disorders, were they not fomented from without? Is this the last attack upon a small state or is it to be followed by others? Is this, in effect, a step toward an attempt

to dominate the world by force? No greater mistake could be made than to suppose that this nation has so lost its fiber that it will not take part in resisting such a challenge if it ever were made."

It was obvious to anyone who had read *Mein Kampf*, or who glanced at a map and saw the new positions of the German Army in Slovakia, just which of the "small states" would be next on the Fuehrer's list. Chamberlain, like almost everyone else, knew perfectly well.

On March 31, sixteen days after Hitler entered Prague, Chamberlain spoke in the House of Commons:

"In the event of any action which clearly threatened Polish independence and which the Polish government considered it vital to resist with their national forces, His Majesty's government would feel themselves bound to lend the Polish government all support in their power. I may add that the French government has authorized me to make it plain that they take the same position." The turn of Poland had come.

Top: German police arrest Nazi opponents in the Sudetenland.

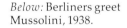

Below: Berliners greet Mussolini, 1938.

The "Pact of Steel"

The news of Chamberlain's guarantee of Poland threw the German dictator into one of his characteristic rages. According to an eyewitness he stormed about the room, pounding his fists on a marble tabletop, his face contorted with fury, shouting against the British, "I'll cook them a stew they'll choke on!"

The next day, April 1, he was in such a belligerent mood that apparently he did not quite trust himself, for at the last moment he ordered that the direct radio broadcast of a speech he was to make be canceled, and that it be broadcast later from recordings, which could be edited. Even the broadcast version was spotted with warnings to Britain and Poland. But, as so often before, Hitler ended on a note of "peace": "Germany has no intention of attacking other people."

That was for public consumption. In the greatest secrecy Hitler gave his real answer to Chamberlain two days later, on April 3. In a top-secret directive to the armed forces, of which only five copies were made, he inaugurated "Case White" – the attack on Poland. "Preparations," it stipulated, "must be made so that the operation can be carried out any time from September 1, 1939."

As in the case of the date Hitler gave planned in advance for getting the Sudetenland, this more important date would also be kept.

The question now was whether Hitler could wear down the Poles to the point of accepting his demands, as he had done the Austrians and the Czechs, or whether Poland would resist the Nazi aggression – and if so, with what.

This writer spent the first week of April in Poland in search of answers. They were, as far as he could see, that the Poles would not give in to Hitler's threats, but that militarily and politically they were in a disastrous position. Their air force was obsolete, their army cumbersome, their strategic position – surrounded by the Germans on three sides – almost hopeless.

Events now moved quickly. On April 7, Mussolini sent his troops into Albania. In the tense atmosphere of Europe this served to make the small countries which dared to defy the Axis more jittery. On April 13, France and Britain countered with a guarantee to Greece and Rumania. The two sides were beginning to line up.

Although the top brass of the Wehrmacht had a low opinion of Italian military power, Hitler now pressed for a military alliance with Italy, which Mussolini had been in no hurry to conclude. But on May 6, on a sudden impulse, Mussolini committed himself irrevocably to Hitler's fortunes, by agreeing to sign an alliance. The consequences for Mussolini would soon prove disastrous; this was, indeed, one of the first signs that the Italian dictator – like the German – was beginning to lose that iron self-control which until this year had enabled them both to pursue their own national interests with ice-cold clarity.

The "Pact of Steel," as it came to be known, was signed with considerable pomp at the Reich chancellery in Berlin on May 22. The core of the treaty was Article III:

"If one of the High Contracting Parties should become involved in warlike complications with another Power, the other High Contracting Party would immediately come to its assistance with all its military forces."

Article V provided that in the event of war neither nation would conclude a separate armistice or peace. In the beginning, as it would turn out, Mussolini did not honor the one article; nor, at the end, did Italy abide by the other.

Right: After the "Reichskristallnacht," a burned out synagogue in Munich. On the night of 9/10 November 1938, Jewish homes, businesses and synagogues throughout Germany were attacked by Nazi thugs, supposedly in retaliation for the murder of a German diplomat in Paris.

"Attack at the First Opportunity"

Above: Hitler Jungvolk on parade.

The day after the signing of the Pact of Steel, on May 23, Hitler summoned his military chiefs to the study in the Chancellery in Berlin and told them bluntly that further successes could not be won without the shedding of blood and that war therefore was inevitable.

This was a somewhat larger gathering than a similar one on November 5, 1937, when the Fuehrer had first imparted his decision to go to war to the commanders in chief of the three armed services. Altogether fourteen officers were present, including Field Marshal Goering, Grand Admiral Raeder (as he now was), General von Brauchitsch, General Halder, General Keitel, General Erhard Milch, Inspector General of the Lutwaffe, and Rear Admiral Otto Schniewind, naval Chief of Staff. The Fuehrer's adjutant, Lieutenant Colonel Rudolf Schmundt, was also present and, luckily for history, took notes. His minutes of the meeting are among the captured German documents. Apparently Hitler's words on this occasion were regarded as such a top secret that no copies of the minutes were made; the one we have is in Schmundt's own handwriting.

It is one of the most revealing and important of the secret papers which depict Hitler's road to war. Here, before the handful of men who will have to direct the military forces in an armed conflict, Hitler cuts through his own propaganda and diplomatic deceit and utters the truth about why he must attack Poland and, if necessary, take on Great Britain and France as well. He predicts with uncanny accuracy the course the war will take – at least in its first year. And yet for all its bluntness his discourse – for the dictator did all the talking – discloses more uncertainty and confusion of mind than he has shown up to this point. Above all, Britain and the British continue to baffle him, as they did to the end of his life.

But about the coming of war and his aims in launching it he is clear and precise, and no general or admiral could have left the Chancellery on May 23 without knowing exactly what was coming at the summer's end.

Germany's economic problems, he began, could be solved only by obtaining more *Lebensraum* in Europe, and "this is impossible without invading other countries or attacking other people's possessions. Further successes can no longer be attained without the shedding of blood. It is a question of expanding our living space in the East, of securing our food supplies and also of solving the problem of the Baltic states. There is no other possibility in Europe. If fate forces us into a

Left: S.A. and S.S. parade at Nuremberg.

showdown with the West it is invaluable to possess a large area in the East.''

Besides, Hitler adds, the population of non-German territories in the East will be available as a source of labor – an early hint of the slave-labor program he was later to put into effect.

The choice of the first victim was obvious.

''There is no question of sparing Poland, and we are left with the decision: *To attack Poland at the first suitable opportunity.* We cannot expect a repetition of the Czech affair. There will be war.'' So there will be war. With an ''isolated'' Poland alone? Here the Fuehrer is not so clear. In fact, he becomes confused and contradictory. He must reserve to himself, he says, the final order to strike. ''It must not come to a simultaneous showdown with the West – France and England. If it is not certain that a German-Polish conflict will not lead to war with the West, then the fight must be primarily against England and France.

''Fundamentally, therefore: conflict with Poland – beginning with an attack on Poland – will be successful only if the West keeps out of it. If that is not possible it is better to fall upon the West and to finish off Poland at the same time.''

In the face of such rapid-fire contradictions the generals must have winced, perhaps prying their monocles loose, though there is no evidence in the minutes that anyone in the audience even dared to ask a question to straighten matters out.

But then Hitler came down to earth again and outlined a strategic plan which later would be carried out with amazing success. ''The aim must be to deal the enemy a smashing blow right at the start. Considerations of right or wrong, or of treaties, do not enter into the matter.

''The army must occupy the positions important for the fleet and the Luftwaffe. If we succeed in occupying and securing Holland and Belgium, as well as defeating France, the basis for a successful war against England has been created.

''The Luftwaffe can then closely blockade England from France and the fleet undertake the wider blockade with submarines.''

That is precisely what would be done a little more than a year later.

On May 23, 1939, Hitler, as he himself said, burned his boats. There would be war. Germany needed *Lebensraum* in the East. To get it Poland would be attacked at the first opportunity. Britain stood in the way; very well, she would be taken on, too, and France. It would be a life-and-death struggle.

As May 1939 came to an end German preparations for war were well along. The great armament works were humming, turning out guns, tanks, planes and warships. The able staffs of the army, navy and air force had reached the final stage of planning. The ranks were being swelled by new men called up for ''summer training.''

But formidable as German military power was at the beginning of the summer of 1939, Germany was still not strong enough, and probably never would be, to take on France, Britain *and* Russia in addition to Poland. As the fateful summer commenced, all depended upon the Fuehrer's ability to limit the war – above all, to keep Russia from forming a military alliance with the West.

Below: Jews arrested after the ''Kristallnacht.''

Stalin, the Fuehrer's Partner

There was reason for Hitler's concern in this respect. On July 23, France and Britain agreed to Russia's proposal that military staff talks be held at once to draw up a convention which would spell out specifically how Hitler's armies were to be met by the three nations. But the Western powers did not think highly of Russia's military prowess, and when they finally sent a mission to negotiate with the Russians, it was sent on a passenger-cargo vessel which was extremely slow. The mission sailed for Leningrad on August 5 and did not arrive in Moscow until August 11. By that time it was too late. Hitler had already begun the diplomatic approaches that were to lead to the Nazi-Soviet non-aggression pact.

And so as the second half of August 1939 began, the German military chiefs pushed forward with their plans to annihilate Poland and to protect the western Reich just in case the democracies, contrary to all evidence, did intervene. On August 15 the annual Nuremberg Party Rally, which Hitler on April 1 had proclaimed as the "Party Rally of Peace" and which was scheduled to begin the first week in September, was secretly canceled. A quarter of a million men were called up for the armies of the west. Advance mobilization orders to the railways were given. Plans were made to move Army headquarters to Zossen, east of Berlin. And on the same day, August 15, the Navy reported that the pocket battleships *Graf Spee* and *Deutschland* and twenty-one submarines were ready to sail for their stations in the Atlantic.

On August 17 General Halder made a strange entry in his diary: "Canaris checked with Section I [Operations]. Himmler, Heydrich, Obersalzberg: 150 Polish uniforms with accessories for Upper Silesia."

What did it mean? It was only after the war that it became clear. It concerned one of the most bizarre incidents ever arranged by the Nazis. Just as Hitler and his Army chiefs, it will be remembered, had considered cooking up an "incident," such as the assassination of the German minister, in order to justify their invading Austria and Czechoslovakia, so now they concerned themselves, as time began to run out, with concocting an incident which would, at least in their opinion, justify before the world the planned aggression against Poland.

The code name was "Operation Himmler" and the idea was quite simple – and crude. The S.S.-Gestapo would stage a faked attack on the German radio station at Gleiwitz, near the Polish border, using condemned concentration camp inmates outfitted in Polish Army uniforms. Thus Poland could be blamed for attacking Germany. Early in August Admiral Canaris, chief of the Abwehr Section of OKW, had received an order from Hitler himself to deliver to Himmler and Heydrich 150 Polish uniforms and some Polish small arms. This struck him as a strange business and on August 17 he asked General Keitel about it.

While the spineless OKW Chief declared he did not think much of "actions of this kind," he nevertheless told the Admiral that "nothing could be done," since the order had come from the Fuehrer. Repelled though he was, Canaris obeyed his instructions and turned the uniforms and arms over to Heydrich.

The chief of the S.D. chose as the man to carry out the operation a young S.S. secret-service veteran by the name of Alfred Helmut Naujocks.

This was not the first of such assignments given this weird individual nor would it be the last. Early in March of 1939, shortly before the German occupation of Czechoslovakia, Naujocks, at Heydrich's instigation, had busied himself running explosives into Slovakia, where they were used, as he later testified, to "create incidents."

Alfred Naujocks was a typical product of the S.S.-Gestapo, a sort of intellectual gangster. He had studied engineering at Kiel University, where he got his first taste of brawling with anti-Nazis; on one occasion he had his nose bashed in by Communists. He had joined the S.S. in 1931 and was attached to the S.D. from its inception in 1934. Like so many other young men around Heydrich he dabbled in what passed as intellectual pursuits in the S.S. – "history" and "philosophy" especially – while rapidly emerging as a tough young man (Skorzeny was another) who could be entrusted with the carrying out of the less savory projects dreamed up by Himmler and Heydrich. On October 19, 1944, Naujocks deserted to the Americans and at Nuremberg a year later made a number of sworn affidavits, in one of which he preserved for history the account of the "incident" which Hitler used to justify his attack on Poland.

"On or about August 10, 1939, the chief of the S.D., Heydrich, personally ordered me to simulate an attack on the radio station near Gleiwitz near the Polish border [Naujocks related in an affidavit signed in Nuremberg November 20, 1945]

Above: Jewish shops looted in Berlin. The broken glass from such episodes gave the "Kristallnacht" its name.

and to make it appear that the attacking force consisted of Poles. Heydrich said: 'Practical proof is needed for these attacks on the Poles for the foreign press as well as for German propaganda.'

"My instructions were to seize the radio station and to hold it long enough to permit a Polish-speaking German who would be put at my disposal to broadcast a speech in Polish. Heydrich told me that this speech should state that the time had come for conflict between Germans and Poles . . . Heydrich also told me that he expected an attack on Poland by Germany in a few days.

"I went to Gleiwitz and waited there fourteen days . . . Between the 25th and 31st of August, I went to see Heinrich Mueller, head of the Gestapo, who was then nearby at Oppeln. In my presence, Mueller discussed with a man named Mehlhorn plans for another border incident, in which it should be made to appear that Polish soldiers were attacking German troops . . . Mueller stated that he had 12 to 13 condemned criminals who were to be dressed in Polish uniforms and left dead on the ground of the scene of the incident to show they had been killed while attacking. For this purpose they were to be given fatal injections by a doctor employed by Heydrich. Then they were also to be given gunshot wounds. After the incident members of the press and other persons were to be taken to the spot of the incident . . .

"Mueller told me he had an order from Heydrich to make one of those criminals available to me for the action at Gleiwitz. The code name by which he referred to these criminals was 'Canned Goods.'"

While Himmler, Heydrich and Mueller, at Hitler's command, were arranging for the use of "Canned Goods" to fake an excuse for Germany's aggression against Poland, the Fuehrer made his first decisive move to deploy his armed forces for a possibly bigger war. On August 19 – another fateful day – orders to sail were issued to the German

Above: Front cover of a Nazi women's magazine.

Right: Hitler inspects an S.S. guard at a 1938 parade.

Navy. Twenty-one submarines were directed to put out for positions north and northwest of the British Isles, the pocket battleship *Graf Spee* to depart for waters off the Brazilian coast and her sister ship, the *Deutschland*, to take a position athwart the British sea lanes in the North Atlantic.

The date of the order to dispatch the warships for possible action against Britain is significant. For on August 19, after a hectic week of frantic appeals from Berlin, the Soviet government finally gave Hitler the answer he wanted.

At 7:10 P.M. on August 19 came the anxiously awaited telegram from the German ambassador in Moscow:

SECRET. MOST URGENT. THE SOVIET GOVERNMENT AGREE TO THE REICH FOREIGN MINISTER COMING TO MOSCOW ON AUGUST 26 OR 27. MOLOTOV HANDED ME A DRAFT OF A NON-AGGRESSION PACT.

But, for the Germans, the date set for the meeting was not soon enough. If Ribbentrop was not received in Moscow before August 26 and then if the Russians stalled a bit, as the Germans feared, the target date of September 1 could not be kept. The whole timetable for the invasion of Poland, indeed the question of whether the attack could take place at all in the brief interval before the autumn rains, depended upon it.

At this crucial stage, Hitler himself intervened with Stalin. Swallowing his pride, he personally begged the Soviet dictator, whom he had for so long maligned, to receive his foreign minister in Moscow at once. During the next 24 hours, from the evening of Sunday, August 20, when Hitler's appeal to Stalin went out over the wires to Moscow, until the following evening, the Fuehrer was in a state bordering on collapse. He could not sleep. In the middle of the night he telephoned Goering to tell of his worries about Stalin's reaction to his message and to fret over the delays.

Next day Stalin's reply came:

THE SOVIET GOVERNMENT HAVE INSTRUCTED ME TO INFORM YOU THAT THEY AGREE TO HERR VON RIBBENTROP'S ARRIVING IN MOSCOW ON AUGUST 23. J. STALIN.

On August 22 Hitler, having received this indication from Stalin himself that Russia would be a friendly neutral, once more convoked his top military commanders and apprised them that he probably would order the attack on Poland to begin four days hence, on Saturday, August 26 – six days ahead of schedule.

Stalin, the Fuehrer's mortal enemy, had made this possible. For sheer cynicism the Nazi dictator had met his match in the Soviet despot. The way was now open to them to get together to dot the i's and cross the t's on one of the crudest deals of this shabby epoch.

What did the new partners sign?

The published treaty carried an undertaking that neither power would attack the other. Should one of them become "the object of belligerent action" by a third power, the other party would "in no manner lend its support to this third power." In a secret additional protocol Germany and Russia agreed to partition Poland.

On August 25 Marshal Kliment Voroshilov met with the French and British military missions in Moscow for the last time. "In view of the changed political situation," he said, "no useful purpose can be served in continuing our conversations."

Mussolini Weasels Out

Buoyed up by the good news from Moscow and confident that Great Britain and France would have second thoughts about honoring their obligations to Poland after the defection of Russia, the Fuehrer on the evening of August 23 set the date for the onslaught on Poland: Saturday, August 26, at 4:30 A.M.

"There will be no more orders regarding Y Day and X Hour," General Halder, chief of the army general staff, noted in his diary. *"Everything is to roll automatically."*

But he was wrong. On August 25 two events occurred which made Hitler shrink back, less than 24 hours before his troops were scheduled to break across the Polish frontier. On the afternoon of that day the Fuehrer had received the British ambassador and told him that he "accepted" the British Empire, and was ready "to pledge himself personally to its continued existence and to commit the power of the German Reich for this."

He desired, Hitler explained, "to make a move toward England which should be as decisive as the move toward Russia. The Fuehrer is ready to conclude agreements with England which not only would guarantee the existence of the British Empire in all circumstances so far as Germany is concerned, but would also assure the British Empire of German assistance regardless of where such assistance should be necessary."

His "large comprehensive offer" to Britain, as he described it, was subject to one condition: that it would take effect only *"after* the solution of the German-Polish problem."* This ridiculous offer was obviously a brainstorm of the moment, for how could the British government, as he requested, take it "very seriously" when Chamberlain would scarcely have time to read it before the Nazi armies hurtled into Poland at dawn on the morrow – the Y Day which still held?

But behind the "offer," no doubt, was a serious

Below: The Nazi Party Congress Hall at Nuremberg.

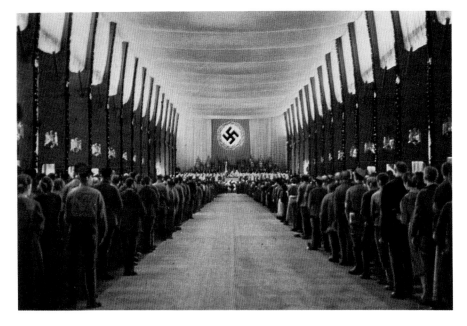

purpose. Hitler apparently believed that Chamberlain, like Stalin, wanted an out by which he could avoid going to war. Could he not buy Britain's non-intervention by assuring the prime minister that the Third Reich would never become a threat to the British Empire?

He got his answer at about 6 P.M. – the news of the signing in London of a formal Anglo-Polish treaty which transformed Britain's unilateral guarantee of Poland into a pact of mutual assistance. This meant that Hitler had failed in his bid to buy off the British as he had bought off the Russians. His interpreter, who was in Hitler's office when the report arrived, remembered later that the Fuehrer after reading it sat brooding at his desk.

Very shortly, his disconsolate brooding was interrupted by equally bad news from Rome. It struck the Fuehrer, according to the interpreter, like a bombshell. Mussolini, after expressing his "complete approval" of the Nazi-Soviet pact and his "understanding concerning Poland," came to the main point:

"If Germany attacks Poland and the latter's allies counterattack, I inform you that it will be opportune for me not to take the initiative in military operations in view of the present state of Italian war preparations. At our meetings the war was envisaged for 1942, and by that time I would have been ready."

Hitler read the Duce's letter and icily dismissed

Below: Hitler inspects panzers in Berlin on his birthday parade, April 20, 1939.

the Italian envoy. That evening the chancellery echoed with unkind words about the "disloyal Axis partner." But words were not enough. The German army was scheduled to hop off against Poland in nine hours. The Nazi dictator had to decide at once whether, in view of the news from London and Rome, to go ahead with the invasion or postpone or cancel it.

Pushed into a corner, Hitler swiftly made his decision: All troop movements would be stopped, the attack called off.

It took some doing to halt the German army, for many units were already on the move. One motorized column was halted on the border by a staff officer who made a quick landing in a small scout-

ing plane. In a few sectors the orders did not arrive until after the shooting had begun, but since the Germans had been provoking incidents all along the border for several days the Polish general staff apparently did not suspect what had really happened.

"Fuehrer considerably shaken." General Halder noted in his diary on August 25, after the news from Rome and London induced Hitler to draw back from the precipice of war. But it was rarely easy, even for his confidants, to penetrate the strange and fantastic workings of Hitler's fevered mind, affected as it was by now with acute megalomania. By the very next afternoon the chief of the general staff noticed an abrupt change in the Leader. "Fuehrer very calm and clear," he jotted in his diary.

There was a reason for this, and the general's journal gave it. "Get everything ready for morning of 7th Mobilization Day. Attack starts September 1."

And what of the Fuehrer's frame of mind that very night, the night of his irrevocable decision to plunge his nation, for the first time under his leadership, into all-out war? Here is an eyewitness description:

"Hitler suddenly got up and, becoming very excited and nervous, walked up and down saying, as though to himself, that Germany was irresistible. Suddenly he stopped in the middle of the room and stood staring. His voice was blurred, and his behavior that of a completely abnormal person. He spoke in staccato phrases: 'If there should be war, then I shall build U-boats, build U-boats, U-boats, U-boats, U-boats.'

"His voice became more indistinct, and finally one could not follow him at all. Then he pulled himself together, raised his voice as though addressing a large audience and shrieked: 'I shall build airplanes, build airplanes, airplanes, airplanes, and I shall annihilate my enemies!' He seemed more like a phantom from a storybook than a real person."

Such was the atmosphere in which World War II was launched.

Above: Hitler with President Hacha of Czechoslovakia in Berlin, March 14, 1939, the day before Hitler announced the establishment of the German 'Protectorate' of Bohemia and Moravia.

Above: German troops enter Prague, March 1939.

Right: Massed ranks of S.A. at Nuremberg.

Hitler Makes His Final Decision

During these last days of peace, the overwrought and exhausted diplomats of all the nations concerned made innumerable scrambling 11th-hour attempts at mediation. They were but a flailing of the air, completely futile, and, in the case of the Germans, entirely and purposely deceptive.

For at half after noon on August 31, Adolf Hitler had taken his final decision and issued the decisive order that was to throw the planet into its bloodiest war.

SUPREME COMMANDER OF THE
ARMED FORCES
MOST SECRET

Berlin, August 31, 1939: Directive No. 1 for the Conduct of the War

1. Now that all the *political possibilities* of disposing by peaceful means of a situation which is intolerable for Germany are exhausted, I have determined on a *solution by force*.
2. The *attack on Poland* is to be carried out.
  Date of attack: Sept. 1, 1939.
  Time of attack: 4:45 a.m.

Hitler was still not quite sure what Britain and France would do. He would refrain from attacking them first. If they took hostile action, he was prepared to meet it. As darkness settled over Europe on the evening of August 31, 1939, and a million and a half German troops began moving forward for the jump-off at dawn, all that remained for Hitler to do was to perpetrate some propaganda trickery to prepare the German people for war.

Above: S.A. standard bearer.

Left: Hitler addressing members of the Condor Legion on their return from Spain, June 7, 1939. The banners on either side of the platform bear the names of Germans killed in Spain.

Above: Czechs protest as German troops enter Prague.

Below: Jews being expelled from Memel, March 1939. Under German pressure, Lithuania ceded the Memel district to Germany in that month.

They were in need of the propaganda treatment which Hitler, abetted by Goebbels and Himmler, had become so expert in applying. I had been about in the streets of Berlin, talking with the ordinary people, and that morning noted in my diary: "Everybody against the war. People talking openly. How can a country go into a major war with a population so dead against it?"

Despite all my experience in the Third Reich I asked such a naïve question! Hitler knew the answer very well. The week before on his Bavarian mountaintop he had promised the generals that he would "give a propagandist reason for starting the war" and admonished them not to "mind whether it was plausible or not." "The victor," he told them, "will not be asked afterward whether he told the truth. In starting and waging a war it is not right that matters, but victory."

Now there remained only the concocting of a deed which would "prove" that not Germany but Poland had attacked first.

For this shady business, it will be remembered, the Germans, at Hitler's direction, had made careful preparation. For six days Alfred Naujocks, the intellectual S.S. ruffian, had been waiting at Gleiwitz on the Polish border to carry out a simulated Polish attack on the German radio station there. The plan had been revised. S.S. men outfitted in Polish Army uniforms were to do the shooting, and drugged concentration camp inmates were to be left dying as "casualties" – this last delectable part of the operation had, as we have seen, the expressive code name "Canned Goods." There were to be several such faked "Polish attacks" but the principal one was to be on the radio station at Gleiwitz.

"At noon on August 31" [Naujocks related in his Nuremberg affidavit] "I received from Heydrich the code word for the attack which was to take place at 8 o'clock that evening. Heydrich said: 'In order to carry out this attack report to Mueller for Canned Goods.' I did this and gave Mueller instructions to deliver the man near the radio station. I received this man and had him laid down at the entrance to the station. He was alive but completely unconscious. I tried to open his eyes. I could not recognize by his eyes that he was alive, only by his breathing. I did not see the gun

wounds but a lot of blood was smeared across his face. He was in civilian clothes.

"We seized the radio station, as ordered, broadcast a speech of three to four minutes over an emergency transmitter, fired some pistol shots and left."

Berlin that evening was largely shut off from the outside world, except for outgoing press dispatches and broadcasts which reported the Fuehrer's "offer" to Poland and the German allegations of Polish "attacks" on German territory. I tried to get through on the telephone to Warsaw, London and Paris but was told that communications with these capitals were cut. Berlin itself was quite normal in appearance. There had been no evacuation of women and children, as there had been in Paris and London, nor any sandbagging of storefront windows, as was reported from the other capitals. Toward 4 A.M. on September 1, after my last broadcast, I drove back from Broadcasting House to the Adlon Hotel. There was no traffic. The houses were dark. The people were asleep and perhaps – for all I knew – had gone to bed hoping for the best, for peace.

Hitler himself had been in fine fettle all day. At 6 P.M. on August 31 General Halder noted in his diary, "Fuehrer calm; has slept well . . . Decision against evacuation [in the west] shows that he expects France and England will not take action."

Admiral Canaris, chief of the Abwehr in OKW and one of the key anti-Nazi conspirators, was in a different mood. Though Hitler was carrying Germany into war, an action which the Canaris circle had supposedly sworn to prevent by getting rid of the dictator, there was no conspiracy in being now that the moment for it had arrived.

Later in the afternoon Gisevius had been summoned to OKW headquarters by Colonel Oster. This nerve center of Germany's military might was humming with activity. Canaris drew Gisevius aside down a dimly lit corridor. In a voice that choked with emotion he said: "This means the end of Germany."

At daybreak next morning, the very date which Hitler had set on April 3, the German armies poured across the Polish frontier and converged on Warsaw from the north, south and west.

In Berlin, the people in the streets were apathetic, despite the immensity of the news which greeted them in the morning newspapers. Perhaps they were simply dazed at waking up to find themselves in a war which they had been sure the Fuehrer somehow would avoid.

There were no such demonstrations as those of 1914 for the troops or for the Nazi warlord, who shortly before 10 A.M. drove from the Chancellery to the Reichstag through empty streets to address the nation on the momentous happenings which he himself, deliberately and cold-bloodedly, had just provoked. Even the robot members of the Reichstag, party hacks, for the most part, whom Hitler had appointed, failed to respond with much enthusiasm as the dictator launched into his explanation of why Germany found itself on this morning engaged in war. There was far less cheering than on previous and less important occasions when the Leader had declaimed from this tribune in the ornate hall of the Kroll Opera House.

Though truculent at times he seemed strangely on the defensive, and throughout the speech, I thought as I listened, ran a curious strain, as though he himself were dazed at the fix he had got himself into and felt a little desperate about it. His explanation of why his Italian ally had reneged on its automatic obligations to come to his aid did not seem to go over even with this hand-picked audience: "I should like here above all to thank Italy, which throughout has supported us, but you will understand that for the carrying out of this struggle we do not intend to appeal for foreign help. We will carry out this task ourselves."

Having lied so often on his way to power and in his consolidation of power, Hitler could not refrain at this serious moment in history from thundering a few more lies to the gullible German people in justification of his wanton act. "You know the endless attempt I made for a peaceful clarification and understanding of the problem of Austria, and later of the problem of the Sudetenland, Bohemia and Moravia. It was all in vain.

"In my talks with Polish statesmen . . . I formulated at last the German proposals and . . . there is nothing more modest or loyal than these proposals. I should like to say this to the world. I alone was in the position to make such proposals, for I know very well that in doing so I brought myself into opposition to millions of Germans. These proposals have been refused."

Now there was no way out. On September 3, Great Britain and France declared war on Germany. That same night, at 9 P.M., the German submarine U-30 torpedoed and sank the British liner *Athenia* some 200 miles west of the Hebrides; 112 passengers, including 28 Americans, lost their lives.

World War II had begun.

Below: The signing of the Nazi-Soviet Non-Aggression Pact August 23, 1939. Molotov replaces his pen in the inkstand while behind, Ribbentrop, center, and Stalin, right, share a joke.

Blitzkrieg!

Brave and valiant and foolhardy though they were – at one point they actually counterattacked Nazi tanks with horse cavalry – the Poles were simply overwhelmed by the German onslaught. This was their, and the world's, first experience of the blitzkrieg: the sudden surprise attack; the fighter planes and bombers roaring overhead, spreading flame and terror; the Stukas screaming as they dived; the tanks, whole divisions of them, breaking through and thrusting forward 30 or 40 miles in a day; the incredible speed of even the infantry, of the whole vast army of a million and a half men on motorized wheels, coordinated through a maze of electronic communications. This was a mechanized juggernaut such as the earth had never seen.

Within 48 hours the Polish air force was destroyed and in one week the Polish army was vanquished, most of its 35 divisions either shattered or caught in a pincer movement that closed around Warsaw. By September 17 all Polish forces, except a handful on the Russian border, were surrounded. All was over except the dying, in the ranks of Polish units which still, with incredible fortitude, held out.

Below: Hitler addresses the Reichstag at the outbreak of war, September 1, 1939.

It was now time for the Russians to move in on the stricken country to grab a share of the spoils.

The Kremlin, like every other seat of government, had been taken by surprise at the rapidity with which the German armies hurtled through Poland. Their success was most embarrassing to the Russians. On what pretext could they now intervene against the fallen state? On September 17 there was disagreement between the two unnatural partners over the text of a joint communiqué which would "justify" the Russo-German destruction of Poland. Stalin objected to the German version because "it presented the facts all too frankly." Whereupon he wrote out his own version, a masterpiece of subterfuge, and forced the Germans to accept it. It stated that the joint aim of Germany and Russia was "to restore peace and order in Poland, which has been destroyed by the disintegration of the Polish state, and to help the Polish people to establish new conditions for its political life." On that shabby pretext, beginning on the morning of September 17, the Soviet Union trampled over a prostrate Poland. The next day Soviet troops met the Germans at Brest Litovsk.

So Poland, like Austria and Czechoslovakia before it, disappeared from the map of Europe. But this time Hitler was aided and abetted in his obliteration of a country by the U.S.S.R., which had posed for so long as the champion of oppressed peoples. Hitler fought and won the war in Poland, but the greater winner was Stalin, whose troops scarcely fired a shot. The Soviet Union got nearly half of Poland and a stranglehold on the Baltic states. It blocked Germany from two

main long-term objectives: Ukrainian wheat and Rumanian oil, both badly needed if Germany was to survive the British blockade. Even Poland's oil region, which Hitler desired, was claimed successfully by Stalin.

Why did Hitler pay such a high price to the Russians? It is true that he had agreed to it in August, in order to keep the Soviet Union out of the Allied camp and out of the war. But he had never been a stickler for keeping agreements and now, with Poland conquered by an incomparable feat of German arms, he might have been expected to welsh, as his army urged, on the August 23 pact. If Stalin objected, the Fuehrer could threaten him with attack by the most powerful army in the world, as the Polish campaign had proved it to be.

Or could he? Not while the British and French stood at arms in the West. To deal with Britain and France he must keep his rear free. This, as subsequent utterances of his would make clear, was the reason why he allowed Stalin to strike such a hard bargain. But he did not forget the Soviet dictator's harsh dealings as he now turned his attention to the western front.

Nothing much had happened there. Hardly a shot had been fired. The German man in the street was beginning to call it the "sit-down war" – *Sitzkrieg*. In the west it would soon be dubbed the "phony war." Here was the French army, "the strongest in the world," as British General J. F. C. Fuller would put it, "facing no more than 26 German divisions, sitting still and sheltering behind steel and concrete while a quixotically valiant ally was being exterminated!"

Above: Racial Germans murdered by Poles at Bromberg, September 3, 1939.

Right: Hitler speaking with General von Reichenau, commander of the German Tenth Army in Poland, September 1939. To the right, behind Reichenau, General Rommel, at that time a member of Hitler's headquarters' staff.

Above: Polish cavalry in action.

For the West, the inaction was costly. As General Halder said at Nuremberg, "The success against Poland was only possible by almost completely baring our western border. The French would have been able to cross the Rhine without our being able to prevent it." Why then did not the French army, which had overwhelming superiority over the German forces in the west, attack, as General Gamelin and the French government had promised the Poles in writing it would?

There were many reasons: defeatism in the French high command, the government and the people; the memories of how France had been bled white in World War I and a determination not to suffer such slaughter again if it could be avoided; the realization by mid-September that the Polish armies were so badly defeated that the Germans would soon be able to move superior forces to the west and thus probably wipe out any initial French advances; the fear of German superiority in arms and in the air.

But now the opportunity for any effective offense had been lost. Hitler could turn his full attention, and the bulk of his forces, to the west.

On October 9, against the advice of his generals, who wanted time to refit the tanks used in Poland, the Fuehrer issued Directive No. 6 for the conduct of the war:

TOP SECRET

Preparations are to be made for an attack through Luxembourg, Belgium and Holland at as early a date as possible.

A secret memorandum which Hitler read to his military chiefs before presenting them the direc-tive showed not only a remarkable grasp of military strategy and tactics but a prophetic sense of how the war in the west would develop. The chief thing, he said, was to avoid the positional warfare of 1914-18. The armored divisions must be used for the crucial breakthrough:

"They are not to be lost among the maze of endless rows of houses in Belgian towns. It is not necessary for them to attack towns at all, but to maintain the flow of the army's advance."

As for the time of the attack, Hitler told his reluctant generals, "The start cannot take place too early. It is to take place in all circumstances (if at all possible) this autumn." But despite his insistence on haste, delay after delay ensued.

As the momentous year of 1939 approached its end Hitler realized, as he had told his generals in his memorandum of October 9, that Soviet neutrality could not be counted on forever. In eight months or a year, he had said, things might change. And in his harangue to them on November 23 he had emphasized that "we can oppose Russia only when we are free in the West." This was a thought which never left his restless mind.

The fateful year faded into history in a curious and even eerie atmosphere. Though there was world war, there was no fighting on land, and in the skies the big bombers carried only propaganda pamphlets, and badly written ones at that. Only at sea was there actual warfare. U-boats continued to take their toll of British and sometimes neutral shipping in the cruel, icy northern Atlantic.

In the South Atlantic the *Graf Spee*, one of Germany's three pocket battleships, had emerged from its waiting area and in three months had sunk nine British cargo vessels totaling 50,000 tons. Then, a fortnight before the first Christmas of the war, on December 14, 1939, the German public was electrified by the news, splashed in flaming headlines and in bulletins flashed over the radio, of a great victory at sea. The *Graf Spee*, it was said, had engaged three British cruisers on the previous day four hundred miles off Montevideo and put them out of action. But elation soon turned to puzzlement. Three days later the press announced that the pocket battleship had scuttled herself in the Plate estuary just outside the Uruguayan capital. What kind of victory was that? On December 21, the High Command of the Navy announced that the *Graf Spee*'s commander, Captain Hans Langsdorff, had "followed his ship" and thus "fulfilled like a fighter and hero the expectations of his Fuehrer, the German people and the Navy."

The wretched German people were never told that the *Graf Spee* had been severely damaged by the three British cruisers, which it outgunned, that it had had to put into Montevideo for repairs, that the Uruguayan government, in accordance with international law, had allowed it to remain for only seventy-two hours, which was not enough, that the "hero," Captain Langsdorff, rather than risk further battle with the British with his crippled ship, had therefore scuttled it, and that he himself, instead of going down with her, had shot himself two days afterward in a lonely hotel room in Buenos Aires.

On January 13, 1940, the Nazi warlord postponed the onslaught on the Low Countries indefinitely "on account of the meteorological situa-

Above: German infantry and tanks in Warsaw.

tion." Weather may have played a part in the calling off of the attack, but we now know that plans for a daring German assault on two other little neutral states farther to the north had in the meantime been ripening in Berlin and now took priority. The phony war, so far as the Germans were concerned, was coming to an end with the approach of spring.

Left: German troops pass dead Poles.

The Strike to the North

The innocent-sounding code name for the latest plan of German aggression was *Weseruebung*, or "Weser Exercise." Its origins and development were unique, quite unlike those for unprovoked attack that have filled so large a part of this narrative. It was not the brain child of Hitler, as were all the others, but of an ambitious admiral and a muddled Nazi party hack. It was the only act of German military aggression in which the German Navy played the decisive role. It was also the only one for which OKW did the planning and co-ordinating of the three armed services. In fact, the Army High Command and its General Staff were not even consulted, much to their annoyance, and Goering was not brought into the picture until the last moment – a slight that infuriated the corpulent chief of the Luftwaffe.

The German Navy had long had its eyes on the north. Germany had no direct access to the wide ocean, a geographical fact which had been imprinted on the minds of its naval officers during the First World War. A tight British net across the narrow North Sea, from the Shetland Islands to the coast of Norway, maintained by a mine bar-

rage and a patrol of ships, had bottled up the powerful Imperial Navy, seriously hampered the attempts of U-boats to break out into the North Atlantic, and kept German merchant shipping off the seas. The German High Seas Fleet never reached the high seas. The British naval blockade stifled Imperial Germany in the first war. Between the wars the handful of German naval officers who commanded the country's modestly sized Navy pondered this experience and this geographical fact and came to the conclusion that in any future war with Britain, Germany must try to gain bases in Norway, which would break the British blockade line across the North Sea, open up the broad ocean to German surface and undersea vessels and indeed offer an opportunity for the Reich to reverse the tables and mount an effective blockade of the British Isles.

It was not surprising, then, that at the outbreak of war in 1939 Admiral Rolf Carls, the third-ranking officer in the German Navy and a forceful personality, should start peppering Admiral Raeder, as the latter noted in his diary and testified at Nuremberg, with letters suggesting "the importance of an occupation of the Norwegian coast by Germany." Raeder needed little urging and on October 3, at the end of the Polish campaign, sent a confidential questionnaire to the Naval War Staff asking it to ascertain the possibility of gaining "bases in Norway under the combined pressure of Russia and Germany." Ribbentrop was consulted about Moscow's attitude and replied that "far-reaching support may be

Below: S.S. soldiers clearing a street in Warsaw.

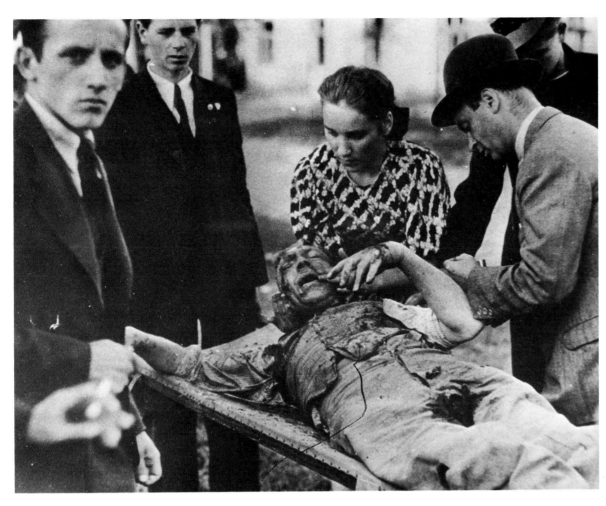

Left: A wounded Pole is taken for medical treatment after a German air raid on Warsaw.

Below: Triumphant, the Fuehrer salutes his troops in Poland.

Above: German troops pose with a Russian motorcyclist on the demarcation line in occupied Poland, September 1939.

preoccupied with launching his attack in the West and with overcoming the hesitations of his generals. Norway apparently slipped out of his mind.

But it came back in two months – for three reasons.

One was the advent of winter. Germany's very existence depended upon the import of iron ore from Sweden. For the first war year the Germans were counting on eleven million tons of it out of a total annual consumption of fifteen million tons. During the warm-weather months this ore was transported from northern Sweden down the Gulf of Bothnia and across the Baltic to Germany, and presented no problem even in wartime, since the Baltic was effectively barred to British submarines and surface ships. But in the wintertime this shipping lane could not be used because of thick ice. During the cold months the Swedish ore had to be shipped by rail to the nearby Norwegian port of Narvik and brought down the Norwegian coast by ship to Germany. For almost the entire journey German ore vessels could sail within Norway's territorial waters and thereby escape destruction by British naval vessels and bombers.

Thus, as Hitler at first pointed out to the Navy, a neutral Norway had its advantages. It enabled Germany to obtain its lifeblood of iron ore without interference from Britain.

In London, Churchill, then First Lord of the Admiralty, perceived this at once and in the very first weeks of the war attempted to persuade the cabinet to allow him to lay mines in Norwegian territorial waters in order to stop the German iron traffic. But Chamberlain and Halifax were most reluctant to violate Norwegian neutrality, and the proposal was for the time being dropped.

Russia's attack on Finland on November 30, 1939, radically changed the situation in Scandinavia, immensely increasing its strategic importance

expected" from that source. Raeder told his staff that Hitler must be informed as soon as possible about the "possibilities."

On October 10, in the course of a lengthy report to the Fuehrer on naval operations, Raeder suggested the importance of obtaining naval bases in Norway, if necessary with the help of Russia. This – so far as the confidential records show – was the first time the Navy had directly called the matter to the attention of Hitler. Raeder says the Leader "saw at once the significance of the Norwegian problem." He asked him to leave his notes on the subject and promised to give the question some thought. But at the moment the Nazi warlord was

Right: Polish prisoners of war being interviewed by the Germans.

Left: Jewish Ghetto Police on a 'razzia' in Warsaw, 1940.

Below: Starving Jewish children in the Warsaw Ghetto.

to both the Western Allies and Germany. France and Britain began to organize an expeditionary force in Scotland to be sent to the aid of the gallant Finns, who, defying all predictions, held out stubbornly against the onslaughts of the Red Army. But it could reach Finland only through Norway and Sweden, and the Germans at once saw that if Allied troops were granted, or took, transit across the northern part of the two Scandinavian lands enough of them would remain, on the excuse of maintaining communications, to completely cut off Germany's supply of Swedish iron ore. Moreover, the Western Allies would outflank the Reich on the north. Admiral Raeder was not backward in reminding Hitler of these threats.

The chief of the German Navy had now found in Norway itself a valuable ally for his designs in the person of Major Vidkun Abraham Lauritz Quisling, whose name would soon become a synonym in almost all languages for a traitor.

Quisling had begun life honorably enough. Born in 1887 of peasant stock, he had graduated first in his class at the Norwegian Military Academy and while still in his twenties had been sent to Petrograd as military attaché. For his services in looking after British interests after diplomatic relations were broken with the Bolshevik government, Great Britain awarded him the C.B.E. At this time he was both pro-British and pro-Bolshevik. He remained in Soviet Russia for some time as assistant to Fridtjof Nansen, the great Norwegian explorer and humanitarian, in relief work.

So impressed had the young Norwegian Army officer been by the success of the Communists in Russia that when he returned to Oslo he offered his services to the Labor Party, which at that time was a member of the Comintern. He proposed that he establish a "Red Guard," but the Labor Party was suspicious of him and his project and turned him down. He then veered to the opposite extreme. After serving as Minister of Defense from 1931 to 1933, he founded in May of the latter year a fascist party called Nasjonal Samling – National Union – appropriating the ideology and tactics of the Nazis, who had just come to power in

Right: Elderly Jews forced to clear rubble in Warsaw.

Below: Hitler with Admiral Raeder, left.

Germany. But Nazism did not thrive in the fertile democratic soil of Norway. Quisling was unable even to get himself elected to Parliament. Defeated at the polls by his own people, he turned to Nazi Germany.

There he established contact with Alfred Rosenberg, the befuddled official philosopher of the Nazi movement, among whose jobs was that of chief of the party's Office for Foreign Affairs. This Baltic dolt, one of Hitler's earliest mentors, thought he saw possibilities in the Norwegian officer, for one of Rosenberg's pet fantasies was the establishment of a Nordic Empire from which the Jews and other "impure" races would be excluded and which eventually would dominate the world under Nazi German leadership. From 1933 on, he kept in touch with Quisling and heaped on him his nonsensical philosophy and propaganda.

In June 1939, as the war clouds gathered over Europe, Quisling took the occasion of his attendance at a convention of the Nordic Society at Luebeck to ask Rosenberg for something more than ideological support. According to the latter's confidential reports, which were produced at Nuremberg, Quisling warned Rosenberg of the danger of Britain's getting control of Norway in the event of war and of the advantages to Germany of occupying it. He asked for substantial aid for his party and press. Rosenberg, a great composer of memoranda, dashed out three of them for Hitler, Goering and Ribbentrop, but the three top men appear to have ignored them – no one in Germany took the "official philosopher" very seriously. Rosenberg himself was able to arrange at least for a fortnight's training course in Germany in August for twenty-five of Quisling's husky storm troopers.

During the first months of the war Admiral Raeder – or so he testified at Nuremberg – had no contact with Rosenberg, whom he scarcely knew, and none with Quisling, of whom he had never heard. But immediately after the Russian attack on Finland Raeder began to get reports from his naval attaché at Oslo, Captain Richard Schreiber, of imminent Allied landing in Norway. He mentioned these to Hitler on December 8 and advised him flatly, "It is important to occupy Norway."

Shortly afterward Rosenberg dashed off a memorandum (undated) to Admiral Raeder "regarding visit of Privy Councilor Quisling – Norway." The Norwegian conspirator had arrived in Berlin and Rosenberg thought Raeder ought to be told who he was and what he was up to. Quisling, he said, had many sympathizers among key officers in the Norwegian Army and, as proof, had shown him a recent letter from Colonel Konrad Sundlo, the commanding officer at Narvik, characterizing Norway's Prime Minister as a "blockhead" and one of his chief ministers as "an old soak" and declaring his willingness to "risk his bones for the national uprising." Later Colonel Sundlo did not risk his bones to defend his country.

Actually, Rosenberg informed Raeder, Quisling had a plan for a coup. It must have fallen upon sympathetic ears in Berlin, for it was copied from the Anschluss. A number of Quisling's storm troopers would be hurriedly trained in Germany "by experienced and diehard National Socialists who are practiced in such operations." The pupils, once back in Norway, would seize strategic points in Oslo, "and at the same time the German Navy with contingents of the German Army will have to put in an appearance at a prearranged bay outside Oslo in answer to a special summons from the new Norwegian Government." It was the Anschluss tactic all over again, with Quisling playing the part of Seyss-Inquart. "Quisling has no doubt [Rosenberg added] that such a coup . . . would meet with the approval of those sections of the Army with which he now has connections . . . As regards the King, he believes that he would accept such a *fait accompli*. Quisling's estimate of the number of German troops needed for the operation coincides with the German estimates."

Admiral Raeder saw Quisling on December 11, the meeting being arranged through Rosenberg by one Viljam Hagelin, a Norwegian businessman whose affairs kept him largely in Germany and who was Quisling's chief liaison there. Hagelin and Quisling told Raeder a mouthful and he duly recorded it in the confidential naval archives. "Quisling stated . . . a British landing is planned in the vicinity of Stavanger, and Christiansand is proposed as a possible British base. The present Norwegian Government as well as the Parliament and the whole foreign policy are controlled by the well-known Jew, Hambro [Carl Hambro, the President of the Storting], a great friend of Hore-Belisha . . . The dangers to Germany arising from a British occupation were depicted in great detail."

To anticipate a British move, Quisling proposed to place "the necessary bases at the disposal of the German Armed Forces. In the whole coastal area men in important positions (railway, post office, communications) have already been bought for this purpose." He and Hagelin had come to Berlin to establish "clear-cut relations with Germany for the future."

It was concern for Germany's supplies of Swedish iron ore that persuaded Hitler to adopt the plan. But when he hastily issued the order to "put units in readiness," no army officer had yet been designated to lead the enterprise. Someone suggested General Nikolaus von Falkenhorst, who had fought in Finland at the end of World War I, and Hitler immediately sent for him.

Falkenhorst later described in an interrogation at Nuremberg their first meeting at the Chancellery on the morning of February 21, which was not without its amusing aspects. Falkenhorst had never even heard of the "North" operation and this was the first time he had faced the Nazi warlord, who apparently did not awe him as he had all the other generals.

"I was made to sit down [he recounted at Nuremberg]. Then I had to tell the Fuehrer about the operations in Finland in 1918 . . . He said: 'Sit down and just tell me how it was,' and I did. Then we got up and he led me to a table that was cov-

Above: U-boat on Atlantic patrol.

ered with maps. He said: ' . . . The Reich Government has knowledge that the British intend to make a landing in Norway . . . '" And the General, to his surprise, found himself appointed then and there to do the carrying out as commander in chief. The Army, Hitler added, would put five divisions at his disposal. The idea was to seize the main Norwegian ports.

At noon the warlord dismissed Falkenhorst and told him to report back at 5 P.M. with his plans for the occupation of Norway.

"I went out and bought a Baedeker, a travel guide [Falkenhorst explained at Nuremberg], in order to find out just what Norway was like. I didn't have any idea . . . Then I went to my hotel room and I worked on this Baedeker . . . At 5 P.M. I went back to the Fuehrer."

The General's plans, worked out from an old Baedeker – he was never shown the plans worked out by OKW – were, as can be imagined, somewhat sketchy, but they seem to have satisfied Hitler. One division was to be allotted to each of Norway's five principal harbors, Oslo, Stavanger, Bergen, Trondheim and Narvik. "There wasn't much else you could do," Falkenhorst said later, "because they were the large harbors." After be-

A King Rallies His People

Above: German cartoon of November 1939 caricaturing Hoare-Belisha and Churchill (then Britain's army and navy minister, respectively) as conspirators in the supposed assassination attempt on Hitler in that month. In fact the plot was faked by the Nazis for their own purposes.

Weseruebung was ordered to begin at 5:15 A.M. on April 9, 1940. At precisely an hour before dawn on that day, the German envoys in Copenhagen and Oslo presented to the Danish and Norwegian governments a German ultimatum demanding that they accept on the instant, and without resistance, the "protection of the Reich." The ultimatum was perhaps the most brazen document yet composed by Hitler and Ribbentrop.

The Danes were in a hopeless position. Their pleasant, flat little country was incapable of defense against Hitler's panzers. The army fought a few skirmishes, but by the time the Danes had finished their hearty breakfasts it was all over. The king, on the advice of his government, capitulated and ordered resistance to cease.

Resistance began in Norway from the outset, though certainly not everywhere. At Narvik, the port and railhead of the iron ore line from Sweden, Colonel Konrad Sundlo, in command of the local garrison, who, as we have seen, was a fanatical follower of Quisling, surrendered to the Germans without firing a shot. The naval commander was of a different caliber. With the approach of ten German destroyers at the mouth of the long fjord, the *Eidsvold*, one of two ancient ironclads in the harbor, fired a warning shot and signaled to the destroyers to identify themselves. Rear Admiral Fritz Bonte, commanding the German destroyer flotilla, answered by sending an officer in a launch to the Norwegian vessel to demand surrender. There now followed a bit of German treachery, though German naval officers later defended it with the argument that in war necessity knows no law. When the officer in the launch signaled the German Admiral that the Norwegians had said they would resist, Bonte waited only until his launch got out of the way and then quickly blew up the *Eidsvold* with torpedoes. The second Norwegian ironclad, the *Norge*, then opened fire but was quickly dispatched. Three hundred Norwegian sailors – almost the entire crews of the two vessels – perished. By 8 A.M. Narvik was in the hands of the Germans, taken by ten destroyers which had slipped through a formidable British fleet, and occupied by a mere two battalions of Nazi troops under the command of Brigadier General Eduard Dietl, an old Bavarian crony of Hitler since the days of the Beer Hall Putsch, who was to prove himself a resourceful and courageous commander when the going at Narvik got rough, as it did beginning the next day.

Trondheim, halfway down the long Norwegian west coast, was taken by the Germans almost as easily. The harbor batteries failed to fire on the German naval ships, led by the heavy cruiser *Hipper*, as they came up the long fjord, and the troops aboard that ship and four destroyers were conveniently disembarked at the city's piers without interference. Some forts held out for a few hours and the nearby airfield at Vaernes for two days, but this resistance did not affect the occupation of

ing sworn to secrecy and urged "to hurry up," the General was again dismissed to set to work.

Of all these goings on, Brauchitsch and Halder, busy preparing the offensive on the Western front, were largely ignorant until Falkenhorst called on the Army General Staff Chief on February 26 and demanded some troops, especially mountain units, to carry out his operation. Halder was not very cooperative; in fact, he was indignant and asked for more information on what was up and what was needed. "Not a single word on this matter has been exchanged between the Fuehrer and Brauchitsch," Halder exclaimed in his diary. "That must be recorded for the history of the war!"

However, Hitler, full of contempt as he was for the old-line generals and especially for his General Staff Chief, was not to be put off. On March 29 he enthusiastically approved Falkenhorst's plans, including his acquisiton of two mountain divisions, and moreover declared that more troops would be necessary because he wanted "a strong force at Copenhagen." Denmark had definitely been added to the list of victims; the Air Force had eyes on bases there to be used against Britain.

The next day, March 1, Hitler issued the formal directive for Weser Exercise.

München, 15. Oktober 1939
44. Jahrgang / Nummer 41

30 Pfennig

SIMPLICISSIMUS

VERLAG KNORR & HIRTH KOMMANDITGESELLSCHAFT, MÜNCHEN

Left: German propaganda on the French border. The sign tells of Hitler's desire "to bury forever the old emnity between Germany and France."

Below: German cartoon of October 1939 showing John Bull isolated on his island and surrounded by U-boats.

Englands Selbsteinkreisung

„Gefahr von unten und oben — eine Situation, aus der man sich schwer herauslügen kann!"

the fine harbor suitable for the largest naval ships as well as submarines and the railhead of a line that ran across north-central Norway to Sweden and over which the Germans expected, and with reason, to receive supplies should the British cut them off at sea.

Bergen, the second port and city of Norway, lying some three hundred miles down the coast from Trondheim and connected with Oslo, the capital, by railway, put up some resistance. The batteries guarding the harbor badly damaged the cruiser *Koenigsberg* and an auxiliary ship, but troops from other vessels landed safely and occupied the city before noon. It was at Bergen that the first direct British aid for the stunned Norwegians arrived. In the afternoon fifteen naval dive bombers sank the *Koenigsberg*, the first ship of that size ever to go down as the result of an air attack. Outside the harbor the British had a powerful fleet of four cruisers and seven destroyers which could have overwhelmed the smaller German naval force. It was about to enter the harbor when it received orders from the Admiralty to cancel the attack because of the risk of mines and bombing from the air, a decision which Churchill, who concurred in it, later regretted. This was the first sign of caution and of half measures which would cost the British dearly in the next crucial days.

Sola airfield, near the port of Stavanger on the southwest coast, was taken by German parachute troops after the Norwegian machine gun emplacements – there was no real antiaircraft protection – were silenced. This was Norway's biggest airfield and strategically of the highest importance to the Luftwaffe, since from here bombers could range not only against the British fleet along the Norwegian coast but against the chief British naval bases in northern Britain. Its seizure gave the Germans immediate air superiority in Norway and spelled the doom of any attempt by the British to land sizable forces.

Kristiansand on the south coast put up considerable resistance to the Germans, its shore batteries twice driving off a German fleet led by the light cruiser *Karlsruhe*. But the forts were quickly reduced by Luftwaffe bombing and the port was

occupied by mid afternoon. The *Karlsruhe*, however, on leaving port that evening was torpedoed by a British submarine and so badly damaged that it had to be sunk.

By noon, then, or shortly afterward, the five principal Norwegian cities and ports and the one big airfield along the west and south coasts that ran for 1,500 miles from the Skagerrak to the Arctic were in German hands. They had been taken by a handful of troops conveyed by a Navy vastly inferior to that of the British. Daring, deceit and surprise had brought Hitler a resounding victory at very little cost.

But at Oslo, the main prize, his military force and his diplomacy had run into some unexpected trouble.

All through the chilly night of April 8-9, a gay welcoming party from the German Legation, led by Captain Schreiber, the naval attaché, and joined occasionally by the busy Dr. Bräuer, the minister, stood at the quayside in Oslo Harbor waiting for the arrival of a German fleet and troop transports. A junior German naval attaché was darting about the bay in a motorboat waiting to act as pilot for the fleet, headed by the pocket battleship *Luetzow* (its name changed from *Deutschland* because Hitler did not want to risk losing a ship by that name) and the brand-new heavy cruiser *Bluecher*, flagship to the squadron.

They waited in vain. The big ships never arrived. They had been challenged at the entrance to the fifty-mile-long Oslo Fjord by the Norwegian mine layer *Olav Trygverson*, which sank a German torpedo boat and damaged the light cruiser *Emden*. After landing a small force to subdue the shore batteries the German squadron, however, continued on its way up the fjord. At a point some fifteen miles south of Oslo where the waters narrowed to fifteen miles, further trouble developed. Here stood the ancient fortress of Oskarsborg, whose defenders were more alert than the Germans suspected. Just before dawn the fort's 28-centimeter Krupp guns opened fire on the *Luetzow* and the *Bluecher*, and torpedoes were also launched from the shore. The 10,000-ton *Bluecher*, ablaze and torn by the explosions of its ammunition, went down, with the loss of 1,600 men, including several Gestapo and administrative officials (and all their papers) who were to arrest the King and the government and take over the administration of the capital. The *Luetzow* was also damaged but not completely disabled. Rear Admiral Oskar Kummetz, commander of the squadron, and General Erwin Engelbrecht, who led the 163rd Infantry Division, who were on the *Bluecher*, managed to swim ashore, where they were made prisoners by the Norwegians. Whereupon the crippled German fleet turned back for the moment to lick its wounds. It had failed in its mission to take the main German objective, the capital of Norway. It did not get there until the next day.

Oslo, in fact, fell to little more than a phantom German force dropped from the air at the local, undefended airport. The catastrophic news from the other seaports and the pounding of the guns fifteen miles down the Oslo Fjord had sent the Norwegian royal family, the government and members of Parliament scurrying on a special train from the capital at 9:30 A.M. for Hamar, eighty miles to the north. Twenty motor trucks laden with the gold of the Bank of Norway and three more with the secret papers of the Foreign Office got away at the same hour. Thus the gallant action of the garrison at Oskarsborg had foiled Hitler's plan to get his hands on the Norwegian King, government and gold.

But Oslo was left in complete bewilderment. There were some Norwegian troops there, but they were not put into a state for defense. Above all, nothing was done to block the airport at nearby Fornebu, which could have been done with a few old automobiles parked along the runway and about the field. Late on the previous night Captain Spiller, the German air attaché in Oslo, had stationed himself there to welcome the airborne troops, which were to come in after the Navy had reached the city. When the ships failed to arrive a frantic radio message was sent from the legation to Berlin apprising it of the unexpected and unhappy situation. The response was immediate. Soon parachute and airborne infantry toops were being landed at Fornebu. By noon about five companies had been assembled. As they were only lightly armed, the available Norwegian troops in the capital could have easily destroyed them. But for reasons never yet made clear – so great was the confusion in Oslo – they were not mustered, much less deployed, and the token German infantry force *marched* into the capital behind a blaring, if makeshift, military band. Thus the last of Norway's cities fell. But not Norway; not yet.

On the afternoon of April 9, the Storting, the Norwegian Parliament, met at Hamar with only five of the two hundred members missing, but adjourned at 7:30 P.M. when news was received that German troops were approaching and moved on to Elverum, a few miles to the east toward the Swedish border. Dr. Bräuer, pressed by Ribbentrop, was demanding an immediate audience with the King, and the Norwegian Prime Minister had assented on condition that German troops withdraw to a safe distance south. This the German minister would not agree to.

Indeed, at this moment a further piece of Nazi treachery was in the making. Captain Spiller, the air attaché, had set out from the Fornebu airport

Below: General Gamelin, the French Commander in Chief, inspecting a British anti-tank unit at Aldershot in 1939.

for Hamar with two companies of German parachutists to capture the recalcitrant King and government. It seemed to them more of a lark than anything else. Since Norwegian troops had not fired a shot to prevent the German entry into Oslo, Spiller expected no resistance at Hamar. In fact the two companies, traveling on commandeered autobuses, were making a pleasant sightseeing jaunt of it. But they did not reckon with a Norwegian Army officer who acted quite unlike so many of the others. Colonel Ruge, Inspector General of Infantry, who had accompanied the King northward, had insisted on providing some sort of protection to the fugitive government and had set up a roadblock near Hamar with two battalions of infantry which he had hastily rounded up. The German buses were stopped and in a skirmish which followed Spiller was mortally wounded. After suffering further casualties the Germans fell back all the way to Oslo.

The next day, Dr. Bräuer set out from Oslo alone along the same road to see the King. An old-school professional diplomat, the German minister did not relish his role, but Ribbentrop had kept after him relentlessly to talk the King and the government into surrender. Bräuer's difficult task had been further complicated by certain political events which had just taken place in Oslo. On the preceding evening Quisling had finally bestirred himself, once the capital was firmly in German hands, stormed into the radio station and broadcast a proclamation naming himself as head of a new government and ordering all Norwegian resistance to the Germans to halt immediately. Though Bräuer could not yet grasp it – and Berlin could never, even later, understand it – this treasonable act doomed the German efforts to induce Norway to surrender. And paradoxically, though

it was a moment of national shame for the Norwegian people, the treason of Quisling rallied the stunned Norwegians to a resistance which was to become formidable and heroic.

Dr. Bräuer met Haakon VII, the only king in the twentieth century who had been elected to the throne by popular vote and the first monarch Norway had had of its own for five centuries, in a schoolhouse at the little town of Elverum at 3 P.M. on April 10. From a talk this writer later had with the monarch and from a perusal of both the Norwegian records and Dr. Bräuer's secret report (which is among the captured German Foreign Office documents) it is possible to give an account of what happened. After considerable reluctance the King had agreed to receive the German envoy in the presence of his Foreign Minister, Dr. Halvdan Koht. When Bräuer insisted on seeing Haakon at first alone the King, with the agreement of Koht, finally consented.

The German minister, acting on instructions, alternately flattered and tried to intimidate the King. Germany wanted to preserve the dynasty. It was merely asking Haakon to do what his brother Christian X of Denmark had done the day before in Copenhagen. It was folly to resist the Wehrmacht. Only useless slaughter for the Norwegians would ensue. The King was asked to approve the government of Quisling and return to Oslo. Haakon, a salty, democratic man and a great stickler, even at this disastrous moment, for constitutional procedure, tried to explain to the German diplomat that in Norway the King did not make political decisions; that was exclusively the business of the government, which he would now consult. Koht then joined the conversation and it was agreed that the answer would be telephoned to Bräuer.

For Haakon, who, though he could not make

Right: Germans unload supplies in Norway, April 1940.

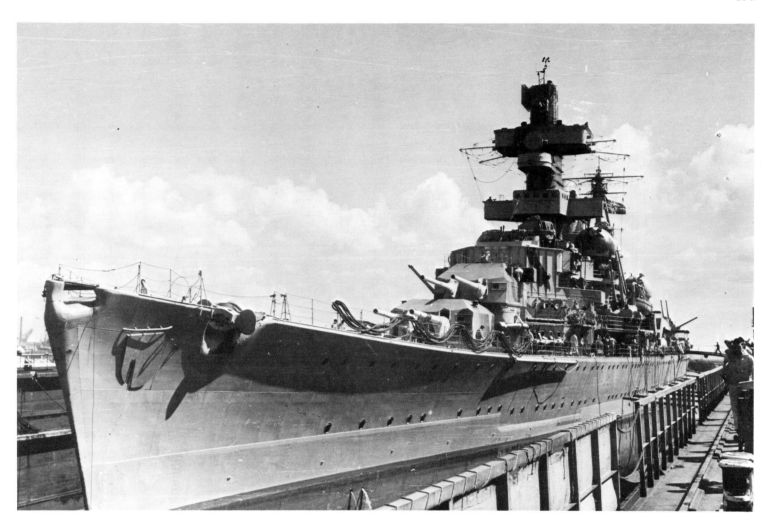

the political decision, could surely influence it, there was but one answer to the Germans. Retiring to a modest inn in the village of Nybergsund near Elverum – just in case the Germans, with Bräuer gone, tried to capture him in another surprise attack – he assembled the members of the government as Council of State.

"For my part" [he told them] "I cannot accept the German demands. It would conflict with all that I have considered to be my duty as King of Norway since I came to this country nearly thirty-five years ago . . . I do not want the decision of the government to be influenced by or based upon this statement. But . . . I cannot appoint Quisling Prime Minister, a man in whom I know neither our people . . . nor its representatives in the Storting have any confidence at all.

"If therefore the government should decide to accept the German demands – and I fully understand the reasons in favor of it, considering the impending danger of war in which so many young Norwegians will have to give their lives – if so, *abdication* will be the only course open to me."

The government, though there may have been some waverers up to this moment, could not be less courageous than the King, and it quickly rallied behind him. By the time Bräuer got to Eidsvold, halfway back to Oslo, Koht was on the telephone line to him with the Norwegian reply. The German minister telephoned it immediately to the legation in Oslo, where it was sped to Berlin: "The King will name no government headed by Quisling and this decision was made upon the unanimous advice of the Government. To my specific question, Foreign Minister Koht replied: 'Resistance will continue as long as possible.'"

That evening from a feeble little rural radio station nearby, the only means of communication to the outside world available, the Norwegian government flung down the gauntlet to the mighty Third Reich. It announced its decision not to accept the German demands and called upon the people – there were only three million of them – to resist the invaders. The King formally associated himself with the appeal.

But the Nazi conquerors could not quite bring themselves to believe that the Norwegians meant what they said. Two more attempts were made to dissuade the King. On the morning of April 11 an emissary of Quisling, a Captain Irgens, arrived to

Above: The German heavy cruiser *Admiral Hipper* in dry dock for repairs to battle damage incurred during the Norwegian campaign.

Below: German troops boarding a ship for the invasion of Norway.

Above: Himmler with Vidkun Quisling, leader of the Norwegian Nazis.

Below: The German destroyer *Friedrich Eckoldt* off the Norwegian coast, April 1940.

urge the monarch to return to the capital. He promised that Quisling would serve him loyally. His proposal was dismissed with silent contempt.

In the afternoon an urgent message came from Bräuer, requesting a further audience with the King to talk over "certain proposals." The hard-pressed German envoy had been instructed by Ribbentrop to tell the monarch that he "wanted to give the Norwegian people one last chance of a reasonable agreement." This time Dr. Koht, after consulting the King, replied that if the German minister had "certain proposals" he could communicate them to the Foreign Minister.

The Nazi reaction to this rebuff by such a small and now helpless country was immediate and in character. The Germans had failed, first, to capture the King and the members of the government and, then, to persuade them to surrender. Now the Germans tried to kill them. Late on April 11, the Luftwaffe was sent out to give the village of Nybergsund the full treatment. The Nazi flyers demolished it with explosive and incendiary bombs and then machine-gunned those who tried to escape the burning ruins. The Germans apparently believed at first that they had succeeded in massacring the King and the members of the government. The diary of a German airman, later captured in northern Norway, had this entry for April 11: "Nybergsund. *Oslo Regierung. Alles vernichtet.*" (Oslo government. Completely wiped out.)

The village had been, but not the King and the government. With the approach of the Nazi bombers they had taken refuge in a nearby wood. Standing in snow up to their knees, they had watched the Luftwaffe reduce the modest cottages of the hamlet to ruins. They now faced a choice of either moving on to the nearby Swedish border and asylum in neutral Sweden or pushing north into their own mountains, still deep in the spring snow. They decided to move on up the rugged Gudbrands Valley, which led past Hamar and Lillehammer and through the mountains to Andalsnes on the northwest coast, a hundred miles southwest of Trondheim. Along the route they might organize the still dazed and scattered Norwegian forces for further resistance. And there was some hope that British troops might eventually arrive to help them.

The Battles for Norway

In the far north at Narvik the British Navy already had reacted sharply to the surprise German occupation. It had been, as Churchill, who was in charge of it, admitted, "completely outwitted" by the Germans. Now in the north at least, out of range of the German land-based bombers, it went over to the offensive. On the morning of April 10, twenty-four hours after ten German destroyers had taken Narvik and disembarked Dietl's troops, a force of five British destroyers entered Narvik harbor, sank two of the five German destroyers then in the port, damaged the other three and sank all the German cargo vessels except one. In this action the German naval commander, Rear Admiral Bonte, was killed. On leaving the harbor, however, the British ships ran into the five remaining German destroyers emerging from nearby fjords. The German craft were heavier gunned and sank one British destroyer, forced the beaching of another on which the British commander, Captain Warburton-Lee, was mortally wounded, and damaged a third. Three of the five British destroyers managed to make the open sea where, in retiring, they sank a large German freighter, laden with ammunition, which was approaching the port.

At noon on April 13 the British, this time with the battleship *Warspite*, a survivor of the First World War Battle of Jutland, leading a flotilla of destroyers, returned to Narvik and wiped out the remaining German war vessels. Vice-Admiral W. J. Whitworth, the commanding officer, in wirelessing the Admiralty of his action urged that since the German troops on shore had been stunned and disorganized – Dietl and his men had in fact taken to the hills – Narvik be occupied at once "by the main landing force." Unfortunately for the Allies, the British Army commander, Major General P. J. Mackesy, was an exceedingly cautious officer and, arriving the very next day with an advance contingent of three infantry battalions, decided not to risk a landing at Narvik but to disembark his troops at Harstad, thirty-five miles to the north, which was in the hands of the Norwegians. This was a costly error.

In the light of the fact that they had prepared a small expeditionary corps for Norway, the British were unaccountably slow in getting their troops under way. On the afternoon of April 8, after news was received of the movement of German fleet units up the Norwegian coast, the British Navy hurriedly *disembarked* the troops that had already been loaded on shipboard for the possible occupation of Stavanger, Bergen, Trondheim and Narvik, on the ground that every ship would be needed for naval action. By the time the British land forces were re-embarked all those port cities were in German hands. And by the time they reached central Norway they were doomed, as were the British naval ships which were to cover them, by the Luftwaffe's control of the air.

Below: German troops land in Oslo, April 27, 1940.

By April 20, one British brigade, reinforced by three battalions of French Chasseurs Alpins, had been landed at Namsos, a small port eighty miles northeast of Trondheim, and a second British brigade had been put ashore at Andalsnes, a hundred miles to the southwest of Trondheim, which was thus to be attacked from north and south. But lacking field artillery, antiaircraft guns and air support, their bases pounded night and day by German bombers which blocked the further landing of supplies or reinforcements, neither force ever seriously threatened Trondheim. The Andalsnes brigade, after meeting a Norwegian unit at Bombas, a rail junction sixty miles to the east, abandoned the proposed attack northward toward Trondheim and pushed southeast down the Gudbrandsdal in order to aid the Norwegian troops which, under the energetic command of Colonel Ruge, had been slowing up the main German drive coming up the valley from Oslo.

At Lillehammer, north of Hamar, the first engagement of the war between British and German troops took place on April 21, but it was no match. The ship laden with the British brigade's artillery had been sunk and there were only rifles and machine guns with which to oppose a strong German force armed with artillery and light tanks. Even worse, the British infantry, lacking air support, was incessantly pounded by Luftwaffe planes operating from nearby Norwegian airfields. Lillehammer fell after a twenty-four-hour battle and the British and Norwegian forces began a retreat of 140 miles up the valley railway to Andalsnes, halting here and there to fight a rearguard action which slowed the Germans but never stopped them. On the nights of April 30 and May 1 the British forces were evacuated from Andalsnes and on May 2 the Anglo-French contingent from Namsos, considerable feats in themselves, for both harbors were blazing shambles from continuous German bombing. On the night of April 29 the King of Norway and the members of his government were taken aboard the British cruiser *Glasgow* at Molde, across the Romsdalsfjord from Andalsnes, itself also a shambles from Luftwaffe bombing, and conveyed to Tromsö, far above the Arctic Circle and north of Narvik, where on May Day the provisional capital was set up.

Above: Ships sunk in Narvik harbor in the course of the battles for the town.

Above right: A German machine gun post at Narvik.

Right: Germans advance through a burning Norwegian village.

By then the southern half of Norway, comprising all the cities and main towns, had been irretrievably lost. But northern Norway seemed secure. On May 28 an Allied force of 25,000 men, including two brigades of Norwegians, a brigade of Poles and two battalions of the French Foreign Legion, had driven the greatly outnumbered Germans out of Narvik. There seemed no reason to doubt that Hitler would be deprived of both his iron ore and his objective of occupying all of Norway and making the Norwegian government capitulate. But by this time the Wehrmacht had struck with stunning force on the Western front and every Allied soldier was needed to plug the gap. Narvik was abandoned, the Allied troops were hastily re-embarked, and General Dietl, who had held out in a wild mountainous tract near the Swedish border, reoccupied the port on June 8 and four days later accepted the surrender of the persevering and gallant Colonel Ruge and his bewildered, resentful Norwegian troops, who felt they had been left in the lurch by the British. King Haakon and his government were taken aboard the cruiser *Devonshire* at Tromsö on June 7 and departed for London and five years of bitter exile. In Berlin Dietl was promoted to Major General, awarded the Ritterkreuz and hailed by Hitler as the *Sieger von Narvik*.

Despite his amazing successes the Fuehrer had

had his bad moments during the Norwegian campaign. General Jodl's diary is crammed with terse entries recounting a succession of the warlord's nervous crises. "Terrible excitement," he noted on April 14 after news had been received of the wiping out of the German naval forces at Narvik. On April 17 Hitler had a fit of hysteria about the loss of Narvik; he demanded that General Dietl's troops there be evacuated by air – an impossibility. "Each piece of bad news," Jodl scribbled that day in his diary, "leads to the worst fears." And two days later: "Renewed crisis. Political action has failed. Envoy Bräuer is recalled. According to the Fuehrer, force has to be used . . ." The conferences at the Chancellery in Berlin that day, April 19, became so embittered, with the heads of the three services blaming each other for the delays, that even the lackey Keitel stalked out of the room. "Chaos of leadership is again threatening," Jodl noted. And on April 22 he added: "Fuehrer is increasingly worried about the English landings."

On April 23 the slow progress of the German forces moving up from Oslo toward Trondheim and Andalsnes caused the "excitement to grow," as Jodl put it, but the next day the news was better and from that day it continued to grow more rosy. By the twenty-sixth the warlord was in such fine fettle that at 3:30 in the morning, during an all-night session with his military advisers, he told them he intended to start "Yellow" between May 1 and 7. "Yellow" was the code name for the attack in the West across Holland and Belgium. Though on April 29 Hitler was again "worried about Trondheim," the next day he was "happy with joy" at the news that a battle group from Oslo had reached the city. He could at last turn his attention back to the West. On May 1 he ordered that preparations for the big attack there be ready by May 5.

The Wehrmacht commanders – Goering, Brauchitsch, Halder, Keitel, Jodl, Raeder and the rest – had for the first time had a foretaste during the Norwegian campaign of how their demonic Leader cracked under the strain of even minor setbacks in battle. It was a weakness which would grow on him when, after a series of further astonishing military successes, the tide of war changed, and it would contribute mightily to the eventual debacle of the Third Reich.

Still, the quick, conquest of Denmark and Norway had been an important victory. It secured the winter iron-ore route, brought Hitler air bases hundreds of miles closer to the main enemy and, perhaps most important of all, it immensely enhanced the military prestige of the Third Reich. Nazi Germany seemed invincible.

But there was one military result of the Scandinavian adventure which could not be evaluated at once. German naval losses were heavy: 10 out of 20 destroyers and three of eight cruisers, plus two battle cruisers and a pocket battleship were damaged so severely that they were out of action for several months. Hitler had no fleet worthy of mention when the time to invade Britain came, as it did so shortly, and this proved an insurmountable handicap.

The possible consequences of the crippling of the German navy, however, did not enter the Fuehrer's thoughts as, at the beginning of May, he worked with his generals on the last-minute preparations for what they were confident would be the greatest conquest of all.

The Wehrmacht Springs a Trap

Shortly after dawn on May 10, 1940, the ambassador of Belgium and the minister of the Netherlands in Berlin were informed that German troops were entering their countries "to safeguard their neutrality against an imminent attack by the Anglo-French armies" – the same hollow excuse that had been made just a month before with Denmark and Norway. A formal German ultimatum called upon the two governments to see to it that no resistance was offered; if it were, it would be crushed.

As the battle began, the two sides were evenly matched in numbers – 136 German divisions against 135 divisions of the French, British, Belgians and Dutch. The defenders had the advantage of vast defensive fortifications: the impenetrable Maginot Line in the south, the Belgian forts in the middle, and fortified water lines in Holland in the north. Even in the number of tanks, the Allies matched the Germans. But they had not concentrated them as had the latter and, because of the Dutch and Belgians' suicidal pre-

Below: German paratroopers jump over Holland, May 1940.

war policy of strict neutrality, there had been no staff consultations which would have enabled the defenders to pool their resources effectively.

The Germans had a unified command, the initiative of the attacker, a contagious confidence in themselves and a daring plan. This was to launch the main German assault in the center, through the Ardennes, with a massive armored force which would then cross the Meuse north of Sedan, break out into the open country and race to the Channel at Abbeville.

Such a strike would hit the Allies where they least expected it, since their generals probably, like most of the Germans, considered this hilly, wooded country unsuitable for tanks. A feint by the right wing of the German forces would bring the British and French armies rushing pell-mell into Belgium. Then by cracking through the French at Sedan and heading west for the Channel, the Germans would entrap the major Anglo-French forces as well as the Belgian army.

It was a daring plan, not without its risks, as several generals emphasized. But by now Hitler, who considered himself a military genius, practically believed that it was his own idea (it had actually been proposed by General Erich von Manstein, against considerable opposition), and the Fuehrer's enthusiasm for it ensured its adoption.

The attack began along a front of 175 miles, from the North Sea to the Maginot Line. For the Germans everything went according to the book, or

Left: Hitler decorating the German paratroop officers who led the capture of Eben Emael.

even better than the book. Hitler's generals were confounded by the lightning rapidity and the extent of their own victories. As for the Allied leaders, they were quickly paralyzed by developments they had not expected and could not – in the utter confusion that ensued – comprehend.

Only one division of panzers could be spared by the Germans for the conquest of the Netherlands, which was accomplished in five days largely by parachutists and by troops landed by air transports behind the great flooded water lines which many in Berlin had believed would hold the Germans up for weeks. To the bewildered Dutch was reserved the experience of being subjected to the first large-scale airborne attack in the history of warfare. Considering their unpreparedness for such an ordeal and the complete surprise by which they were taken they did better than was realized at the time.

The first objective of the Germans was to land a strong force by air on the flying fields near The Hague, occupy the capital at once and capture the Queen and the government, as they had tried to do just a month before with the Norwegians. But

Below: German panzers and infantry advance in France, May 1940.

at The Hague, as at Oslo, the plan failed, though due to different circumstances. Recovering from their initial surprise and confusion, Dutch infantry, supported by artillery, was able to drive the Germans – two regiments strong – from the three airfields surrounding The Hague by the evening of May 10. This saved the capital and the government momentarily, but it tied down the Dutch reserves, desperately needed elsewhere.

The key to the German plan was the seizure by airborne troops of the bridges just south of Rotterdam over the Nieuwe Maas and those farther southeast over the two estuaries of the Maas (Meuse) at Dordrecht and Moerdijk. It was over these bridges that General Georg von Kuechler's Eighteenth Army driving from the German border nearly a hundred miles away hoped to force his way into Fortress Holland. In no other way could this entrenched place, lying behind formidable water barriers and comprising The Hague, Amsterdam, Utrecht, Rotterdam and Leyden, be taken easily and quickly.

The bridges were seized on the morning of May 10 by airborne units – including one company that landed on the river at Rotterdam in antiquated seaplanes – before the surprised Dutch guards

Above: German troops in the streets of a Dutch town.

Right: German motor cyclists in France, May 1940.

Left: Hitler's headquarters' staff for the Western Campaign. On Hitler's left General Jodl and Reichsleiter Bormann, and on his right, General Keitel.

could blow them. Desperate efforts were made by improvised Netherlands units to drive the Germans away and they almost succeeded. But the Germans hung on tenuously until the morning of May 12, when the one armored division assigned to Kuechler arrived, having smashed through the Grebbe-Peel Line, a fortified front to the east strengthened by a number of water barriers, on which the Dutch had hoped to hold out for several days.

There was some hope that the Germans might be stopped short of the Moerdijk bridges by General Giraud's French Seventh Army, which had raced up from the Channel and reached Tilburg on the afternoon of May 11. But the French, like the hard-pressed Dutch, lacked air support, armor, and antitank guns, and were easily pushed back to Breda. This opened the way for the German 9th Panzer Division to cross the bridges at Moerdijk and Dordrecht and, on the afternoon of May 12, arrive at the south bank of the Nieuwe Maas across from Rotterdam, where the German airborne troops still held the bridges.

But the tanks could not get across the Rotterdam bridges. The Dutch in the meantime had sealed them off at the northern ends. By the morning of May 14, then, the situation for the Netherlands was desperate but not hopeless. Fortress Holland had not been cracked. The strong German airborne forces around The Hague had been either captured or dispersed into nearby villages. Rotterdam still held. The German High Command, anxious to pull the armored division and supporting troops out of Holland to exploit a new opportunity which had just been opened to the south in France, was not happy. Indeed, on the morning of the fourteenth Hitler issued Directive No. 11 stating: "The power of resistance of the Dutch Army has proved to be stronger than was anticipated. Political as well as military considerations require that this resistance be broken *speedily*." How? He commanded that detachments of the Air Force be taken from the Sixth Army front in Belgium "to facilitate the rapid conquest of Fortress Holland."

Specifically he and Goering ordered a heavy bombing of Rotterdam. The Dutch would be induced to surrender by a dose of Nazi terror – the kind that had been applied before at Warsaw.

On the morning of May 14 a German staff officer from the XXXIXth Corps had crossed the bridge at Rotterdam under a white flag and demanded the surrender of the city. He warned that unless it capitulated it would be bombed. While surrender negotiations were under way – a Dutch officer had come to German headquarters near the bridge to discuss the details and was returning with the German terms – bombers appeared and wiped out the heart of the great city. Some eight hundred persons, almost entirely civilians, were massacred, several thousand wounded and 78,000 made homeless. This bit of treachery, this act of calculated ruthlessness, would long be remembered by the Dutch, though at Nuremberg both Goering and Kesselring of the Luftwaffe defended it on the grounds that Rotterdam was not an open city but stoutly defended by the Dutch. Both denied that they knew that surrender negotiations were going on when they dispatched the bombers, though there is strong evidence from German Army archives that they did. At any rate, OKW made no excuses at the time. I myself heard over the Berlin radio on the evening of May 14 a special OKW communiqué: "Under the tremendous impression of the attacks of German dive bombers and the imminent attack of German tanks, the city of Rotterdam has capitulated and thus saved itself from destruction."

Rotterdam surrendered, and then the Dutch armed forces. Queen Wilhelmina and the government members had fled to London on two British destroyers. At dusk on May 14 General H. G. Winkelmann, the Commander in Chief of the Dutch forces, ordered his troops to lay down their arms and at 11 A.M. on the next day he signed the official capitulations. Within five days it was all over. The fighting, that is. For five years a night of savage German terror would henceforth darken this raped, civilized little land.

The Nazis Pierce the Center

It was on May 14 that the avalanche began. An army of tanks unprecedented in warfare for size, concentration, mobility and striking power, broke through the French armies and headed swiftly for the Channel, behind the Allied forces in Belgium. So enormous was the striking force that when it started through the Ardennes Forest from the German frontier on May 10, it stretched in three columns back for 100 miles behind the Rhine.

Preceded by waves of Stuka dive bombers, this phalanx of steel and fire could not be stopped by any means in the hands of the bewildered defenders.

On both sides of Dinant on the Meuse the French gave way to General Hermann Hoth's XVth Armored Corps, one of whose two tank divisions was commanded by a daring young brigadier general, Erwin Rommel. Farther south along the river, at Monthermé, the same pattern was being executed by General Reinhardt's XLIst Armored Corps of two tank divisions.

But it was around Sedan, of disastrous memory to the French, that the greatest blow fell. Here on the morning of May 14 two tank divisions of General Heinz Guderian's XIXth Armored Corps poured across a hastily constructed pontoon bridge set up during the night over the Meuse and struck toward the west. Though French armor and British bombers tried desperately to destroy the bridge – forty of seventy-one R.A.F. planes were shot down in one single attack, mostly by flak, and seventy French tanks were destroyed – they could not damage it. By evening the German bridgehead at Sedan was thirty miles wide and fifteen miles deep and the French forces in the vital center of the Allied line were shattered. Those who were not surrounded and made prisoners were in disorderly retreat. The Franco-British armies to the north, as well as the twenty-two divisions of Belgians, were placed in dire danger of being cut off.

The first couple of days had gone fairly well for the Allies, or so they thought. To Churchill, plunging with new zest into his fresh responsibilities as Prime Minister, "up until the night of the twelfth," as he later wrote, "there was no reason to suppose that the operations were not going well." Gamelin, the generalissimo of the Allied forces, was highly pleased with the situation. The evening before, the best and largest part of the French forces, the First, Seventh and Ninth armies, along with the B.E.F. (British Expeditionary Force), nine divisions strong under Lord Gort, had joined the Belgians, as planned, on a strong defensive line running along the Dyle River from Antwerp through Louvain to Wavre and thence across the Gembloux gap to Namur and south along the Meuse to Sedan. Between the formid-

Below: General Guderian in his command vehicle during the fighting in France.

able Belgian fortress of Namur and Antwerp, on a front of only sixty miles, the Allies actually outnumbered the oncoming Germans, having some thirty-six divisions against the twenty in General Reichenau's Sixth Army.

The Belgians, though they had fought well along the reaches of their northeast frontier, had not held out there as long as had been expected, certainly not as long as in 1914. They, like the Dutch to the north of them, had simply not been able to cope with the revolutionary new tactics of the Wehrmacht. Here, as in Holland, the Germans seized the vital bridges by the daring use of a handful of specially trained troops landed silently at dawn in gliders. They overpowered the guards at two of the three bridges over the Albert Canal behind Maastricht before the defenders could throw the switches to blow them up.

They had even greater success in capturing Fort Eben Emael, which commanded the junction of the Meuse River and the Albert Canal. This modern, strategically located fortress was regarded by both the Allies and the Germans as the most impregnable fortification in Europe, stronger than anything the French had built in the Maginot Line or the Germans in the West Wall. Constructed in a series of steel-and-concrete galleries deep underground, its gun turrets protected by heavy armor and manned by 1,200 men, it was expected to hold out indefinitely against the pounding of the heaviest bombs and artillery shells. It fell in thirty hours to eighty German soldiers who under the command of a sergeant had landed in nine gliders on its roof and whose total casualties amounted to six killed and nineteen wounded. In Berlin, I remember, OKW made the enterprise look very mysterious, announcing in a special communiqué on the evening of May 11 that Fort Eben Emael had been taken by a "new method of attack," an announcement that caused rumors to spread – and Dr. Goebbels was delighted to fan them – that the Germans had a deadly new "secret weapon," perhaps a nerve gas that temporarily paralyzed the defenders.

Above: German engineers crossing the River Meuse.

Left: German troops take cover under French shell fire.

Above: French Char B destroyed, May 1940.

Below: German panzers advance in France, a photograph from Rommel's personal collection. The radio antenna of his command vehicle appears at the top of the picture.

The truth was much more prosaic. With their usual flair for minute preparation, the Germans during the winter of 1939-40 had erected at Hildesheim a replica of the fort and of the bridges across the Albert Canal and had trained some four hundred glider troops on how to take them. Three groups were to capture the three bridges, the fourth Eben Emael. This last unit of eighty men landed on the top of the fortress and placed a specially prepared ''hollow'' explosive in the armored gun turrets which not only put them out of action but spread flames and gas in the cham-

bers below. Portable flame throwers were also used at the gun portals and observation openings. Within an hour the Germans were able to penetrate the upper galleries, render the light and heavy guns of the great fort useless and blind its observation posts. Belgian infantry behind the fortification tried vainly to dislodge the tiny band of attackers but they were driven off by Stuka attacks and by reinforcements of parachutists. By the morning of May 11 advance panzer units, which had raced over the two intact bridges to the north, arrived at the fort and surrounded it, and, after further Stuka bombings and hand-to-hand fighting in the underground tunnels, a white flag was hoisted at noon and the 1,200 dazed Belgian defenders filed out and surrendered.

This feat, along with the capture of the bridges and the violence of the attack mounted by General von Reichenau's Sixth Army, which was sustained by General Hoepner's XVIth Armored Corps of two tank divisions and one mechanized infantry division, convinced the Allied High Command that now, as in 1914, the brunt of the German offensive was being carried out by the enemy's right wing and that they had taken the proper means to stop it. In fact, as late as the evening of May 15 the Belgian, British and French forces were holding firm on the Dyle line from Antwerp to Namur.

This was just what the German High Command wanted. It had now become possible for it to spring the Manstein plan and deliver the haymaker in the center. General Halder, the Chief of the Army General Staff, saw the situation – and his opportunities - very clearly on the evening of May 13. ''North of Namur [he wrote in his diary] we can count on a completed concentration of some 24 British and French and about 15 Belgian divisions. Against this our Sixth Army has 15 divisions on the front and six in reserve . . . We are strong enough there to fend off any enemy attack. No need to bring up any more forces. South of Namur we face a weaker enemy. About half our strength. Outcome of Meuse attack will decide if, when and where we will be able to exploit this superiority. The enemy has no force worth mentioning behind this front.''

No force worth mentioning *behind* this front, which, the next day, was broken?

On May 16 Prime Minister Churchill flew to Paris to find out. By the afternoon, when he drove to the Quai d'Orsay to see Premier Reynaud and General Gamelin, German spearheads were sixty miles west of Sedan, rolling along the undefended open country. Nothing very much stood between them and Paris, or between them and the Channel, but Churchill did not know this. "Where is the strategic reserve?" he asked Gamelin and, breaking into French, *"Où est la masse de manoeuvre?"* The Commander in Chief of the Allied armies turned to him with a shake of the head and a shrug and answered, *"Aucune* – there is none."

"I was dumfounded," Churchill later related. It was unheard of that a great army, when attacked, held no troops in reserve. "I admit," says Churchill, "that this was one of the greatest surprises I have had in my life."

It was scarcely less a surprise to the German High Command, or at least to Hitler and the generals at OKW if not to Halder. Twice during this campaign in the West, which the Fuehrer himself directed, he hesitated. The first occasion was on May 17 when a crisis of nerves overcame him. That morning Guderian, who was a third of the way to the Channel with his panzer corps, received an order to halt in his tracks. Intelligence had been received from the Luftwaffe that the

French were mounting a great counterattack to cut off the thin armored German wedges which extended westward from Sedan. Hitler conferred hastily with his Army Commander in Chief, Brauchitsch, and with Halder. He was certain that a serious French threat was developing from the south. Rundstedt, commander of Army Group A, the main force which had launched the breakthrough over the Meuse, backed him up when they conferred later in the day. He expected, he said, "a great surprise counteroffensive by strong French forces from the Verdun and Châlons-sur-Marne areas." The specter of a second Marne rose in Hitler's feverish mind. "I am keeping an eye on this," he wrote Mussolini the next day. "The miracle of the Marne of 1914 will not be repeated!"

"A very unpleasant day [Halder noted in his diary the evening of May 17]. The Fuehrer is terribly nervous. He is worried over his own success, will risk nothing and insists on restraining us. Puts forward the excuse that it is all because of his concern with the left flank . . . [He] has brought only bewilderment and doubts."

The Nazi warlord showed no improvement during the next day despite the avalanche of news about the French collapse. Halder recorded the crisis in his diary of the eighteenth: "The Fuehrer has an unaccountable worry about the south flank. He rages and screams that we are on the way to ruining the whole operation and that we are courting the danger of a defeat. He won't have any part in continuing the drive westward, let alone southwest, and clings always to the idea of a thrust to the northwest. This is the subject of a most unpleasant dispute between the Fuehrer on the one side and Brauchitsch and me on the other."

General Jodl of OKW, for whom the Fuehrer was nearly always right, also noted the discord at the top. "Day of great tension [he wrote on the

Left: Fraternisation. A French girl talking to German soldiers.

Right: "France's Responsibility." Nazi propaganda blaming France for the war complete with the stereotype Jewish financier and "racially inferior" soldiers from France's African colonies.

Below: A Nazi cartoon in 1940 showing a desperate John Bull trying to auction his naval bases.

forces with which to stage a counterattack from the south. And though the panzer divisions, chafing at the bit as they were, received orders to do no more than proceed with "a reconnaissance in force" this was all they needed to press toward the Channel. By the morning of May 19 a mighty wedge of seven armored divisions, driving relentlessly westward north of the Somme River past the storied scenes of battle of the First World War, was only some fifty miles from the Channel. On the evening of May 20, to the surprise of Hitler's headquarters, the 2nd Panzer Division reached Abbeville at the mouth of the Somme. The Belgians, the B.E.F. and three French armies were trapped. "Fuehrer is beside himself with joy [Jodl scribbled in his diary that night]. Talks in words of highest appreciation of the German Army and its leadership. Is working on the peace treaty, which shall express the tenor: return of territory robbed over the last 400 years from the German people, and of other values . . . A special memorandum is in the files containing the emotion-choked words of the Fuehrer when receiving the telephone report from the Commander in Chief of the Army about the capture of Abbeville."

The only hope of the Allies to extricate themselves from this disastrous encirclement was for the armies in Belgium to immediately turn southwest, disengage themselves from the German Sixth Army attacking them there, fight their way across the German armored wedge that stretched across northern France to the sea and join up with fresh French forces pushing northward from the Somme. This was in fact what General Gamelin ordered on the morning of May 19, but he was replaced that evening by General Maxime Weygand, who immediately canceled the order. Weygand, who had a formidable military reputation gained in the First World War, wanted to confer first with the Allied commanders in Belgium before deciding what to do. As a result, three days were lost before Weygand came up with precisely the same plan as his predecessor. The delay proved costly. There were still forty French, British and Belgian battle-tested divisions in the north, and had they struck south across the thin armored German line on May 19 as Gamelin ordered, they might have succeeded in breaking through. By the time they moved, communications between the various national commands had become chaotic and the several Allied armies, hard pressed as they were, began to act at cross-purposes. At any rate, the Weygand plan existed only in the General's mind; no French troops ever moved up from the Somme.

In the meantime the German High Command had thrown in all the infantry troops that could be rushed up to strengthen the armored gap and enlarge it. By May 24 Guderian's tanks, driving up the Channel from Abbeville, had captured Boulogne and surrounded Calais, the two main ports, and reached Gravelines, some twenty miles down the coast from Dunkirk. The front in Belgium had moved southwestward as the Allies attempted to detach themselves there. By the 24th, then, the British, French and Belgian armies in the north were compressed into a relatively small triangle with its base along the Channel from Gravelines to Terneuzen and its apex at Valenciennes, some seventy miles inland. There was now no hope of breaking out of the trap. The only hope, and it

eighteenth]. The Commander in Chief of the Army [Brauchitsch] has not carried out the intention of building up as quickly as possible a new flanking position to the south . . . Brauchitsch and Halder are called immediately and ordered peremptorily to adopt the necessary measures immediately."

But Halder had been right; the French had no

seemed a slim one, was possible evacuation by sea from Dunkirk.

It was at this juncture, on May 24, that the German armor, now within sight of Dunkirk and poised along the Aa Canal between Gravelines and St.-Omer for the final kill, received a strange – and to the soldiers in the field inexplicable – order to halt their advance. It was the first of the German High Command's major mistakes in World War II and became a subject of violent controversy, not only between the German generals themselves but among the military historians, as to who was responsible and why . . . Whatever the reasons for this stop order, it provided a miraculous reprieve to the Allies, and especially to the British, leading as it did to the miracle of Dunkirk. But it did not save the Belgians.

King Leopold III of the Belgians surrendered early on the morning of May 28. The headstrong young ruler, who had taken his country out of its alliance with France and Britain into a foolish neutrality, who had refused to restore the alliance even during the months when he knew the Germans were preparing a massive assault across his border, who at the last moment, after Hitler had struck, called on the French and British for military succor and received it, now deserted them in a desperate hour, opening the dyke for German divisions to pour through on the flank of the

Above: Mussolini, Hitler and Ritter von Epp.

Left: Destruction on the outskirts of Paris.

Right: German 3.7 cm anti-tank gun outside La Gare de l'Est, one of the principal stations in Paris, June 14, 1940.

Below: Sunken British ships and destroyed vehicles at Dunkirk.

sorely pressed Anglo-French troops. Moreover, he did it, as Churchill told the Commons on June 4, "without prior consultation, with the least possible notice, without the advice of his ministers and upon his own personal act."

Actually he did it *against* the unanimous advice of his government, which he was constitutionally sworn to follow. At 5 A.M. on May 25 there was a showdown meeting at the King's headquarters between the monarch and three members of the cabinet, including the Prime Minister and the Foreign Minister. They urged him for the last time not to surrender personally and become a prisoner of the Germans, for if he did he "would be degraded to the role of Hácha" in Prague. They also reminded him that he was head of state as well as Commander in Chief, and that if matters came to the worst he could exercise his first office in exile, as the Queen of Holland and the King of Norway had decided to do, until eventual Allied victory.

"I have decided to stay," Leopold answered. "The cause of the Allies is lost."

At 5 P.M. on May 27 he dispatched General

Derousseaux, Deputy Chief of the Belgian General Staff, to the Germans to ask for a truce. At 10 o'clock the General brought back the German terms: "The Fuehrer demands that arms be laid down unconditionally." The King accepted unconditional surrender at 11 P.M. and proposed that fighting cease at 4 A.M., which it did.

Despite this additional setback, the British nation and its leaders were still determined to fight to the end. But Hitler and his generals, ignorant of the sea as they were – and remained – did not dream that the sea-minded British could evacuate a third of a million men from a small battered port and from the exposed beaches of Dunkirk right under their noses in the operation code-named Dynamo.

An armada of 850 vessels of all sizes, shapes and methods of propulsion, from cruisers and destroyers to small sailboats and Dutch *skoots*, many of them manned by civilian volunteers from the English coastal towns, converged on Dunkirk. The first day, May 27, they took off 7,669 troops; the next day, 17,804; the following day, 47,310; and on May 30, 53,823, for a total of 126,606 during the first four days. This was far more than the Admiralty had hoped to get out. When the operation began it counted on evacuating only about 45,000 men in the two days' time it then thought it would have.

It was not until this fourth day of Operation

Above: German supply wagons in front of the Cathedral of Notre Dame, Paris. Note how the entrances to the church have been protected with sandbags.

Dynamo, on May 30, that the German High Command woke up to what was happening. For four days the communiques of OKW had been reiterating that the encircled enemy armies were doomed. A communique of May 29, which I noted in my diary, stated flatly: "The fate of the French army in Artois is sealed . . . The British army, which has been compressed into the territory . . . around Dunkirk, is also going to its destruction before our concentric attack."

But it wasn't; it was going to sea. Without its heavy arms and equipment, to be sure, but with the certainty that the men would live to fight another day.

As late as the morning of May 30, Halder was noting confidentially in his diary that "the disintegration of the enemy which we have encircled continues." Some of the British, he conceded, were "fighting with tooth and nail": the others were "fleeing to the coast and trying to get across the Channel on anything that floats. *Le Débâcle,*" he concluded, alluding to Zola's famous novel of the French collapse in the Franco-Prussian War.

By afternoon, after a session with Brauchitsch, the General Staff Chief had awakened to the significance of the swarms of miserable little boats on which the British were fleeing. "Brauchitsch is angry . . . The pocket would have been closed at the coast if only our armor had not been held back. The bad weather has grounded the Luftwaffe and we must now stand by and watch countless thousands of the enemy get away to England right under our noses."

That was, in fact, what they watched. Despite increased pressure which was immediately applied by the Germans on all sides of the pocket, the British lines held and more troops were evacuated. The next day, May 31, was the biggest day of all. Some 68,000 men were embarked for England, a third of them from the beaches, the rest from the Dunkirk harbor. A total of 194,620 men had now been taken out, more than four times the number originally hoped for.

Where was the famed Luftwaffe? Part of the time, as Halder noted, it was grounded by bad weather. The rest of the time it encountered unexpected opposition from the Royal Air Force, which from bases just across the Channel successfully challenged it for the first time. Though outnumbered, the new British Spitfires proved more than a match for the Messerschmitts and they mowed down the cumbersome German bombers. On a few occasions Goering's planes arrived over Dunkirk between British sorties and did such extensive damage to the port that for a time it was unusable and the troops had to be lifted exclusively from the beaches. The Luftwaffe also pressed several strong attacks on the shipping and accounted for most of the 243 – out of 861 – vessels sunk. But it failed to achieve what Goering had promised Hitler: the annihilation of the B.E.F. On June 1, when it carried out its heaviest attack (and suffered its heaviest losses – each side lost thirty planes), sinking three British destroyers and a number of small transports, the second-highest day's total was evacuated – 64,429 men. By dawn of the next day, only 4,000 British troops remained in the perimeter, protected by 100,000 French who now manned the defenses.

Medium German artillery had in the meantime come within range and daytime evacuation operations had to be abandoned. The Luftwaffe at that time did not operate after dark and during the nights of June 2 and 3 the remainder of the B.E.F. and 60,000 French troops were successfully brought out. Dunkirk, still defended stubbornly by 40,000 French soldiers, held out until the morning of June 4. By that day 338,226 British and French soldiers had escaped the German clutches. They were no longer an army; most of them, understandably, were for the moment in a pitiful shape. But they were battle-tried; they knew that if properly armed and adequately covered from the air they could stand up to the Germans. Most of them, when the balance in armament was achieved, would prove it – and on beaches not far down the Channel coast from where they had been rescued.

A deliverance Dunkirk was to the British. But Churchill reminded them in the House on June 4 that "wars are not won by evacuations." The predicament of Great Britain was indeed grim, more dangerous than it had been since the Nor-

Below: General de Gaulle's appeal from exile in London for continued French resistance, June 1940.

A TOUS LES FRANÇAIS

La France a perdu une bataille!
Mais la France n'a pas perdu la guerre!

Des gouvernants de rencontre ont pu capituler, cédant à la panique, oubliant l'honneur, livrant le pays à la servitude. Cependant, rien n'est perdu!

Rien n'est perdu, parce que cette guerre est une guerre mondiale. Dans l'univers libre, des forces immenses n'ont pas encore donné. Un jour, ces forces écraseront l'ennemi. Il faut que la France, ce jour-là, soit présente à la victoire. Alors, elle retrouvera sa liberté et sa grandeur. Tel est mon but, mon seul but!

Voilà pourquoi je convie tous les Francais, où qu'ils se trouvent, à s'unir à moi dans l'action, dans le sacrifice et dans l'espérance.

Notre patrie est en péril de mort.
Luttons tous pour la sauver!

VIVE LA FRANCE !

Signature: G. de Gaulle

GÉNÉRAL DE GAULLE

QUARTIER-GÉNÉRAL,
4, CARLTON GARDENS,
LONDON, S.W.1.

man landings nearly a millennium before. It had no army to defend the islands. The Air Force had been greatly weakened in France. Only the Navy remained, and the Norwegian campaign had shown how vulnerable the big fighting ships were to land-based aircraft. Now the Luftwaffe bombers were based but five or ten minutes away across the narrow Channel. France, to be sure, still held out below the Somme and the Aisne. But its best troops and armament had been lost in Belgium and in northern France, its small and obsolescent Air Force had been largely destroyed, and its two most illustrious generals, Marshal Pétain and General Weygand, who now began to dominate the shaky government, had no more stomach for battle against such a superior foe.

These dismal facts were very much on the mind of Winston Churchill when he rose in the House of Commons on June 4, 1940, while the last transports from Dunkirk were being unloaded, determined, as he wrote later, to show not only his own people but the world – and especially the U.S.A. – "that our resolve to fight on was based on serious grounds." It was on this occasion that he uttered his famous peroration, which will be long remembered and will surely rank with the greatest ever made down the ages: "Even though large tracts of Europe and many old and famous States have fallen or may fall into the grip of the Gestapo and all the odious apparatus of Nazi rule, we shall not flag or fail. We shall go on to the end, we shall fight in France, we shall fight in the seas and oceans, we shall fight with growing confidence and growing strength in the air, we shall defend our island, whatever the cost may be, we shall fight on the beaches, we shall fight on the landing grounds, we shall fight in the fields and in the streets, we shall fight in the hills; we shall never surrender, and even if, which I do not for a moment believe, this island or a large part of it were subjugated and starving, then our Empire beyond the seas, armed and guarded by the British Fleet, would carry on the struggle, until, in God's good time, the New World, with all its power and might, steps forth to the rescue and the liberation of the Old."

The determination of the British to fight on does not seem to have troubled Hitler's thoughts. He was sure they would see the light after he had finished off France, which he now proceeded to do. The morning after Dunkirk fell, on June 5, the Germans launched a massive assault on the Somme and soon they were attacking in overwhelming strength all along a 400-mile front that stretched across France from Abbeville to the Upper Rhine. The French were doomed. Against 143 German divisions, including ten armored, they could deploy only 65 divisions, most of them second-rate, for the best units and most of the armor had been expended in Belgium. Little was left of the weak French Air Force. The British could contribute but one infantry division, which had been in the Saar, and parts of an armored division. The R.A.F. could spare few planes for this battle unless it were to leave the British Isles themselves defenseless. Finally, the French High Command, now dominated by Pétain and Weygand, had become sodden with defeatism. Nevertheless some French units fought with great bravery and tenacity, temporarily stopping even the German armor here and there, and standing up resolutely to the incessant pounding of the Luftwaffe.

Above: Luftwaffe pilots relax between sorties.

But it was an unequal struggle. In "victorious confusion," as Telford Taylor has aptly put it, the German troops surged across France like a tidal wave, the confusion coming because there were so many of them and they were moving so fast and often getting in each other's way. On June 10 the French government hastily departed Paris and on June 14 the great city, the glory of France, which was undefended, was occupied by General von Kuechler's Eighteenth Army. The swastika was immediately hoisted on the Eiffel Tower. On June 16, Premier Reynaud, whose government had fled to Bordeaux, resigned and was replaced by Pétain, who the next day asked the Germans, through the Spanish ambassador, for an armistice. Hitler replied the same day that he would first have to consult his ally, Mussolini. For this strutting warrior, after making sure that the French armies were hopelessly beaten, had, like a jackal, hopped into the war on June 10, to try to get in on the spoils.

The Duce's campaign was ludicrous. By June 18, when Hitler summoned his junior partner to Munich to discuss an armistice with France, some 32 Italian divisions, after a week of "fighting," had been unable to budge a scanty French force of six divisions, though the defenders were now threatened by assault in the rear from the Germans sweeping down the Rhône Valley.

Mussolini was unable even to get Hitler to agree to joint armistice negotiations with the French. The Fuehrer was not going to share his triumph with this Johnny-come-lately, and the Duce left Munich bitter and frustrated.

Celebrating Victory in the West

Left: German troops parade past the Arc de Triomphe in Paris at the height of the victory parade in the French capital.

Below: German troops remove the railroad car used for the Armistice negotiations in November 1918 from its museum so that it can be readied for the French surrender ceremony.

Right: The French representatives wait at Compiègne for the Fuehrer's arrival.

Bottom: The German delegation arrives to accept the French surrender. From left, Brauchitsch, Raeder, Hitler, Hess, Goering and Ribbentrop.

Bottom right: The dejected French representatives leave after having signed the Armistice.

The Guns Fall Silent

I followed the German army into Paris that June, always the loveliest of months in the majestic capital, and on June 19 got wind of where Hitler was going to lay down his armistice terms. It was to be on the same spot where Germany had capitulated to France and her allies on November 11, 1918: in the little clearing in the woods at Compiègne. There the Nazi warlord would get his revenge, and the place itself would add to the sweetness of it for him. Late on the afternoon of June 19 I drove there and found German army engineers pulling the old railway car or *wagon-lit* in which the World War I armistice had been signed out to the tracks in the center of the clearing, on the exact spot, they said, where it had stood at 5 a.m. on November 11, 1918.

And on the afternoon of June 21 I stood by the edge of the forest at Compiègne to observe the latest and greatest of Hitler's triumphs, of which I had seen so many over the last turbulent years. It was one of the loveliest summer days I ever remember in France. A warm June sun beat down on the stately trees, casting pleasant shadows on the wooded avenues leading to the little circular clearing. At 3:15 p.m. precisely, Hitler arrived in his big Mercedes.

Right: Hitler's victory parade in Berlin, filmed for the benefit of propaganda newsreels.

Below: Smiling and victorious German troops parade through Berlin.

"I observed his face," I wrote in my diary. "It was grave, solemn, yet brimming with revenge. There was also in it, as in his springy step, a note of the triumphant conqueror, the defier of the world. There was something else, a sort of scornful inner joy at being present at this great reversal of fate."

When he reached the little opening in the forest and his personal standard had been run up, his attention was attracted by a large granite block.

"Hitler, followed by others, walks slowly over to it (I am quoting my diary), steps up, and reads the inscription engraved, in French, in great high letters:

HERE ON THE ELEVENTH OF NOVEMBER 1918 SUCCUMBED THE CRIMINAL PRIDE OF THE GERMAN EMPIRE – VANQUISHED BY THE FREE PEOPLES WHICH IT TRIED TO ENSLAVE.

"Hitler reads it and Goering reads it. I look for the expression in Hitler's face. I have seen that face many times at the great moments of his life. But today! It is afire with scorn, anger, hate, revenge, triumph.

"He steps off the monument and contrives to make even this gesture a masterpiece of contempt. He glances back at it, contemptuous, angry – angry, you almost feel, because he cannot wipe out the awful, provoking lettering with one sweep of his high Prussian boot. He glances slowly around the clearing, and now, as his eyes meet yours, you grasp the depth of his hatred. But there is triumph there, too – revengeful, triumphant hate.

"Suddenly, as though his face were not giving quite complete expression to his feelings, he

Right: Petals being strewn on the streets of Berlin before the victory parade.

Below: Hitler and Goering respond to a cheering crowd from the Reich Chancellery.

throws his whole body into harmony with his mood. He swiftly snaps his hands on his hips, arches his shoulders, plants his feet wide apart. It is a magnificent gesture of defiance, of burning contempt for this place now and all that it has stood for in the 22 years since it witnessed the humbling of the German Empire.''

Hitler and his party then entered the armistice railway car, the Fuehrer seating himself in the chair occupied by Foch in 1918. Five minutes later the French delegation arrived, headed by Gen. Charles Huntziger. They looked shattered, but retained a tragic dignity. They had not been told that they would be led to this proud French shrine to undergo such a humiliation, and the shock was no doubt just what Hitler had calculated.

Hitler and his entourage left the *wagon-lit* as soon as General Keitel had read the preamble to the armistice terms. The conditions were hard and merciless, and on the second day of the negotiations the French delegates continued to bicker and delay. Finally, at 6:30 p.m. Keitel issued an ultimatum: The French must accept or reject the German armistice terms within an hour. Within the allotted time the French government capitulated. At 6:50 p.m. on June 22, 1940, Huntziger and Keitel signed the treaty. France was now destined to become a German vassal.

A light rain began to fall as the delegates left the armistice car and drove away. Down the road through the woods you could see an unbroken line of refugees making their way home on weary feet, on bicycles, on carts, a few fortunate ones on old trucks. I walked out to the clearing. A gang of German army engineers, shouting lustily, had already started to move the old *wagon-lit*.

"Where to?" I asked.

"To Berlin," they said.

The Franco-Italian armistice was signed in Rome two days later. Mussolini was able to occupy only what his troops had conquered, which meant a few hundred yards of French territory, and to impose a 50-mile demilitarized zone opposite him in France and Tunisia. The armistice was signed at 7:35 p.m. on June 24. Six hours later the guns in France lapsed into silence.

France, which had held out unbeaten for four years the last time, was out of the war after six weeks. German troops stood guard over most of Europe, from the North Cape above the Arctic Circle to Bordeaux, from the English Channel to the River Bug in eastern Poland. Adolf Hitler had reached the pinnacle. The former Austrian waif, this corporal of World War I, had become the greatest of German conquerors.

All that stood between him and establishment of German hegemony in Europe under his dictatorship was one indomitable Englishman, Winston Churchill, and the determined people Churchill led, who did not recognize defeat when it stared them in the face and who now stood alone, virtually unarmed, their island home besieged by the mightiest military machine the world had ever seen.

Below: German gains 1939-40.

3. Reaping the Whirlwind

The Last Days of the Third Reich

Britain Fights On

After the fall of France in June 1940, Adolf Hitler seems to have had no doubt that Britain would be anxious to make peace. The mighty German army had smashed everything that opposed it, had conquered the greater part of Europe for the Fuehrer, and now stood poised for the assault upon England's nearly defenseless shores. Why should the British fight on alone against hopeless odds?

Even when Prime Minister Winston Churchill stated publicly that Britain was not quitting, Hitler apparently did not believe it. On the evening of July 19 I watched him as he rose in the Reichstag to make his peace offer to Britain. In sharp contrast to his frequently hysterical orations, his talk that night was moderate, delivered in a tone of calm confidence.

"I feel it my duty," he said, "to appeal to reason and common sense in Great Britain. I consider myself in a position to make this appeal, since I am not the vanquished begging favors but the victor speaking in the name of reason. I can see no reason why this war must go on."

Not one of the many officials with whom I mingled at the close of the session had the slightest doubt that the British would accept the Fuehrer's magnanimous offer. But they were not to be deceived for long.

I had hardly arrived at Broadcasting House to report the speech to the United States when I picked up a BBC broadcast, in German, giving the British answer to Hitler. Already, within the hour, it was a determined No!

"Can you understand those British fools?" a German ministry official said to me then. "They're crazy!"

But despite their overweening confidence in their military supremacy, neither Hitler, the high command nor the general staffs of the army, navy and air force had ever seriously considered *how* a war with Great Britain could be fought and won. This is one of the great paradoxes of the Third Reich. At the very moment when Hitler stood at the zenith of his military power, his victorious armies stretched from the Pyrenees to the Arctic Circle, from the Atlantic to beyond the Vistula, he had no idea how to exploit his glittering success and bring the war to a victorious conclusion. This fateful neglect would ultimately prove his downfall.

Previous page: The ruins of the Reichstag in Berlin surrounded by the debris of war, May 1945.

Below: RAF Hurricane fighter planes on patrol.

The Air War Begins

Goering's great air offensive against Britain, Operation Eagle (*Adlerangriffe*), was launched on August 13 with the objective of driving the British Air Force from the skies and thus achieving the one condition on which the . . . invasion of the British Isles, Operation Sea Lion, depended. The fat Reich Marshal, as he now was, had no doubts about victory. By mid-July he had become confident that British fighter defenses in southern England could be smashed within four days by an all-out assault, thus opening the way for the invasion. To destroy the R.A.F. completely would take a little longer, Goering told the Army High Command: from two to four weeks. In fact, the bemedaled German Air Force chief thought that the Luftwaffe alone could bring Britain to her knees and that an invasion by land forces probably would not be necessary.

To obtain this mighty objective he had three great air fleets (*Luftflotten*): Number 2 under Field Marshal Kesselring, operating from the Low Countries and northern France, Number 3 under Field Marshal Sperrle, based on northern France, and Number 5 under General Stumpff, stationed in Norway and Denmark. The first two had a total of 929 fighters, 875 bombers and 316 dive bombers; Number 5 was much smaller, with 123 bombers and 34 twin-engined ME-110 fighters. Against this vast force the R.A.F. had for the air defense of the realm at the beginning of August between 700 and 800 fighters.

Throughout July the Luftwaffe gradually stepped up its attacks on British shipping in the Channel and on Britain's southern ports. This was a probing operation. Though it was necessary to clear the narrow waters of British ships before an invasion could begin, the main object of these preliminary air assaults was to lure the British fighters to battle. This failed. The R.A.F. Command shrewdly declined to commit more than a fraction of its fighters, and as a result considerable damage was done to shipping and to some of the ports. Four destroyers and eighteen merchant ships were sunk, but this preliminary sparring cost the Luftwaffe 296 aircraft destroyed and 135 damaged. The R.A.F. lost 148 fighters.

On August 12, Goering gave orders to launch Eagle the next day. As a curtain raiser heavy attacks were made on the twelfth on enemy radar stations, five of which were actually hit and damaged and one knocked out, but the Germans at this stage did not realize how vital to Britain's defenses radar was and did not pursue the attack. On the thirteenth and fourteenth the Germans put in the air some 1,500 aircraft, mostly against R.A.F. fighter fields, and though they claimed five of them had been "completely destroyed" the damage was actually negligible and the Luftwaffe lost forty-seven planes against thirteen for the R.A.F.

August 15 brought the first great battle in the skies. The Germans threw in the bulk of their

Above: Prime Minister Winston Churchill.

planes from all three air fleets, flying 810 bombing and 1,149 fighter sorties. Luftflotte 5, operating from Scandinavia, met disaster. By sending some 800 planes in a massive attack on the south coast the Germans had expected to find the northeast coast defenseless. But a force of a hundred bombers, escorted by thirty-four twin-engined Me-110 fighters, was surprised by seven squadrons of Hurricanes and Spitfires as it approached the Tyneside and severely mauled. Thirty German planes, mostly bombers, were shot down without loss to the defenders. That was the end of Air Fleet 5 in the Battle of Britain. It never returned to it.

In the south of England that day the Germans were more successful. They launched four massive attacks, one of which was able to penetrate almost to London. Four aircraft factories at Croydon were hit and five R.A.F. fighter fields damaged. In all, the Germans lost seventy-five planes, against thirty-four for the R.A.F. At this rate, despite their numerical superiority, the Germans could scarcely hope to drive the R.A.F. from the skies.

Now Goering made the first of his two tactical

164

Right: Goering inspects
Luftwaffe units in
northern France, August
1940.

Below: German observers
watch a Stuka dive-
bomber returning after a
raid on Britain.

errors. The skill of British Fighter Command in committing its planes to battle against vastly superior attacking forces was based on its shrewd use of radar. From the moment they took off from their bases in Western Europe the German aircraft were spotted on British radar screens, and their course so accurately plotted that Fighter Command knew exactly where and when they could best be attacked. This was something new in warfare and it puzzled the Germans, who were far behind the British in the development and use of this electronic device. "We realized [Adolf Galland, the famous German fighter ace, later testified] that the R.A.F. fighter squadrons must be controlled from the ground by some new procedure because we heard commands skillfully and accurately directing Spitfires and Hurricanes on to German formations . . . For us this radar and fighter control was a surprise and a very bitter one."

Yet the attack on British radar stations which on August 12 had been so damaging had not been continued and on August 15, they day of his first major setback, Goering called them off entirely, declaring: "It is doubtful whether there is any point in continuing the attacks on radar stations, since not one of those attacked has so far been put out of action."

A second key to the successful defense of the skies over southern England was the sector station. This was the underground nerve center from

which the Hurricanes and Spitfires were guided by radiotelephone into battle on the basis of the latest intelligence from radar, from ground observation posts and from pilots in the air. The Germans, as Galland noted, could hear the constant chatter over the air waves between the sector stations and the pilots aloft and finally began to understand the importance of these ground control centers. On August 24 they switched their tactics to the destruction of the sector stations, seven of which on the airfields around London were crucial to the protection of the south of England and of the capital itself. This was a blow against the very vitals of Britain's air defenses.

Until that day the battle had appeared to be going against the Luftwaffe. On August 17 it lost seventy-one aircraft against the R.A.F.'s twenty-seven. The slow Stuka dive bomber, which had helped to pave the way for the Army's victories in Poland and in the West, was proving to be a sitting duck for British fighters and on that day, August 17, was withdrawn by Goering from the battle, reducing the German bombing force by a third. Between August 19 and 23 there was a five-day lull in the air due to bad weather. Goering, reviewing the situation at Karinhall, his country show place near Berlin, on the nineteenth, ordered that as soon as the weather improved, the Luftwaffe was to concentrate its attacks exclusively on the Royal Air Force.

"We have reached the decisive period of the air war against England," he declared. "The vital task is the defeat of the enemy air force. Our first aim is to destroy the enemy's fighters."

From August 24 to September 6 the Germans sent over an average of a thousand planes a day to achieve this end. For once the Reich Marshal was right. The Battle of Britain had entered its decisive

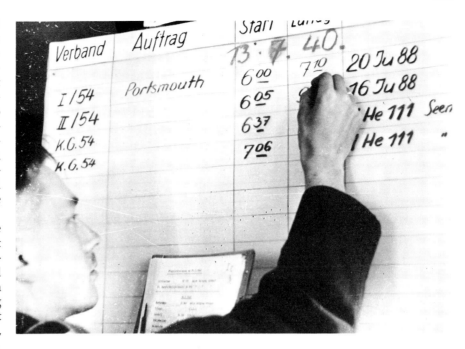

Above: Luftwaffe raid indicator board during the Battle of Britain.

stage. Though the R.A.F. pilots, already strained from a month of flying several sorties a day, put up a valiant fight, the German preponderance in sheer numbers began to tell. Five forward fighter fields in the south of England were extensively damaged and, what was worse, six of the seven key sector stations were so severely bombed that the whole communications system seemed to be on the verge of being knocked out. This threatened disaster to Britain.

Worst of all, the pace was beginning to tell on the R.A.F. fighter defense. In the crucial fortnight between August 23 and September 6 the British lost 466 fighters destroyed or badly damaged, and though they did not know it at the time the Luft-

Left: Luftwaffe aircrew preparing for a raid on Britain in a Ju-88.

166

Top: German fighter
aircraft being refuelled on
the Channel Island of
Guernsey. The Channel
Islands were the only part
of Britain held by the
Nazis, being occupied
from the end of June 1940
to 1945.

waffe losses were less: 385 aircraft, of which 214 were fighters and 138 bombers. Moreover, the R.A.F. had lost 103 pilots killed and 128 seriously wounded – a quarter of all those available.

"The scales," as Churchill later wrote, "had tilted against Fighter Command . . . There was much anxiety." A few more weeks of this and Britain would have had no organized defense of its skies. The invasion would almost certainly be successful.

And then suddenly Goering made his second tactical error, this one comparable in its consequences to Hitler's calling off the armored attack on Dunkirk on May 24. It saved the battered, reeling R.A.F. and marked one of the major turning points of history's first great battle in the air.

With the British fighter defense suffering losses in the air and on the ground which it could not for long sustain, the Luftwaffe switched its attack on September 7 to massive night bombing of London. The R.A.F. fighters were reprieved.

What had happened in the German camp to cause this change in tactics which was destined to prove so fatal to the ambitions of Hitler and Goering? The answer is full of irony.

To begin with, there was a minor navigational error by the pilots of a dozen German bombers on the night of August 23. Directed to drop their loads on aircraft factories and oil tanks on the outskirts of London, they missed their mark and dropped bombs on the center of the capital, blowing up some homes and killing some civilians. The British thought it was deliberate and as retaliation bombed Berlin the next evening.

It didn't amount to much. There was a dense cloud cover over Berlin that night and only about half of the eighty-one R.A.F. bombers dispatched found the target. Material damage was negligible. But the effect on German morale was tremendous. *For this was the first time that bombs had ever fallen on Berlin.*

"The Berliners are stunned," I wrote in my diary the next day, August 26. "They did not think it could ever happen. When this war began, Goering assured them it couldn't . . . They believed him. Their disillusionment today therefore is all the greater. You have to see their faces to measure it."

Berlin was defended by two great rings of anti-aircraft guns and for three hours while the visiting bombers droned above the clouds, which prevented the hundreds of searchlight batteries from picking them up, the flak fire was the most intense I had ever seen. But not a single plane was brought down. The British also dropped a few leaflets saying that "the war which Hitler started will go on, and it will last as long as Hitler does." This was good propaganda, but the thud of exploding bombs was better.

The R.A.F. came over in greater force on the night of August 28-29 and, as I noted in my diary,

Far right: Firefighting in
London during the blitz,
October 1940.

Right: Luftwaffe aircrew
enjoying the hot summer
weather.

Right: Anti-aircraft guns firing from Hyde Park, London, during a night air raid.

Below: Germans practise landing from a make-shift landing craft, September 1940.

"for the first time killed Germans in the capital of the Reich." The official count was ten killed and twenty-nine wounded. The Nazi bigwigs were outraged. Goebbels, who had ordered the press to publish only a few lines on the first attack, now gave instructions to cry out at the "brutality" of the British flyers in attacking the defenseless women and children of Berlin. Most of the capital's dailies carried the same headline: COWARDLY BRITISH ATTACK. Two nights later, after the third raid, the headlines read: BRITISH AIR PIRATES OVER BERLIN!

"The main effect of a week of constant British night bombings," I wrote in my diary on September 1, has been to spread great disillusionment among the people and sow doubt in their minds . . . Actually the bombings have not been very deadly."

September 1 was the first anniversary of the beginning of the war. I noted the mood of the people, aside from their frayed nerves at having been robbed of their sleep and frightened by the surprise bombings and the terrific din of the flak. "In this year German arms have achieved victories never equaled even in the brilliant military history of this aggressive, militaristic nation. And yet the war is not yet over or won. And it was on this aspect that people's minds were concentrated today. They long for peace. And they want it before the winter comes."

And so on the late afternoon of September 7 the great air attack on London began. At about 5 P.M. that Saturday the first wave of 320 bombers, protected by every fighter the Germans had, flew up the Thames and began to drop their bombs on Woolwich Arsenal, various gas works, power stations, depots and mile upon mile of docks. The whole vast area was soon a mass of flames. At one locality, Silvertown, the population was surrounded by fire and had to be evacuated by water. At 8:10 P.M., after dark, a second wave of 250 bombers arrived and resumed the attack, which was kept up by successive waves until dawn at 4:30 on Sunday morning. The next evening at 7:30, the attack was renewed by two hundred bombers and continued throughout the night. Some 842 persons were killed and 2,347 wounded, according to the official British historian, during these first two nights, and vast damage was inflicted on the sprawling city. The assault went on all the following week, night after night.

And then, stimulated by its successes, or what it thought were such, the Luftwaffe decided to carry out a great daylight assault on the battered, burning capital. This led on Sunday, September 15, to one of the decisive battles of the war.

Some two hundred German bombers, escorted by three times as many fighters, appeared over the Channel about midday, headed for London. Fighter Command had watched the assembling of the attackers on its radar screens and was ready.

The Germans were intercepted before they approached the capital, and though some planes got through, many were dispersed and others shot down before they could deliver their bomb load. Two hours later an even stronger German formation returned and was routed. Though the British claimed to have shot down 185 Luftwaffe planes, the actual figure, as learned after the war from the Berlin archives, was much lower – fifty-six, but thirty-four of these were bombers. The R.A.F. lost only twenty-six aircraft.

The day had shown that the Luftwaffe could not for the moment, anyway, now that it had given Fighter Command a week to recover, carry out a successful major daylight attack on Britain. That being so, the prospect of an effective landing was dim. September 15 therefore was a turning point, "the crux," as Churchill later judged, of the Battle of Britain. Though Goering the next day, in ordering a change of tactics that provided for the use of bombers in daylight no longer to bomb but merely to serve as decoys for British fighters, boasted that the enemy's fighters "ought to be finished off within four or five days," Hitler and the Army and Navy commanders knew better and two days after the decisive air battle, on September 17, the Fuehrer called off Sea Lion indefinitely.

Although London was to take a terrible pounding for fifty-seven consecutive nights from September 7 to November 3 from a daily average of two hundred bombers, so that it seemed certain to

Below: Rhine barges being towed along the French coast, ready for the planned invasion of Britain.

Above: The German propaganda film *Sieg im Westen (Victory in the West)* being screened in a Channel Islands' cinema.

make clear, never fully recovered from the blow it received in the skies over Britain that late summer and fall.

The German Navy, crippled by the losses off Norway in the early spring, was unable, as its chiefs admitted all along, to provide the sea power for an invasion of Britain. Without this, and without air supremacy, the German Army was helpless to move across the narrow Channel waters. For the first time in the war Hitler had been stopped, his plans of further conquest frustrated, and just at the moment, as we have seen, when he was certain that final victory had been achieved.

He had never conceived – nor had anyone else up to that time – that a decisive battle could be decided in the air. Nor perhaps did he yet realize as the dark winter settled over Europe that a handful of British fighter pilots, by thwarting his invasion, had preserved England as a great base for the possible reconquest of the Continent from the west at a later date. His thoughts were perforce turning elsewhere; in fact, as we shall see, had already turned.

Britain was saved. For nearly a thousand years it had successfully defended itself by sea power. Just in time, its leaders, a very few of them, despite all the bungling (of which these pages have been so replete) in the interwar years, had recognized that air power had become decisive in the mid-twentieth century and the little fighter plane and its pilot the chief shield for defense. As Churchill told the Commons in another memorable peroration on August 20, when the battle in the skies still raged and its outcome was in doubt, "never in the field of human conflict was so much owed by so many to so few."

Churchill, as he later revealed, that the city would soon be reduced to a rubble heap, and though most of Britain's other cities, Coventry above all, were to suffer great damage throughout the grim fall and winter, British morale did not collapse nor armament production fall off, as Hitler had so confidently expected. Just the opposite. Aircraft factories in England, one of the prime targets of the Luftwaffe bombers, actually outproduced the Germans in 1940 by 9,924 to 8,070 planes. Hitler's bomber losses over England had been so severe that they could never be made up, and in fact the Luftwaffe, as the German confidential records

Right: Signing the Tripartite Pact between Germany, Italy and Japan, September 27, 1940.

The Thieves Fall Out

Above: Japanese naval delegation meeting Hitler, 1940.

During the summer of 1940, Soviet Premier Joseph Stalin took advantage of German preoccupations by moving into the Baltic states and the Balkans. From now on relations between Berlin and Moscow began to sour. It was one thing for Stalin and Hitler to double-cross third parties, but quite another when they began to double-cross each other. Hitler, his armies engaged in the West, had been helpless to prevent the Russians from grabbing Lithuania, Latvia and Estonia, plus two Rumanian provinces, and his frustration added to his growing resentment. The Russian drive westward would have to be stopped, and first of all in Rumania – for the Wehrmacht was desperately dependent on Rumanian oil.

To complicate Hitler's problem, Hungary and Bulgaria also demanded slices of Rumanian territory. If a Balkan war broke out, Hitler realized, it would probably bring the Russians in to occupy *all* of Rumania.

By August 28 the situation had become so threatening that Hitler dispatched Foreign Minister Joachim von Ribbentrop to Vienna, where he was to lay down the law to the foreign ministers of Hungary and Rumania and make them accept Axis arbitration. This mission was accomplished without much trouble after Ribbentrop had browbeaten both sides, but the solution infuriated the Russians, who accused the German government of violating the Nazi-Soviet Pact, which called for consultation about questions of common interest. The thieves, as is almost inevitable in such cases, had begun to quarrel over the spoils.

As recriminations became more heated in the following days, Hitler grew exasperated. "Stalin is clever and cunning," the Fuehrer told his top military chiefs. "He demands more and more. A German victory has become unbearable for Russia. Therefore she must be brought to her knees as soon as possible."

The cold-blooded Nazi blackmailer had met his match, and the realization infuriated him. On December 18, 1940, Hitler issued Directive No. 21, headed "Operation Barbarossa." "TOP SECRET," it began. "The German armed forces must be prepared to *crush Soviet Russia in a quick campaign* before the end of the war against England. Preparations are to be completed by May 15, 1941."

But before Barbarossa could get under way, the southern flank, which lay in the Balkans, had to be secured. And here the Fuehrer ran into unexpected trouble from his Axis stooge, Benito Mussolini.

Left: Mussolini, Hitler and Ciano, Italian Foreign Minister, meet at the Brenner Pass, October 4, 1940.

Mussolini Deceives His Partner

Hitler and Mussolini had conferred on October 4, at the Brenner Pass. Hitler, as usual, had done most of the talking, but had *not* mentioned that he was sending troops to Rumania, which Italy also coveted. When the Duce learned of this a few days later, he was indignant.

"Hitler always faces me with a *fait accompli*," he fumed to his son-in-law, Foreign Minister Galeazzo Ciano. "This time I am going to pay him back in his own coin. He will find out from the newspapers that I have occupied Greece. In this way the equilibrium will be re-established."

On October 22 Mussolini set the date for a surprise Italian assault on Greece for October 28, and on the same day he wrote Hitler a letter (predated October 19) alluding to his contemplated action but making it vague as to the exact date. He feared, Ciano noted that day in his diary, that the Fuehrer might "order" him to halt. Hitler and Ribbentrop got wind of the Duce's plans, and at the Fuehrer's orders the Nazi foreign minister urged an immediate meeting of the Axis leaders. Mussolini suggested October 28 at Florence and, when

his German visitor alighted from the train that morning, greeted him full of glee: "Fuehrer, we are on the march! Victorious Italian troops crossed the Greco-Albanian frontier at dawn today!"

According to all accounts, Mussolini greatly enjoyed this revenge on his friend for all the previous occasions when the Nazi dictator had marched into a country without previously informing his Italian ally. Hitler was furious. This rash act against a sturdy foe at the worst possible time of year threatened to upset the applecart in the Balkans.

Hardly had the Fuehrer returned to Berlin before disaster overtook the Duce's armies in Greece. Within a week, the "victorious" Italian attack had been turned into a rout. Worse still, the British, by sending troops to the Greek mainland, threatened the whole German position in the Balkans.

To counter this danger, Hitler ordered the army to prepare immediate plans to invade Greece through Bulgaria and Rumania.

By the third week in February 1941, the Germans had massed a formidable army of 680,000 troops in Rumania. On the night of February 28, German army units crossed the Danube from Rumania and took up strategic positions in Bulgaria, which the next day joined the Tripartite Pact.

Above: Hitler and Prince Paul, Regent of Yugoslavia, 1941.

Left: General Erwin Rommel, commander of the Afrika Korps, 1941-2.

Right: "Il Duce," Benito Mussolini, 1941.

Hitler's Most Catastrophic Decision

The hardier Yugoslavs were not quite so accommodating. But after the usual threats and browbeating, the Yugoslav premier and foreign minister signed up Yugoslavia in the Tripartite Pact. Hitler was highly pleased, for this would facilitate his attack on Greece.

But the Yugoslav ministers had no sooner returned to Belgrade after signing the pact than they, the government and the prince regent were overthrown on the night of March 26, by a popular uprising. The new regime immediately offered to sign a nonaggression pact with Germany, but it was obvious that it would not accept the puppet status for Yugoslavia that the Fuehrer had assigned. Indeed, during the celebrations in Belgrade, a crowd spat on the German minister's car.

The coup in Belgrade threw Adolf Hitler into one of the wildest rages of his entire life. He took it as a personal affront and in his fury made sudden decisions which would prove utterly disastrous to the fortunes of the Third Reich.

He hurriedly summoned his military chieftains to the Chancellery in Berlin on March 27 – the

meeting was so hastily called that Brauchitsch, Halder and Ribbentrop arrived late – and raged about the revenge he would take on the Yugoslavs. The Belgrade coup, he said, had endangered both Marita (code name for the Balkan campaign) and, even more, Barbarossa. He was therefore determined, "without waiting for possible declarations of loyalty of the new government, to destroy Yugoslavia militarily and as a nation. No diplomatic inquiries will be made," he ordered, "and no ultimatums presented." Yugoslavia, he added, would be crushed with "unmerciful harshness." He ordered Goering then and there to "destroy Belgrade in attacks by waves," with bombers operating from Hungarian air bases. He issued Directive No. 25 for the immediate invasion of Yugoslavia and told Keitel and Jodl to work out that very evening the military plans. He instructed Ribbentrop to advise Hungary, Rumania and Italy that they would all get a slice of Yugoslavia, which would be divided up among them, except for a Croatian puppet state.

And then, according to an underlined passage in the top-secret OKW notes of the meeting, Hitler announced the most fateful decision of all.

"The beginning of the Barbarossa operation," he told his generals, "will have to be postponed up to four weeks."

Above: German assault gun in Athens, April 1941.

174

Above: Serbian troops surrender, April 1941.

This postponement of the attack on Russia in order that the Nazi warlord might vent his personal spite against a small Balkan country which had dared to defy him was probably the most catastrophic single decision in Hitler's career. It is hardly too much to say that by making it that March afternoon in the Chancellery in Berlin during a moment of convulsive rage he tossed away his last golden opportunity to win the war and to make of the Third Reich, which he had created with such stunning if barbarous genius, the greatest empire in German history and himself the master of Europe. Field Marshal von Brauchitsch, the Commander in Chief of the German Army, and General Halder, the gifted Chief of the General Staff, were to recall it with deep bitterness but also with more understanding of its consequences than they showed at the moment of its making, when later the deep snow and subzero temperatures of Russia hit them three or four weeks short of what they thought they needed for final victory. For ever afterward they and their fellow generals would blame that hasty, ill-advised decision of a vain and infuriated man for all the disasters that ensued.

Military Directive No. 25, which the Supreme Commander issued to his generals before the meeting broke up, was a typical Hitlerian document. "The military putsch in Yugoslavia has altered the political situation in the Balkans. Yugoslavia, in spite of her protestations of loyalty, must be considered for the time being as an enemy and

therefore crushed as speedily as possible. It is my intention to force my way into Yugoslavia . . . and to annihilate the Yugoslav Army . . ."

Jodl, as Chief of the Operations Staff of OKW, was told to prepare the plans that very night. "I worked the whole night at the Reich Chancellery," Jodl later told the Nuremberg tribunal. "At four o'clock in the morning of March 28, I put an *aide-mémoire* into the hand of General von Rintelen, our liaison officer with the Italian High Command."

For Mussolini, whose sagging armies in Albania were in danger of being taken in the rear by the Yugoslavs, had to be told immediately of the German operational plans and asked to co-operate with them. To make sure that the Duce understood what was expected of him and without waiting for General Jodl to concoct the military plans, Hitler dashed off a letter at midnight of the twenty-seventh and ordered it wired to Rome so that it would reach Mussolini that same night:

DUCE, events force me to give you by this quickest means my estimation of the situation and the consequences which may result from it.

From the beginning I have regarded Yugoslavia as a dangerous factor in the controversy with Greece . . . Today's reports leave no doubt as to the imminent turn in the foreign policy of Yugoslavia.

Therefore I have already arranged for all necessary measures . . . with military means. Now, I would cordially request you, Duce, not to undertake any further operations in Albania in the course of the next few days. I consider it necessary that you should cover and screen the most important passes from Yugoslavia into Albania with all available forces . . .

Accept my heartfelt and friendly greetings,
Yours,
ADOLF HITLER

For this short-range objective, the Nazi warlord was again right in his prediction, but he seems to have had no inkling how costly his successful revenge on Yugoslavia would be in the long run. At dawn on April 6, his armies in overwhelming strength fell on Yugoslavia and Greece, smashing across the frontiers of Bulgaria, Hungary and Germany itself with all their armor and advancing rapidly against poorly armed defenders dazed by the usual preliminary bombing.

Belgrade itself, as Hitler ordered, was razed to the ground. For three successive days and nights Goering's bombers ranged over the little capital at rooftop level – for the city had no antiaircraft guns – killing 17,000 civilians, wounding many more and reducing the place to a mass of smoldering rubble. "Operation Punishment," Hitler called it, and he obviously was satisfied that his commands had been so effectively carried out. The Yugoslavs, who had not had time to mobilize their tough little army and whose General Staff made the mistake of trying to defend the whole country, were overwhelmed. On April 13 German and Hungarian troops entered what was left of Belgrade and on the seventeenth the remnants of the Yugoslav Army, still twenty-eight divisions strong, surrendered at Sarajevo, the King and the Prime Minister escaping by plane to Greece.

The Greeks, who had humiliated the Italians in six months of fighting, could not stand up to Field Marshal List's Twelfth Army of fifteen divisions, four of which were armored. The British had hurriedly sent to Greece some four divisions from Libya – 53,000 men in all – but they, like the Greeks, were overwhelmed by the German panzers and by the murderous strikes of the Luft-

Below: German soldiers sight-seeing in Athens, April 1941.

Above: Dead German paratrooper on Crete, May 1941.

Below: German paratroopers on the attack during the fighting for Crete.

waffe. The northern Greek armies surrendered to the Germans and – bitter pill – to the Italians on April 23. Four days later Nazi tanks rattled into Athens and hoisted the swastika over the Acropolis. By this time the British were desperately trying once again to evacuate their troops by sea – a minor Dunkirk and almost as successful.

By the end of April – in three weeks – it was all over except for Crete, which was taken by the Germans from the British in an airborne assault toward the end of May. Where Mussolini had failed so miserably all winter, Hitler had succeeded in a few days in the spring. Though the Duce was relieved to be pulled off the hook, he

was humiliated that it had to be done by the Germans. Nor were his feelings assuaged by Italy's disappointing share in the Yugoslav spoils, which Hitler now began to divide up.

The Balkans was not the only place where the Fuehrer pulled his muddling junior partner off the hook. After the annihilation of the Italian armies in Libya Hitler, although reluctantly, had finally consented to sending a light armored division and some Luftwaffe units to North Africa, where he arranged for General Erwin Rommel to be in overall command of the Italo-German forces. Rommel, a dashing resourceful tank officer, who had distinguished himself as commander of a panzer division in the Battle of France, was a type of general whom the British had not previously met in the North African desert and he was to prove an immense problem to them for two years. But he was not the only problem. The sizable army and air force which the British had sent to Greece from Libya had greatly weakened them in the desert. At first they were not unduly worried, not even after their intelligence reported the arrival of German armored units in Tripolitania at the end of February. But they should have been.

Rommel, with his German panzer division and two Italian divisions, one of which was armored, struck suddenly at Cyrenaica on the last day of March. In twelve days he recaptured the province, invested Tobruk and reached Bardia, a few miles from the Egyptian border. The entire British position in Egypt and the Suez was again threatened; in fact, with the Germans and Italians in Greece the British hold on the eastern Mediterranean had become gravely endangered.

Another spring, the second of the war, had brought more dazzling German victories, and the predicament of Britain, which now held out alone,

battered at home by nightly Luftwaffe bombings, its armies overseas chased out of Greece and Cyrenaica, seemed darker and more hopeless than ever before. Its prestige, so important in a life-and-death struggle where propaganda was so potent a weapon, especially in influencing the United States and Russia, had sunk to a new low point.

Hitler was not slow or backward in taking advantage of this in a victory speech to the Reichstag in Berlin on May 4. It consisted mostly of a venomous and sarcastic personal attack on Churchill as the instigator (along with the Jews) of the war and as the man who was masterminding the losing of it.

As to the Yugoslavian coup which had provoked him to such fury, Hitler made no attempt to hide his true feelings. "We were all stunned by that coup, carried through by a handful of bribed conspirators . . . You will understand, gentlemen, that when I heard this I at once gave orders to attack Yugoslavia. *To treat the German Reich in this way is impossible* . . . "

Arrogant though he was over his spring victories and especially those over the British, Hitler did not fully realize what a blow they had been to Britain nor how desperate was the predicament of the Empire. On the very day he was addressing the Reichstag, Churchill was writing President Roosevelt about the grave consequences of the loss of Egypt and the Middle East and pleading for America to enter the war. The Prime Minister was in one of the darkest moods he was to know throughout the war. "I adjure you, Mr. President," he wrote, "not to underestimate the gravity of the consequences which may follow from a Middle-East collapse."

The German Navy urged the Fuehrer to make the most of this situation. To further improve mat-

ters for the Axis, the newly appointed premier of Iraq, Rashid Ali, who was pro-German, had led an attack against the British airbase of Habbaniya, outside Bagdad, and appealed to Hitler for aid in driving the British out of the country. This was at the beginning of May. With Crete conquered by May 27, Admiral Raeder, who had always been lukewarm to Barbarossa, appealed to Hitler on May 30 to prepare a decisive offensive against Egypt and Suez, and Rommel, eager to continue his advance as soon as he had received reinforcements, sent similar pleas from North Africa. "This stroke," Raeder told the Fuehrer "would be more deadly to the British Empire than the capture of London!" A week later the Admiral handed Hitler a memorandum prepared by the Operations Division of the Naval War Staff which warned that, while Barbarossa "naturally stands in the foreground of the OKW leadership, it must under no circumstances lead to the abandonment of, or to delay in, the conduct of the war in the Mediterranean."

But the Fuehrer already had made up his mind; in fact, he had not changed it since the Christmas holidays when he had promulgated Barbarossa and told Admiral Raeder that Russia must be "eliminated first." His landlocked mind simply did not comprehend the larger strategy advocated by the Navy. Even before Raeder and the Naval Staff pleaded with him at the end of May he laid down the law in Directive No. 30 issued on May 25. He ordered a military mission, a few planes and some arms to be dispatched to Bagdad to help Iraq. "I have decided," he said, "to encourage developments in the Middle East by supporting Iraq." But he saw no further than this small inadequate step. As for the larger, bold strategy championed by the admirals and Rommel, he declared: "Whether – and if so, by what means – it would be possible afterward to launch an offensive against the Suez Canal and eventually oust the British finally from their position between the Mediterranean and the Persian Gulf cannot be decided until Operation Barbarossa is completed." The destruction of the Soviet Union came first; all else must wait. This, we can now see, was a staggering blunder. At this moment, the end of May 1941,

Above: General Ramcke awarding medals to veterans of the battle for Crete. Casualties among the German paratroop force were high and it was never used in as adventurous a fashion again.

Right: General von Kleist. Panzer forces under Kleist's command played a lead role in the campaign in France in 1940 and later in Yugoslavia and Russia in 1941.

Hitler, with the use of only a fraction of his forces, could have dealt the British Empire a crushing blow, perhaps a fatal one. No one realized this better than the hard-pressed Churchill. In his message to President Roosevelt on May 4, he had admitted that, were Egypt and the Middle East to be lost, the continuation of the war "would be a hard, long and bleak proposition," even if the United States entered the conflict. But Hitler did not understand this. His blindness is all the more incomprehensible because his Balkan campaign had delayed the commencement of Barbarossa by several weeks and thereby jeopardized it. The conquest of Russia would have to be accomplished in a shorter space of time than originally planned. For there was an inexorable deadline: the Russian winter, which had defeated Charles XII and Napoleon. That gave the Germans only six months to overrun, before the onset of winter, an immense country that had never been conquered from the west. And though June had arrived, the vast army which had been turned southeast into Yugoslavia and Greece had to be brought back great distances to the Soviet frontier over unpaved roads and run-down single-track railway lines that were woefully inadequate to handle so swarming a traffic.

The delay, as things turned out, was fatal. Defenders of Hitler's military genius have contended that the Balkan campaign did not set back the timetable for Barbarossa appreciably and that in any case the postponement was largely due to the late thaw that year which left the roads in Eastern Europe deep in mud until mid-June. But the testimony of the key German generals is otherwise. Field Marshal Friedrich Paulus, whose name will always be associated with Stalingrad, and who at this time was the chief planner of the Russian campaign on the Army General Staff, testified on the stand at Nuremberg that Hitler's decision to destroy Yugoslavia postponed the

beginning of Barbarossa by "about five weeks." The Naval War Diary gives the same length of time. Field Marshal von Rundstedt, who led Army Group South in Russia, told Allied interrogators after the war that because of the Balkan campaign "we began at least four weeks late. That," he added, "was a very costly delay."

At any rate, on April 30, when his armies had completed their conquest of Yugoslavia and Greece, Hitler set the new date for Barbarossa. It was to begin on June 22, 1941.

Right: Hitler at a conference at Army headquarters, August 1941. Left to right, Keitel, an aide, Brauchistch, Hitler and Halder.

The Planning of the Terror

No holds were to be barred in the taking of Russia. Hitler insisted that the generals understand this very clearly. Early in March 1941, he convoked the chiefs of the three armed services and the key Army field commanders and laid down the law. Halder took down his words. "The war against Russia will be such that it cannot be conducted in a knightly fashion. This struggle is one of ideologies and racial differences and will have to be conducted with unprecedented, unmerciful and unrelenting harshness. All officers will have to rid themselves of obsolete ideologies. I know that the necessity for such means of waging war is beyond the comprehension of you generals but . . . I insist absolutely that my orders be executed without contradiction. The commissars are the bearers of ideologies directly opposed to National Socialism. Therefore the commissars will be liquidated. German soldiers guilty of breaking international law . . . will be excused. Russia has not participated in the Hague Convention and therefore has no rights under it."

Thus was the so-called "Commissar Order" issued; it was to be much discussed at the Nuremberg trial when the great moral question was posed to the German generals whether they should have obeyed the orders of the Fuehrer to commit war crimes or obeyed their own consciences.

According to Halder, as he later remembered it, the generals were outraged at this order and, as soon as the meeting was over, protested to their Commander in Chief, Brauchitsch. This spineless Field Marshal promised that he would "fight against this order in the form it was given." Later, Halder swears, Brauchitsch informed OKW in writing that the officers of the Army "could never execute such orders." But did he?

In his testimony on direct examination at Nuremberg Brauchitsch admitted that he took no such action with Hitler "because nothing in the world could change his attitude." What the head of the Army did, he told the tribunal, was to issue a written order that "discipline in the Army was to be strictly observed along the lines and regulations that applied in the past."

"You did not give any order directly referring to the Commissar Order?" Lord Justice Lawrence, the peppery president of the tribunal, asked Brauchitsch.

"No," he replied. "I could not rescind the order directly."

The old-line Army officers, with their Prussian traditions, were given further occasion to struggle with their consciences by subsequent directives issued in the name of the Fuehrer by General Keitel on May 13. The principal one limited the functions of German courts-martial. They were to give way to a more primitive form of law. "Punishable

Below: German panzers being shipped to North Africa.

Above: Rommel discussing tactics in North Africa.

tive said, the occupied areas in Russia were to be sealed off while Himmler went to work. Not even the "highest personalities of the Government and Party," Hitler stipulated, were to be allowed to have a look. The same directive named Goering for the "exploitation of the country and the securing of its economic assets for use by German industry." Incidentally, Hitler also declared in this order that as soon as military operations were concluded Russia would be "divided up into individual states with governments of their own."

Just how this would be done was to be worked out by Alfred Rosenberg, the befuddled Balt and officially the leading Nazi thinker, who had been, as we have seen, one of Hitler's early mentors in the Munich days. On April 20 the Fuehrer appointed him "Commissioner for the Central Control of Questions Connected with the East-European Region" and immediately this Nazi dolt, with a positive genius for misunderstanding history, even the history of Russia, where he was born and educated, went to work to build his castles in his once native land. Rosenberg's voluminous files were captured intact; like his books, they make dreary reading.

By early May, Rosenberg had drawn up his first wordy blueprint for what promised to be the greatest German conquest in history. To begin with, European Russia was to be divided up into so-called Reich Commissariats. Russian Poland would become a German protectorate called Ostland, the Ukraine "an independent state in alliance with Germany." Caucasia, with its rich oil fields, would be ruled by a German "plenipotentiary," and the three Baltic States and White Russia would form a German protectorate preparatory to being annexed outright to the Greater German Reich. This last feat, Rosenberg explained in one of the endless memoranda which he showered on Hitler and the generals in order, as he said, to elucidate "the historical and racial conditions" for his decisions, would be accomplished by Germanizing the racially assimilable Balts and "banishing the undesirable elements." In Latvia and Estonia, he cautioned "banishment on a large scale will have to be envisaged." Those driven out would be replaced by Germans, preferably war veterans. "The Baltic Sea," he ordained, "must become a Germanic inland sea."

Two days before the troops jumped off, Rosenberg addressed his closest collaborators who were to take over the rule of Russia: "The job of feeding the German people stands at the top of the list of Germany's claims on the East. The southern [Russian] territories will have to serve . . . for the feeding of the German people. We see absolutely no reason for any obligation on our part to feed also the Russian people with the products of that surplus territory. We know that this is a harsh necessity, bare of any feelings . . . The future will hold very hard years in store for the Russians."

Very hard years indeed, since the Germans were deliberately planning to starve to death millions of them!

Goering, who had been placed in charge of the economic exploitation of the Soviet Union, made this even clearer than Rosenberg did. In a long directive of May 23, 1941, his Economic Staff, East, laid it down that the surplus food from Russia's black-earth belt in the south must not be diverted

offenses committed by enemy civilians [in Russia] do not, until further notice, come any longer under the jurisdiction of the courts-martial . . . *persons suspected of criminal action will be brought at once before an officer. This officer will decide whether they are to be shot.* With regard to *offenses* committed against *enemy civilians by members of the Wehrmacht, prosecution is not obligatory* even where the deed is at the same time a military crime or offense."

The Army was told to go easy on such offenders, remembering in each case all the harm done to Germany since 1918 by the "Bolsheviki." Courts-martial of German soldiers would be justified only if "maintenance of discipline or security of the Forces calls for such a measure." At any rate, the directive concluded, "only those court sentences are confirmed which are in accordance with the political intentions of the High Command." The directive was to "be treated as 'most secret.'"

A second directive of the same date signed by Keitel on behalf of Hitler entrusted Himmler with *"special tasks"* for the preparation of the political administration in Russia – "tasks," it said, "which result from the struggle which has to be carried out between two opposing political systems." The Nazi secret-police sadist was delegated to act "independently" of the Army, "under his own responsibility." The generals well knew what the designation of Himmler for "special tasks" meant, though they denied that they did when they took the stand at Nuremberg. Furthermore, the directo the people in the industrial areas, where, in any case, the industries would be destroyed. The workers and their families in these regions would simply be left to starve – or, if they could, to emigrate to Siberia. Russia's great food production must go to the Germans . . .

How many Russian civilians would die as the result of this deliberate German policy? A meeting of state secretaries on May 2 had already given a general answer. *"There is no doubt,"* a secret memorandum of the conference declared, *"that as a result, many millions of persons will be starved to death if we take out of the country the things necessary for us."*

Did any German, even one single German, protest against this planned ruthlessness, this well-thought-out scheme to put millions of human beings to death by starvation? In all the memoranda concerning the German directives for the spoliation of Russia, there is no mention of anyone's objecting – as at least some of the generals did in regard to the Commissar Order. These plans were not merely wild and evil fantasies of distorted minds and souls of men such as Hitler, Goering, Himmler and Rosenberg. For weeks and months, it is evident from the records, hundreds of German officials toiled away at their desks in the cheerful light of the warm spring days, adding up figures and composing memoranda which coldly calculated the massacre of millions. By starvation, in this case. Heinrich Himmler, the mild-faced ex-chicken farmer, also sat at his desk at S.S. headquarters in Berlin those days, gazing through his pince-nez at plans for the massacre of other millions in a quicker and more violent way.

Well pleased with the labors of his busy minions, both military and civilian, in planning the onslaught on the Soviet Union, her destruction, her exploitation and the mass murder of her citizenry, Hitler on April 30 set the date for the attack – June 22 – made his victory speech in the Reichstag on May 4 and then retired to his favorite haunt, the Berghof above Berchtesgaden, where

Left: Hitler speaking to a wounded soldier on Heroes' Remembrance Day.

he could gaze at the splendor of the Alpine mountains, their peaks still covered with spring snow, and contemplate his next conquest, the greatest of all, at which, as he had told his generals, the world would hold its breath.

It was here on the night of Saturday, May 10, 1941, that he received strange and unexpected news which shook him to the bone and forced him, as it did almost everyone else in the Western world, to take his mind for the moment off the war. His closest personal confidant, the deputy leader of the Nazi Party, the second in line to succeed him after Goering, the man who had been his devoted and fanatically loyal follower since 1921 and, since Roehm's murder, the nearest there was to a friend, had literally flown the coop and on his own gone to parley with the enemy!

Below: The New Order for Europe; a Serb hanged in Belgrade by the Germans, July 1941.

The Flight of Rudolf Hess

The first report late that evening of May 10 that Rudolf Hess had taken off alone for Scotland in a Messerschmitt-110 fighter plane hit Hitler, as Dr. Schmidt recalled, "as though a bomb had struck the Berghof." General Keitel found the Fuehrer pacing up and down his spacious study pointing a finger at his forehead and mumbling that Hess must have been crazy. "I've got to talk to Goering right away," Hitler shouted. The next morning there was an agitated powwow with Goering and all the party gauleiters as they sought to "figure out" – the words are Keitel's – how to present this embarrassing event to the German public and to the world. Their task was not made easier, Keitel later testified, by the British at first keeping silent about their visitor, and for a time Hitler and his conferees hoped that perhaps Hess had run out of gasoline, fallen into the North Sea and drowned.

The Fuehrer's first information had come in a somewhat incoherent letter from Hess which was delivered by courier a few hours after he took off at 5:45 P.M. on May 10 from Augsburg. "I can't recognize Hess in it. It's a different person. Something must have happened to him – some mental disturbance," Hitler told Keitel. But the Fuehrer was also suspicious. Messerschmitt, from whose company airfield Hess had taken off, was ordered arrested, as were dozens of men on the deputy leader's staff.

If Hitler was mystified by Hess's abrupt departure, so was Churchill by his unexpected arrival. Stalin was highly suspicious. For the duration of the war, the bizarre incident remained a mystery, and it was cleared up only at the Nuremberg trial, in which Hess was one of the defendants. The facts may be briefly set down.

Hess, always a muddled man though not so doltish as Rosenberg, flew on his own to Britain under the delusion that he could arrange a peace settlement. Though deluded, he was sincere – there seems to be no reason to doubt that. He had met the Duke of Hamilton at the Olympic games in Berlin in 1936, and it was within twelve miles of the Duke's home in Scotland – so efficient was his navigation – that he baled out of his Messerschmitt, parachuted safely to the ground and asked a farmer to take him to the Scottish lord. As

Below: Nazi leaders. On Hitler's left Hess and Streicher and, far right, Bormann.

it happened, Hamilton, a wing commander in the R.A.F., was on duty that Saturday evening at a sector operations room and had spotted the Messerschmitt plane off the coast as it came in to make a landfall shortly after 10 P.M. An hour later it was reported to him that the plane had crashed in flames, that the pilot, who had baled out and who gave his name as Alfred Horn, had claimed to be on a "special mission" to see the Duke of Hamilton. This meeting was arranged by British authorities for the next morning.

To the Duke, Hess explained that he was on "a mission of humanity and that the Fuehrer did not want to defeat England and wished to stop the fighting." The fact, Hess said, that this was his fourth attempt to fly to Britain – and that he was, after all, a Reich cabinet minister, showed "his sincerity and Germany's willingness for peace." In this interview, as in later ones with others, Hess was not backward in asserting that Germany would win the war and that if it continued the plight of the British would be terrible. Therefore, his hosts had better take advantage of his presence and negotiate peace. So confident was this Nazi fanatic that the British would sit down and parley with him, that he asked the Duke to request "the King to give him 'parole,' as he had come unarmed and of his own free will." Later he demanded that he be treated with the respect due to a cabinet member.

The subsequent talks, with one exception, were conducted on the British side by Ivone Kirkpatrick, the knowing former First Secretary of the British Embassy in Berlin, whose confidential reports were later made available at Nuremberg. To this sophisticated student of Nazi Germany Hess, after parroting Hitler's explanations of all the Nazi aggressions, from Austria to Scandinavia and the Lowlands, and having insisted that Britain was responsible for the war and would certainly lose it if she didn't bring a stop to it now, divulged his proposals for peace. They were none other than those which Hitler had urged on Chamberlain – unsuccessfully – on the eve of his attack on Poland: namely, that Britain should give Germany a free hand in Europe in return for Germany's giving Britain "a completely free hand in the Empire." The former German colonies would have to be returned and of course Britain would have to make peace with Italy.

"Finally, as we were leaving the room," Kirkpatrick reported, "Hess delivered a parting shot. He had forgotten, he declared, to emphasize that the proposal could only be considered on the understanding that it was negotiated by Germany with an English government other than the present one. Mr. Churchill, who had planned the war since 1936, and his colleagues who had lent themselves to his war policy, were not persons with whom the Fuehrer could negotiate."

For a German who had got so far in the jungle warfare within the Nazi Party and then within the Third Reich, Rudolf Hess, as all who knew him could testify, was singularly naive. He had expected, it is evident from the record of these interviews, to be received immediately as a serious negotiator – if not by Churchill, then by the "opposition party," of which he thought the Duke of Hamilton was one of the leaders. When his contacts with British officialdom continued to be restricted to Kirkpatrick, he grew bellicose and

threatening. At an interview on May 14, he pictured to the skeptical diplomat the dire consequences to Britain if she continued the war. There would soon be, he said, a terrible and absolutely complete blockade of the British Isles.

Hess urged that the conversations, which he had risked so much to bring about, get under way at once. "His own flight," as explained to Kirkpatrick, "was intended to give us a chance of opening conversations without loss of prestige. If we rejected this chance it would be clear proof that we desire no understanding with Germany, and Hitler would be entitled – in fact, it would be his duty – to destroy us utterly and to keep us after the war in a state of permanent subjection." Hess insisted that the number of negotiators be kept small. "As a Reich Minister he could not place himself in the position of being a lone individual subjected to a crossfire of comment and questions from a large number of people."

On this ridiculous note, the conversations ended, so far as Kirkpatrick was concerned. But –

Above: The border between German and Soviet occupied Poland on the eve of Operation Barbarossa.

184

Above: Waffen S.S. soldiers relaxing during the initial advance into Russia, June 1941.

Russian prosecutor told the tribunal that he was sure of it. And so was Joseph Stalin, whose mighty suspicions at this critical time seem to have been concentrated not on Germany, as they should have been, but on Great Britain. The arrival of Hess in Scotland convinced him that there was some deep plot being hatched between Churchill and Hitler which would give Germany the same freedom to strike the Soviet Union which the Russian dictator had given her to assault Poland and the West. When three years later the British Prime Minister, then on his second visit to Moscow, tried to convince Stalin of the truth, he simply did not believe it. It is fairly clear from the interrogations conducted by Kirkpatrick, who tried to draw the Nazi leader out on Hitler's intentions regarding Russia, that either Hess did not know of Barbarossa or, if he did, did not know that it was imminent.

The days following Hess's sudden departure were among the most embarrassing of Hitler's life. He realized that the prestige of his regime had been severely damaged by the flight of his closest collaborator. How was it to be explained to the German people and the outside world? The

surprisingly – the British cabinet, according to Churchill, "invited" Lord Simon to interview Hess on June 10. According to the Nazi deputy leader's lawyer at Nuremberg, Simon promised that he would bring Hess's peace proposals to the attention of the British government.

Hess's motives are clear. He sincerely wanted peace with Britain. He had not the shadow of doubt that Germany would win the war and destroy the United Kingdom unless peace were concluded at once. There were, to be sure, other motives. The war had brought his personal eclipse. Running the Nazi Party as Hitler's deputy during the war was dull business and no longer very important. What mattered in Germany now was running the war and foreign affairs. These were the things which engaged the attention of the Fuehrer to the exclusion of almost all else, and which put the limelight on Goering, Ribbentrop, Himmler, Goebbels and the generals. Hess felt frustrated and jealous. How better restore his old postion with his beloved Leader and in the country than by pulling off a brilliant and daring stroke of statesmanship such as singlehandedly arranging peace between Germany and Britain?

Finally, the beetle-browed deputy leader, like some of the other Nazi bigwigs – Hitler himself and Himmler – had come to have an abiding belief in astrology. At Nuremberg he confided to the American prison psychiatrist, Dr. Douglas M. Kelley, that late in 1940 one of his astrologers had read in the stars that he was ordained to bring about peace. He also related how his old mentor, Professor Haushofer, the Munich *Geopolitiker*, had seen him in a dream striding through the tapestried halls of English castles, bringing peace between the two great "Nordic" nations. For a man who had never escaped from mental adolescence, this was heady stuff and no doubt helped impel Hess to undertake his weird mission to England.

At Nuremberg one of the British prosecutors suggested still another reason: that Hess flew to England to try to arrange a peace settlement so that Germany would have only a one-front war to fight when she attacked the Soviet Union. The

The Invasion of Russia

questioning of the arrested members of Hess's entourage convinced the Fuehrer that his trusted lieutenant had simply cracked up. It was decided at the Berghof, after the British had confirmed Hess's arrival, to offer this explanation to the public. Soon the German press was dutifully publishing brief accounts that this once great star of National Socialism had become "a deluded, deranged and muddled idealist, ridden with hallucinations traceable to World War [I] injuries . . . It seemed that Party Comrade Hess lived in a state of hallucination, as a result of which he felt he could bring about an understanding between England and Germany . . . This, however, will have no effect on the continuance of the war, which has been forced on the German people."

Privately, Hitler gave orders to have Hess shot at once if he returned, and publicly he stripped his old comrade of all his offices, replacing him as deputy leader of the party by Martin Bormann, a more sinister and conniving character. The Fuehrer hoped that the bizarre episode would be forgotten as soon as possible; his own thoughts quickly turned again to the attack on Russia, which was not far off.

On Sunday morning, June 22, Adolf Hitler's armored, mechanized and hitherto invincible armies poured across the Niemen and various other rivers and penetrated swiftly into Russia. The Red Army was "surprised along the entire front." Within a few days tens of thousands of prisoners began to pour in; whole armies were quickly encircled. Indeed, by the beginning of autumn, Hitler believed that Russia was finished.

So according to plan was the German progress along a 1,000-mile front from the Baltic to the Black Sea, and so confident was the Nazi dictator that it would continue at an accelerated pace, that by the end of September he instructed the high command to prepare to disband 40 infantry divisions so that the manpower could be used by industry.

Below: Destroyed Soviet aircraft. Huge numbers of Soviet aircraft were hit on their bases by the initial Luftwaffe attacks.

Right: Panzer crewmen in
Russia, summer 1941.

Russia's two greatest cities, Leningrad and
Moscow, seemed to Hitler about to fall. On September 18 he issued strict orders: "A capitulation
of Leningrad or Moscow is not to be accepted,
even if offered." What was to happen to them he
made clear to his commanders in a directive of
September 29:

"The Fuehrer has decided to have Leningrad
wiped off the face of the earth. Requests that the
city be taken over will be turned down, for the
problem of the survival of the population and of
supplying it with food is one which should not be
solved by us. In this war for existence we have no
interest in keeping even part of this great city's
population."

The same week, on October 3, Hitler said in an
address to the German people, "I declare without
any reservation that the enemy in the East has
been struck down and will never rise again."

This boast was, to say the least, premature. In
reality the Russians, despite the entrapment and
loss of some of their best armies, had begun in July
to put up a mounting resistance such as the Wehrmacht had never before encountered. The reports
of front-line commanders began to be peppered –
and then laden – with accounts of severe fighting,
desperate Russian stands and counterattacks.
And there proved to be more Russians, with better
equipment, than Adolf Hitler had dreamed was
possible.

Fresh Soviet divisions of which German intelligence had no inkling were continually being
thrown into battle. "At the beginning," Halder
wrote in his diary on August 11, "we reckoned
with some 200 enemy divisions, and we have
already identified 360. When a dozen of them are
destroyed, the Russians throw in another dozen."
Field Marshal Gerd von Rundstedt put it bluntly

to Allied interrogators after the war. "I realized," he said, "soon after the attack was begun that everything that had been written about Russia was nonsense."

Several generals, Heinz Guderian, Guenther Blumentritt and Sepp Dietrich among them, have left reports expressing astonishment at their first encounter with the Russian T-34 tank, of which they had not previously heard and which was so heavily armored that the shells from the German antitank guns bounced harmlessly off it. The appearance of this panzer, Blumentritt said later, marked the beginning of what came to be called the "tank terror." Also, for the first time in the war, the Germans did not have the benefit of overwhelming superiority in the air to protect their ground troops and scout ahead. Despite the heavy losses on the ground in the first day of the campaign and in early combat, Soviet fighter planes kept appearing, like the fresh divisions, out of nowhere. Moreover, the swiftness of the German advance and the lack of suitable airfields in Russia left the German fighter bases too far back to provide effective cover at the front. "At several stages in the advance," General von Kleist later reported, "my panzer forces were handicapped through lack of cover overhead."

There was another German miscalculation about the Russians which Kleist mentioned to the British military writer Liddell Hart and which, of course, was shared by most of the other peoples of the West that summer.

"Hopes of victory," Kleist said, "were largely built on the prospect that the invasion would produce a political upheaval in Russia . . . Too high hopes were built on the belief that Stalin would be overthrown by his own people if he suffered heavy defeats. The belief was fostered by the Fuehrer's political advisers."

Indeed Hitler had told Jodl, "We have only to kick in the door and the whole rotten structure will come crashing down."

Above: NCO of a German cavalry unit on the Eastern front, 1941.

Left: German horse-drawn supply train in Russia. Throughout the war the German Army's transport units were never fully mechanized.

A Vital Question of Objectives

The opportunity to kick in the door seemed to the Fuehrer to be at hand halfway through July when there occurred the first great controversy over strategy in the German High Command and led to a decision by the Fuehrer, over the protests of most of the top generals, which Halder thought proved to be "the greatest strategic blunder of the Eastern campaign." The issue was simple but fundamental. Should Field Marshal Fedor von Bock's Army Group Center, the most powerful and so far the most successful of the three main German armies, push on the two hundred miles to Moscow from Smolensk, which it had reached on July 16? Or should the original plan, which Hitler had laid down in the December 18 directive, and which called for the main thrusts on the north and south flanks, be adhered to? In other words, was Moscow the prize goal, or Leningrad and the Ukraine?

The Army High Command, led by Brauchitsch and Halder and supported by Bock, whose central army group was moving up the main highway to Moscow, and by Guderian, whose panzer forces were leading it, insisted on an all-out drive for the Soviet capital. There was much more to their argument than merely stressing the psychological value of capturing the enemy capital. Moscow, they pointed out to Hitler, was a vital source of armament production and, even more important, the center of the Russian transportation and communications system. Take it, and the Soviets would be unable to move troops and supplies to the distant fronts, which thereafter would weaken, wither and collapse.

This, we learn from Halder's diary, was recommended by the Army High Command on August 18. "The effect," says Halder, "was explosive." Hitler had his hungry eyes on the food belt and

Below: A group of German soldiers crowds round to take ghoulish souvenir photographs of hanged Soviet partisans.

industrial areas of the Ukraine and on the Russian oil fields just beyond in the Caucasus. Besides, he thought he saw a golden opportunity to entrap Marshal Semën Budënny's armies east of the Dnieper beyond Kiev, which still held out. He also wanted to capture Leningrad and join up with the Finns in the north. To accomplish these twin aims, several infantry and panzer divisions from Army Group Center would have to be detached and sent north and especially south. Moscow could wait.

On August 21, Hitler hurled a new directive at his rebellious General Staff. Halder copied it out word for word in his diary the next day. "The proposals of the Army for the continuation of the operations in the East do not accord with my intentions. The most important objective to attain before the onset of winter is not the capture of Moscow but the taking of the Crimea, the industrial and coal-mining areas of the Donets basin and the cutting off of Russian oil supplies from the

Above: German public execution of Soviet officials.

Caucasus. In the north it is the locking up of Leningrad and the union with the Finns."

The Soviet Fifth Army on the Dnieper in the south, whose stubborn resistance had annoyed Hitler for several days, must, he laid it down, be utterly destroyed, the Ukraine and the Crimea occupied, Leningrad surrounded and a junction with the Finns achieved. "Only then," he concluded, "will the conditions be created whereby Marshal Semën Timoshenko's army can be attacked and successfully defeated."

"Thus," commented Halder bitterly, "the aim of defeating decisively the Russian armies in front of Moscow was subordinated to the desire to obtain a valuable industrial area and to advance in the direction of Russian oil . . . Hitler now became obsessed with the idea of capturing both Leningrad and Stalingrad, for he persuaded himself that if these two 'holy cities of Communism' were to fall, Russia would collapse."

To add insult to injury to the field marshals and the generals who did not appreciate his strategic genius, Hitler sent what Halder called a "countermemorandum" (to that of the Army on the eighteenth), which the General Staff Chief described as "full of insults," such as stating that the Army High Command was full of "minds fossilized in out-of-date theories."

"Unbearable! Unheard of! The limit!" Halder snorted in his diary the next day. He conferred all afternoon and evening with Field Marshal von Brauchitsch about the Fuehrer's "inadmissible" mixing into the business of the Army High Command and General Staff, finally proposing that the head of the Army and he himself resign their posts. "Brauchitsch refused," Halder noted, "because it wouldn't be practical and would change nothing." The gutless Field Marshal had already, as on so many other occasions, capitulated to the onetime corporal.

When General Guderian arrived at the Fuehrer's headquarters the next day, August 23, and was egged on by Halder to try to talk Hitler out of his disastrous decision, though the hard-bitten panzer leader needed no urging, he was met by Brauchitsch. "I forbid you," the Army Commander in Chief said, "to mention the question of Moscow to the Fuehrer. The operation to the south has been ordered. The problem now is simply how it is to be carried out. Discussion is pointless."

Nevertheless, when Guderian was ushered into the presence of Hitler – neither Brauchitsch nor Halder accompanied him – he disobeyed orders and argued as strongly as he could for the immediate assault on Moscow.

Guderian later wrote, "Hitler let me speak to the end. He then described in detail the considerations which had led him to make a different decision. He said that the raw materials and agriculture of the Ukraine were vitally necessary for the future prosecution of the war. He spoke of the need of neutralizing the Crimea, 'that Soviet aircraft carrier for attacking the Rumanian oil fields.' For the first time I heard him use the phrase: 'My generals know nothing about the economic aspects of war.' . . . He had given strict orders that the attack on Kiev was to be the immediate strategic objective and all actions were to be carried out with that in mind. I here saw for the first time a spectacle with which I was later to become very familiar: all those present – Keitel, Jodl and others – nodded in agreement with every sentence that Hitler uttered, while I was left alone with my point of view . . ."

But Halder had at no point in the previous dis-

Above: Maintenance on a Panzer Mark IV in Russia.

Right: German anti-tank gunners destroy Soviet armor.

cussions nodded his agreement. When Guderian saw him the next day and reported his failure to get Hitler to change his mind, Guderian says the General Staff Chief "to my amazement suffered a complete nervous collapse, which led him to make accusations and imputations which were utterly unjustified."

This was the most severe crisis in the German military High Command since the beginning of the war. Worse were to follow, with adversity.

In itself Rundstedt's offensive in the south, made possible by the reinforcement of Guderian's panzer forces and infantry divisions withdrawn from the central front, was, as Guderian put it, a great tactical victory. Kiev itself fell on September 19 – German units had already penetrated 150 miles beyond it – and on the twenty-sixth the Battle of Kiev ended with the encirclement and surrender of 665,000 Russian prisoners, according to the German claim. To Hitler it was "the greatest battle in the history of the world," but though it was a singular achievement some of his generals were more skeptical of its strategic significance. Bock's armorless army group in the center had been forced to cool its heels for two months along the Desna River just beyond Smolensk. The autumn rains, which would turn the Russian roads into quagmires, were drawing near. And after them – the winter, the cold and the snow.

Left: German infantry in Russia.

Below: German military column on the line of march in the Ukraine.

The Great Drive on Moscow

Reluctantly Hitler gave in to the urging of Brauchitsch, Halder and Bock and consented to the resumption of the drive on Moscow. But too late! Halder saw him on the afternoon of September 5 and now the Fuehrer, his mind made up, was in a hurry to get to the Kremlin. "Get started on the central front within eight to ten days," the Supreme Commander ordered. ("Impossible!" Halder exclaimed in his diary.) "Encircle them, beat and destroy them," Hitler added, promising to return to Army Group Center Guderian's panzer group, then still heavily engaged in the Ukraine, and add General Georg-Hans Reinhardt's tank corps from the Leningrad front. But it was not until the beginning of October that the armored forces could be brought back, refitted and made ready. On October 2 the great offensive was finally launched. "Typhoon" was the code name. A mighty wind, a cyclone, was to hit the Russians, destroy their last fighting forces before Moscow and bring the Soviet Union tumbling down.

But here again the Nazi dictator became a victim of his megalomania. Taking the Russian capital before winter came was not enough. He gave orders that Field Marshal von Leeb in the north was *at the same time* to capture Leningrad, make contact with the Finns beyond the city and drive on and cut the Murmansk railway. Also, at the same time, Rundstedt was to clear the Black Sea coast, take Rostov, seize the Maikop oil fields and push forward to Stalingrad on the Volga, thus severing Stalin's last link with the Caucasus. When Rundstedt tried to explain to Hitler that this meant an advance of more than four hundred miles beyond the Dnieper, with his left flank dangerously exposed, the Supreme Commander told him that the Russians in the south were now

incapable of offering serious resistance. Rundstedt, who says that he "laughed aloud" at such ridiculous orders, was soon to find the contrary.

The German drive along the old road which Napoleon had taken to Moscow at first rolled along with all the fury of a typhoon. In the first fortnight of October, in what later Blumentritt called a "textbook battle," the Germans encircled two Soviet armies between Vyazma and Bryansk and claimed to have taken 650,000 prisoners along with 5,000 guns and 1,200 tanks. By October 20 German armored spearheads were within forty miles of Moscow and the Soviet ministries and foreign embassies were hastily evacuating to Kuibyshev on the Volga. Even the sober Halder, who had fallen off his horse and broken a collarbone and was temporarily hospitalized, now believed that with bold leadership and favorable weather Moscow could be taken before the severe Russian winter set in.

The fall rains, however, had commenced. *Rasputitza*, the period of mud, set in. The great army, moving on wheels, was slowed down and often forced to halt. Tanks had to be withdrawn from battle to pull guns and ammunition trucks out of the mire. Chains and couplings for this job were lacking and bundles of rope had to be dropped by Luftwaffe transport planes which were badly needed for lifting other military supplies. The rains began in mid-October and, as Guderian later remembered, "the next few weeks were dominated by the mud." General Blumentritt, chief of staff of Field Marshal von Kluge's Fourth Army, which was in the thick of the battle for Moscow, has vividly described the predicament. "The infantryman slithers in the mud, while many teams of horses are needed to drag each gun forward. All wheeled vehicles sink up to their axles in the slime. Even tractors can only move with great difficulty. A large portion of our heavy artillery was soon stuck fast . . . The strain that all this caused our already exhausted troops can perhaps be imagined."

For the first time there crept into the diary of Halder and the reports of Guderian, Blumentritt and other German generals signs of doubt and then of despair. It spread to the lower officers and the troops in the field – or perhaps it stemmed from them. "And now, when Moscow was already almost in sight," Blumentritt recalled, "the mood both of commanders and troops began to change. Enemy resistance stiffened and the fighting became more bitter . . . Many of our companies were reduced to a mere sixty or seventy men." There was a shortage of serviceable artillery and tanks. "Winter," he says, "was about to begin, but there was no sign of winter clothing . . . Far behind the front the first partisan units were beginning to make their presence felt in the vast forests and swamps. Supply columns were frequently ambushed . . ."

Now, Blumentritt remembered the ghosts of the Grand Army, which had taken this same road to Moscow, and the memory of Napoleon's fate began to haunt the dreams of the Nazi conquerors. The German generals began to read, or reread, Caulaincourt's grim account of the French conqueror's disastrous winter in Russia in 1812.

Far to the south, where the weather was a little warmer but the rain and the mud were just as bad, things were not going well either. Kleist's tanks had entered Rostov at the mouth of the Don on

Top right: Mixed columns of horse and mechanized vehicles in Russia.

Bottom right: Destroyed Soviet T-34 tanks in a marsh.

Below: German troops pose for the camera in Lappland besides a sign marking the edge of the Arctic Circle.

November 21 amidst much fanfare from Dr. Goebbel's propaganda band that the "gateway to the Caucasus" had been opened. It did not remain open very long. Both Kleist and Rundstedt realized that Rostov could not be held. Five days later the Russians retook it and the Germans, attacked on both the northern and southern flanks, were in headlong retreat back fifty miles to the Mius River where Kleist and Rundstedt had wished in the first place to establish a winter line.

The retreat from Rostov is another little turning point in the history of the Third Reich. Here was the first time that any Nazi army had ever suffered a major setback. "Our misfortunes began with Rostov," Guderian afterward commented; "that was the writing on the wall." It cost Field Marshal von Rundstedt, the senior officer in the German Army, his command. As he was retreating to the Mius, he subsequently told Allied interrogators, "Suddenly an order came to me from the Fuehrer: 'Remain where you are, and retreat no further.' I immediately wired back: 'It is madness to attempt to hold. In the first place the troops cannot do it and in the second place if they do not retreat they will be destroyed. I repeat that this order be rescinded or that you find someone else.' That same night the Fuehrer's reply arrived: 'I am acceding to your request. Please give up your command.'"

"I then," said Rundstedt, "went home."

This mania for ordering distant troops to stand fast no matter what their peril perhaps saved the German Army from complete collapse in the shattering months ahead, though many generals dispute it, but it was to lead to Stalingrad and other disasters and to help seal Hitler's fate.

"This Winter of Our Misery"

Heavy snows and subzero temperatures came early that winter in Russia. Guderian noted the first snow on the night of October 6-7, just as the drive on Moscow was being resumed. It reminded him to ask headquarters again for winter clothing, especially for heavy boots and heavy wool socks. On October 12 he recorded the snow as still falling. On November 3 came the first cold wave, the thermometer dropping below the freezing point and continuing to fall. By the seventh Guderian was reporting the first "severe cases of frostbite" in his ranks and on the thirteenth that the temperature had fallen to 8 degrees below zero, Fahrenheit, and that the lack of winter clothing "was becoming increasingly felt." The bitter cold affected guns and machines as well as men. "Ice was causing a lot of trouble since the calks for the tank tracks had not yet arrived. The cold made the telescopic sights useless. In order to start the engines of the tanks fires had to be lit beneath them. Fuel was freezing on occasions and the oil became viscous . . . Each regiment [of the 112th Infantry Division] had already lost some 500 men from frostbite. As a result of the cold the machine guns were no longer able to fire and our 37-mm. antitank guns had proved ineffective against the [Russian] T-34 tank.

"The result," says Guderian, "was a panic which reached as far back as Bogorodsk. This was the first time that such a thing had occurred during the Russian campaign, and it was a warning that the combat ability of our infantry was at an end."

But not only of the infantry. On November 21 Halder scribbled in his diary that Guderian had telephoned to say that his panzer troops "had reached their end." This tough, aggressive tank commander admits that on this very day he

decided to visit the commander of Army Group Center, Bock, and request that the orders he had received be changed, since he "could see no way of carrying them out." He was in a deep mood of depression, writing on the same day: "The icy cold, the lack of shelter, the shortage of clothing, the heavy losses of men and equipment, the wretched state of our fuel supplies – all this makes the duties of a commander a misery, and the longer it goes on the more I am crushed by the enormous responsibility I have to bear."

In retrospect Guderian added: "Only he who saw the endless expanse of Russian snow during this winter of our misery and felt the icy wind that blew across it, burying in snow every object in its path; who drove for hour after hour through that no-man's land only at last to find too thin shelter with insufficiently clothed, half-starved men; and who also saw by contrast the well-fed, warmly clad and fresh Siberians, fully equipped for winter fighting . . . can truly judge the events which now occurred."

Those events may now be briefly narrated, but not without first stressing one point: terrible as the Russian winter was and granted that the Soviet troops were naturally better prepared for it than the German, the main factor in what is now to be set down was not the weather but the fierce fighting of the Red Army troops and their indomitable will not to give up. The diary of Halder and the reports of the field commanders, which constantly express amazement at the extent and severity of Russian attacks and counterattacks and despair at the German setbacks and losses, are proof of that. The Nazi generals could not understand why the Russians, considering the nature of their tyrannical regime and the disastrous effects of the first German blows, did not collapse, as had the French and so many others with less excuse.

"With amazement and disappointment," Blumentritt wrote, "we discovered in late October and early November that the beaten Russians seemed quite unaware that as a military force they had almost ceased to exist." Guderian tells of meeting an old retired Czarist general at Orel on the road to Moscow, who said to him, "If only you had come twenty years ago, we should have welcomed you with open arms. But now it's too late. We were just beginning to get on our feet, and now you arrive and throw us back twenty years so that we will have to start from the beginning all over again. Now we are fighting for Russia and in that cause we are all united."

Yet, as November approached its end amidst fresh blizzards and continued subzero temperatures, Moscow seemed within grasp to Hitler and most of his generals. North, south and west of the capital German armies had reached points within twenty to thirty miles of their goal. To Hitler poring over the map at his headquarters far off in East Prussia the last stretch seemed no distance at all. His armies had advanced five hundred miles; they had only twenty to thirty miles to go. "One final heave," he told Jodl in mid-November, "and we shall triumph." On the telephone to Halder on November 22, Field Marshal von Bock, directing Army Group Center in its final push for Moscow, compared the situation to the Battle of the Marne, "where the last battalion thrown in decided the battle." Despite increased enemy resistance Bock told the General Staff Chief he believed "every-

Below: Finnish troops near Leningrad. Finland joined the German attack on Russia at the end of June 1941 in an attempt to regain territory lost in the Winter War of 1939-40.

ARCTIC OCEAN

ICELAND
REYKJAVIK

Barents Sea

PETSAMO
MURMANSK
NARVIK
ARCHANGEL
White Sea

NORWAY
SWEDEN
FINLAND
TRONDHEIM
PETROZAVODSK

15 Sept 1941
Siege of Leningrad
begins

HELSINKI
VIIPURI
L. Ladoga

BERGEN
OSLO
STOCKHOLM
TALLINN
LENINGRAD
DEMYANSK

5/6 Dec 1941-end April 1942
Russian counteroffensive
on Moscow axis

22 June 1941
("Barbarossa")
Germany invades
Russia

NORTH
SEA

EDINBURGH
DENMARK COPENHAGEN

PSKOV
RIGA
MOSCOW
R U S S I A

EIRE GREAT
DUBLIN
LIVERPOOL
BRITAIN
LONDON
AMSTERDAM
NETH.

KAUNAS
KÖNIGSBERG
DANZIG
E.PRUSSIA

SMOLENSK
TULA
Volga

19 Nov 1942
High-tide of German expansion,
Russian counteroffensive begins

ATLANTIC
OCEAN

HAMBURG
BERLIN
BRUSSELS BELG.

MINSK
WARSAW
POLAND

VORONEZH
KHARKOV
STALINGRAD

Caspian Sea

COLOGNE
Rhine
PARIS LUX.
Vistula

6-17 April 1941
Germany invades
Yugoslavia

GERMANY
LVOV
KIEV
Dnieper
ZAPOROZHYE
ROSTOV
Don

FRANCE
MUNICH VIENNA
BERNE SWITZ.
SLOVAKIA
BUDAPEST
HUNGARY
ODESSA
GROZNY
NOVOROSSIISK

Bay of Biscay
VICHY
MILAN
TURIN
VENICE
FLORENCE

RUMANIA
BUCHAREST
SEVASTOPOL
TIFLIS

BORDEAUX

BELGRADE
YUGOSLAVIA
Danube
BLACK SEA

LISBON
MADRID
Corsica
11 November 1942
Germans occupy
Vichy France

ROME
BULGARIA
SOFIA
ALBANIA

IRAN

PORTUGAL
SPAIN
Sardinia
NAPLES
ISTANBUL
ANKARA
T U R K E Y

8 Nov 1942
US/British forces land
in Morocco & Algeria

9 Nov 1942
German forces
land in Tunisia

6-28 April 1941
Germany invades
Greece invaded

GREECE
ATHENS
SYRIA
(Free French)
IRAQ
(Br)

PORT LYAUTEY
SP.MOR. (Br)
GIBRALTAR

ORAN
ALGIERS BÔNE
TUNIS
MALTA (Br)

20-29 May 1941
Crete invaded
Crete
Dodecanese
(Italian)
Cyprus
(Br)
DAMASCUS

CASABLANCA
SAFI
MEDITERRANEAN
PALESTINE
(Br)
JERUSALEM
AMMAN
TRANSJORDAN
(Br)

MOROCCO
(Vichy French)
ALGERIA
(Vichy French)
TUNISIA
(Vichy French)

1941-1942
Axis forces & Brit Eighth Army
engaged in battles across the desert

SEA
ALEXANDRIA
Suez Canal
CAIRO
SAUDI ARABIA

TRIPOLI
BENGHAZI
Tripoli
EL ALAMEIN

23 Oct-4 Nov 1942
Battle of El Alamein

LIBYA
(Italian)
SIRTE
EL AGHEILA
Nile
EGYPT

GERMAN OCCUPIED, 1 JAN 1941
ALLIED WITH AXIS
GERMAN OCCUPIED, 1 JAN – 29 MAY 1941
22 JUNE 1941 – 19 NOV 1942
GERMAN FRONT LINES
16 JULY 1941
5 DECEMBER 1941
END-APRIL 1942
19 NOVEMBER 1942
MILES 500
KILOMETERS 800

Above: German expansion 1941-42.

thing was attainable." By the last day of November he was literally throwing in his last battalion. The final all-out attack on the heart of the Soviet Union was set for the next day, December 1, 1941.

It stumbled on a steely resistance. The greatest tank force ever concentrated on one front: General Hoepner's Fourth Tank Group and General Hermann Hoth's Third Tank Group just north of Moscow and driving south, Guderian's Second Panzer Army just to the south of the capital and pushing north from Tula, Kluge's great Fourth Army in the middle and fighting its way due east through the forests that surrounded the city – on this formidable array were pinned Hitler's high hopes. By December 2 a reconnaissance battalion of the 258th Infantry Division had penetrated to Khimki, a suburb of Moscow, within sight of the spires of the Kremlin, but was driven out the next morning by a few Russian tanks and a motley force of hastily mobilized workers from the city's factories.

This was the nearest the German troops ever got to Moscow; it was their first and last glimpse of the Kremlin. Already on the evening of December 1, Bock, who was now suffering severe stomach cramps, had telephoned Halder to say that he could no longer "operate" with his weakened troops. The General Staff Chief had tried to cheer him on. "One must try," he said, "to bring the enemy down by a last expenditure of force. If that proves impossible then we will have to draw new conclusions." The next day Halder jotted in his diary: "Enemy resistance has reached its peak." On the following day, December 3, Bock was again on the phone to the Chief of the General Staff, who noted his message in his diary: "Spearheads of the Fourth Army again pulled back because the flanks could not come forward . . . The moment must be faced when the strength of our troops is at an end."

When Bock spoke for the first time of going over

Above: German troops in snow clothing. Good winter clothing was in very short supply for the Germans in Russia in 1941.

Below: German machine gun post in Russia, winter 1942.

December 5 was the critical day. Everywhere along the 200-mile semi-circular front around Moscow the Germans had been stopped. By evening Guderian was notifying Bock that he was not only stopped but must pull back, and Bock was telephoning Halder that "his strength was at an end," and Brauchitsch was telling his Chief of the General Staff in despair that he was quitting as Commander in Chief of the Army. It was a dark and bitter day for the German generals. "This was the first time," Guderian later wrote, "that I had to take a decision of this sort, and none was more difficult . . . Our attack on Moscow had broken down. All the sacrifices and endurance of our brave troops had been in vain. We had suffered a grievous defeat."

At Kluge's Fourth Army headquarters, Blumentritt, the chief of staff, realized that the turning point had now been reached. Recalling it later, he wrote: "Our hopes of knocking Russia out of the war in 1941 had been dashed at the very last minute.

The next day, December 6, General Georgi Zhukov, who had replaced Marshal Timoshenko as commander of the central front but six weeks before, struck. On the 200-mile front before Moscow he unleashed seven armies and two cavalry corps – 100 divisions in all – consisting of troops that were either fresh or battle-tried and were equipped and trained to fight in the bitter cold and the deep snow. The blow which this relatively unknown general now delivered with such a formidable force of infantry, artillery, tanks, cavalry

to the defensive Halder tried to remind him that "the best defense was to stick to the attack."

It was easier said than done, in view of the Russians and the weather. The next day, December 4, Guderian, whose Second Panzer Army had been halted in its attempt to take Moscow from the south, reported that the thermometer had fallen to 31 degrees below zero. The next day it dropped another five degrees. His tanks, he said, were "almost immobilized" and he was threatened on his flanks and in the rear north of Tula.

and planes, which Hitler had not faintly suspected existed, was so sudden and so shattering that the German Army and the Third Reich never fully recovered from it. For a few weeks during the rest of that cold and bitter December and on into January it seemed that the beaten and retreating German armies, their front continually pierced by Soviet breakthroughs, might disintegrate and perish in the Russian snows, as had Napoleon's Grand Army just 130 years before. At several crucial moments it came very close to that. Perhaps it was Hitler's granite will and determination and certainly it was the fortitude of the German soldier that saved the armies of the Third Reich from a complete debacle.

But the failure was great. The Red armies had been crippled but not destroyed. Moscow had not been taken, nor Leningrad nor Stalingrad nor the oil fields of the Caucasus; and the lifelines to Britain and America, to the north and to the south, remained open. For the first time in more than two years of unbroken military victories the armies of Hitler were retreating before a superior force.

That was not all. The failure was greater than that. Halder realized this, at least later. "The myth of the invincibility of the German Army," he wrote, "was broken." There would be more German victories in Russia when another summer came around, but they could never restore the myth. December 6, 1941, then, is another turning point in the short history of the Third Reich and one of the most fateful ones. Hitler's power had reached its zenith; from now on it was to decline, sapped by the growing counterblows of the nations against which he had chosen to make aggressive war.

The Fuehrer Honors a Promise

On Sunday, December 7, 1941, one day after Zhukov had launched his vast surprise counterattack, an event occurred on the other side of the earth that transformed the European war into a world war. Japanese bombers attacked Pearl Harbor. The next day Hitler hurried back by train to Berlin from his field headquarters in the East. He had made a solemn secret promise to Japan, and the time had come to keep it.

The Japanese onslaught on the U.S. Pacific Fleet at Pearl Harbor at 7:30 a.m. on Sunday, December 7, 1941, caught Berlin as completely by surprise as it did Washington. Though Hitler had made an oral promise that Germany would join Japan in a war against the United States, the assurance had not yet been signed, and the Japanese had not breathed a word to the Germans about Pearl Harbor. Besides, at this moment, Hitler was fully occupied trying to rally his faltering generals and retreating troops in Russia.

But there is no doubt that Japan's sneaky blow against the American fleet at Pearl Harbor kindled the Fuehrer's admiration – all the more so because it was the kind of "surprise" he had been so proud of pulling off so often himself. He expressed this to the Japanese ambassador: "You gave the right declaration of war! This method is the only proper one."

The Fuehrer quickly decided to honor his unwritten promise to the Japanese. He was fed up with Roosevelt's attacks on him and on Nazism; his patience was exhausted by the warlike acts of the U.S. Navy against German U-boats in the Atlantic. Furthermore, he harbored a growing contempt for the United States and disastrously underestimated its potential strength. "I don't see much future for the Americans," he told his cronies at a conference a month later. "It's a decayed country. My feelings against Americanism are feelings of hatred and deep repugnance."

At the same time, he grossly overestimated Japan's military power, and he told some of his followers a few months later that he thought Japan's entry into the war had been "of exceptional value to us, if only because of the date chosen.

"It was, in effect, at the moment when the surprises of the Russian winter were pressing most heavily on the morale of our people, and when everybody in Germany was oppressed by the certainty that sooner or later the United States would come into the conflict. Japanese intervention therefore was, from our point of view, most opportune."

At 2:30 p.m. on December 11, Germany formally declared war on the United States. Adolf Hitler, who a bare six months before had faced only a beleaguered Britain in a war which seemed to him as good as won, now, by deliberate choice, had arrayed against him the three greatest industrial powers in the world in a struggle in which military might depended largely, in the long run, on economic strength. Moreover, those three enemy countries together had a great preponderance of manpower over the three Axis nations. At the time, neither Hitler nor his generals nor his admirals seem to have weighed these sobering facts.

Above: U-boat in Brest harbor displays a captured US flag, August 1942. The German U-boats scored many successes off the US East Coast in the first months of 1942.

Left: Admiral Doenitz congratulating U-boat officers on their return from the convoy routes.

Early 1942: False Appearances

Although the Fuehrer's folly in refusing to allow the German armies in Russia to retreat in time had led to heavy losses, there is little doubt that Hitler's fanatical determination to hold on and fight also helped stem the Soviet tide. The traditional courage and endurance of the German soldiers did the rest.

By February 20 the Russian offensive had run out of steam, and at the end of March the season of deep mud set in, bringing a relative quiet to the front. Both sides were exhausted. A German army report of March 30, 1942, revealed what a terrible toll had been paid in the winter fighting: of a total of 162 combat divisions in the East only eight were ready for offensive missions. The 16 armored divisions had among them only 140 serviceable tanks – less than the normal number for one division.

While the troops were resting and refitting, Hitler was busy with plans for the coming summer's offensive. "If I do not get the oil of the Caucasus," Hitler told General Friedrich Paulus, commander of the ill-fated Sixth Army, just before the summer offensive began, "then I must end this war."

Stalin could have said almost the same thing. He, too, had to have the Caucasian oil to stay in the war. That was where the significance of Stalingrad came in. German possession of it would block the last main route over which the oil, as long as the Russians held the wells, could reach central Russia.

Besides oil to propel his planes and tanks and trucks, Hitler needed men to fill out his thinned ranks. Total casualties at the end of winter fighting were 1,167,835, and there were not enough replacements to make up for such losses. The high command turned to Germany's allies – or, rather, satellites – for additional troops. Hitler himself appealed to Mussolini for Italian formations, but the Duce was concerned about his ally's defeats on the Eastern front. Hitler decided it was time for another meeting, to explain how strong Germany still was.

The Fuehrer, as always, did most of the talking.

"Hitler talks, talks, talks," Ciano, the Italian foreign minister, wrote in his diary. "Mussolini suffers – he, who is in the habit of talking himself, and who, instead, practically has to keep quiet. On the second day, after lunch, when everything had been said, Hitler talked uninterruptedly for an hour and 40 minutes. He omitted absolutely no argument: war and peace, religion and philosophy, art and history. The Germans – poor people – have to take it every day, and I am certain there isn't a gesture, a word or a pause, which they don't know by heart. General Jodl, after an epic struggle, finally went to sleep on the divan. Keitel was reeling, but he succeeded in keeping his head up. He was too close to Hitler to let himself go."

Despite the numbing avalanche of talk, Hitler got the promise of more Italian cannon fodder for the Russian front.

At first, that summer of 1942, the fortunes of the Axis prospered. Even before the jump-off toward the Caucasus and Stalingrad, a sensational victory was scored in North Africa. General Rommel had resumed his offensive, and by the end of June he was at El Alamein, 65 miles from the Nile. But he had reached it with just 13 operational tanks, and Hitler, obsessed with his Russian campaign, refused to reinforce him adequately. "Our strength," Rommel wrote in his diary on July 3, "has faded away."

Still, by the end of the summer of 1942, Adolf Hitler seemed to be on top of the world. German U-boats were sinking 700,000 tons of British and American shipping a month in the Atlantic – more than the Allied shipyards could replace. On the map the sum of Hitler's conquests by September 1942 looked staggering. German troops stood guard from the Arctic Ocean to Egypt, from the Atlantic Ocean to the border of Central Asia.

And yet these rosy appearances were deceptive. Almost all the generals saw flaws in the picture. They could be summed up: the Germans simply didn't have the resources – the men or the guns or the tanks or the planes or the means of transportation – to reach the objectives Hitler insisted on setting.

Even the rankest amateur strategist could see the growing danger to the German armies in southern Russia as Soviet resistance stiffened in the Caucasus and at Stalingrad and the season of the autumn rains approached. The long northern flank of the Sixth Army was dangerously exposed along the line of the upper Don for 350 miles from Stalingrad to Voronezh. Here Hitler had stationed three satellite armies: the Hungarian Second, south of Voronezh; the Italian Eighth, farther southeast; and the Rumanian Third, on the right at the bend of the Don just west of Stalingrad. Because of the bitter hostility of Rumanians and Hungarians to each other their armies had to be separated by the Italians. In the steppes south of Stalingrad there was a fourth satellite army, the Rumanian Fourth. Aside from their doubtful fighting qualities, all these armies were inadequately equipped, lacking armored power, heavy artillery and mobility. Furthermore, they were spread out very thinly. The Rumanian Third Army held a front of 105 miles with only sixty-nine

Below: U-boat at St Nazaire in March 1942.

battalions. But these "allied" armies were all Hitler had. There were not enough German units to fill the gap. And since he believed, as he told Halder, that the Russians were "finished," he did not unduly worry about this exposed and lengthy Don flank.

Yet it was the key to maintaining both the Sixth Army and the Fourth Panzer Army at Stalingrad and Army Group A in the Caucasus. Should the Don flank collapse not only would the German forces at Stalingrad be threatened with encirclement but those in the Caucasus would be cut off. Once more the Nazi warlord had gambled. It was not his first gamble of the summer's campaign.

On July 23, at the height of the offensive, he had made another. The Russians were in full retreat between the Donets and upper Don rivers, falling rapidly back toward Stalingrad to the east and toward the lower Don to the south. A decision had to be made. Should the German forces concentrate on taking Stalingrad and blocking the Volga River, or should they deliver their main blow in the Caucasus in quest of Russian oil? Earlier in the month Hitler had pondered this crucial question but had been unable to make up his mind. At first, the smell of oil had tempted him most, and on July 13 he had detached the Fourth Panzer Army from Army Group B, which had been driving down the Don toward the river's bend and Stalingrad just beyond, and sent it south to help Kleist's First Panzer Army get over the lower Don near Rostov and on into the Caucasus toward the oil fields. At

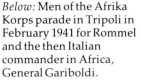

Below: Men of the Afrika Korps parade in Tripoli in February 1941 for Rommel and the then Italian commander in Africa, General Gariboldi.

that moment the Fourth Panzer Army probably could have raced on to Stalingrad, which was then largely undefended, and easily captured it. By the time Hitler realized his mistake it was too late, and then he compounded his error. When the Fourth Panzer Army was shifted back toward Stalingrad a fortnight later, the Russians had recovered sufficiently to be able to check it; and its departure from the Caucasus front left Kleist too weak to complete his drive to the Grozny oil fields.

The shifting of this powerful armored unit back to the drive on Stalingrad was one result of the fatal decision which Hitler made on July 23. His fanatical determination to take *both* Stalingrad *and* the Caucasus at the same time, against the advice of Halder and the field commanders, who did not believe it could be done, was embodied in Directive No. 45, which became famous in the annals of the German Army. It was one of the most fateful of Hitler's moves in the war, for in the end, and in a very short time, it resulted in his failing to achieve either objective and led to the most humiliating defeat in the history of German arms, making certain that he could never win the war and that the days of the thousand-year Third Reich were numbered.

General Halder was appalled, and there was a stormy scene at "Werewolf" headquarters in the Ukraine near Vinnitsa to which Hitler had moved on July 16 in order to be nearer the front. The Chief of the General Staff urged that the main forces be concentrated on the taking of Stalingrad and tried

Left: German Mark IV tanks on the defensive in Tunisia at the end of 1942.

to explain that the German Army simply did not possess the strength to carry out two powerful offensives in two different directions. When Hitler retorted that the Russians were "finished," Halder attempted to convince him that, according to the Army's own intelligence, this was far from the case.

"The continual underestimation of enemy possibilities," Halder noted sadly in his diary that evening, "takes on grotesque forms and is becoming dangerous. Serious work has become impossible here. Pathological reaction to momentary impressions and a complete lack of capacity to assess the situation and its possibilities give this so-called 'leadership' a most peculiar character."

Later the Chief of the General Staff, whose own days at his post were now numbered, would come back to this scene and write: "Hitler's decisions had ceased to have anything in common with the principles of strategy and operations as they have been recognized for generations past. They were the product of a violent nature following its momentary impulses, which recognized no limits to possibility and which made its wish-dreams the father of its acts . . ."

As to what he called the Supreme Commander's "pathological over-estimation of his own strength and criminal underestimation of the enemy's," Halder later told a story: "Once when a quite objective report was read to him showing that still in 1942 Stalin would be able to muster from one to one and a quarter million fresh troops in the region north of Stalingrad and west of the Volga, not to mention half a million men in the Caucasus, and which provided proof that Russian output of front-line tanks amounted to at least 1,200 a month, Hitler flew at the man who was reading with clenched fists and foam in the corners of his mouth and forbade him to read any more of such idiotic twaddle." "You didn't have to have the gift of a prophet," says Halder, "to foresee what would happen when Stalin unleashed those million and a half troops against Stalingrad and the Don flank. I pointed this out to Hitler very clearly.

The result was the dismissal of the Chief of the Army General Staff."

This took place on September 24. Already on the ninth, upon being told by Keitel that Field Marshal List, who had the over-all command of the armies in the Caucasus, had been sacked, Halder learned that he would be the next to go. The Fuehrer, he was told, had become convinced that he "was no longer equal to the psychic demands of his position." Hitler explained this in greater detail to his General Staff Chief at their farewell meeting on the twenty-fourth.

"You and I have been suffering from nerves. Half of my nervous exhaustion is due to you. It is not worth it to go on. We need National Socialist ardor now, not professional ability. I cannot expect this of an officer of the old school such as you."

Below: General von Seydlitz-Kurzbach and General Paulus (right) at Stalingrad in November 1942.

Above: Mussolini inspects the Italian Expeditionary Force in Russia, 1942.

"So spoke," Halder commented later, "not a responsible warlord but a political fanatic."

And so departed Franz Halder. He was not without his faults, which were similar to those of his predecessor, General Beck, in that his mind was often confused and his will to action paralyzed. And though he had often stood up to Hitler, however ineffectually, he had also, like all of the other Army officers who enjoyed high rank during World War II, gone along with him and for a long time abetted his outrageous aggressions and his conquests. Yet he had retained some of the virtues of more civilized times. He was the last of the old-school General Staff chiefs that the Army

of the Third Reich would have. He was replaced by General Kurt Zeitzler, a younger officer of a different stripe who was serving as chief of staff to Rundstedt in the West, and who endured in the post, which once – especially in the First World War – had been the highest and most powerful in the German Army, as little more than the Fuehrer's office boy until the attempt against the dictator's life in July 1944.

A change in General Staff chiefs did not change the situation of the German Army, whose twin drives on Stalingrad and the Caucasus had now been halted by stiffening Soviet resistance itself. All through October bitter street fighting contin-

Right: Stukas bomb Stalingrad. The close-quarter fighting which developed in Stalingrad generally prevented the Luftwaffe from intervening effectively in the battle even when sufficient aircraft were available.

ued in Stalingrad itself. The Germans made some progress, from building to building, but with staggering losses, for the rubble of a great city, as everyone who has experienced modern warfare knows, gives many opportunities for stubborn and prolonged defense and the Russians, disputing desperately every foot of the debris, made the most of them. Though Halder and then his successor warned Hitler that the troops in Stalingrad were becoming exhausted, the Supreme Commander insisted that they push on. Fresh divisions were thrown in and were soon ground to pieces in the inferno.

Instead of a means to an end – the end had already been achieved when German formations reached the western banks of the Volga north and south of the city and cut off the river's traffic – Stalingrad had become an end in itself. To Hitler its capture was now a question of personal prestige. When even Zeitzler got up enough nerve to suggest to the Fuehrer that in view of the danger to the long northern flank along the Don the Sixth Army should be withdrawn from Stalingrad to the elbow of the Don, Hitler flew into a fury. "Where the German soldier sets foot, there he remains!"

Despite the hard going and the severe losses, General Paulus, commander of the Sixth Army, informed Hitler by radio on October 25 that he expected to complete the capture of Stalingrad at the latest by November 10. Cheered up by this assurance, Hitler issued orders the next day that the Sixth Army and the Fourth Panzer Army, which was fighting south of the city, should prepare to push north and south along the Volga as soon as Stalingrad had fallen.

It was not that Hitler was ignorant of the threat to the Don flank. The OKW diaries make clear that it caused him considerable worry. The point is that he did not take it seriously enough and that, as a consequence, he did nothing to avert it. Indeed, so confident was he that the situation was well in hand that on the last day of October he, the staff of OKW and the Army General Staff abandoned their headquarters at Vinnitsa in the Ukraine and returned to Wolfsschanze (Wolf's Lair) at Rastenburg. The Fuehrer had practically convinced himself that if there were to be any Soviet winter offensive at all it would come on the central and northern fronts. He could handle that better from his quarters in East Prussia.

At the same time, bad news reached the Fuehrer from another front. Field Marshal Rommel's Afrika Korps was in serious difficulty.

At long last the British army in Egypt had received strong reinforcements. When it launched a major offensive late that October, Rommel was in Austria on sick leave. By the time he got back to his army, the battle was already lost. The British had too many guns, tanks and planes, and though Rommel made desperate efforts to shift his battered divisions to stem the various attacks, he realized that his situation was hopeless. He had begun to withdraw when a message came from the supreme warlord: "There can be no other consideration save that of holding fast, of not retreating one step, of throwing every gun and every man into the battle. You can show your troops no other way than that which leads to victory or death."

This idiotic order meant, if obeyed, that the Italo-German armies were condemned to annihilation. After a struggle with his conscience, Rommel reluctantly gave the order to halt the withdrawal. But two days later, at the risk of being court-martialed, he decided to save what was left of his forces and retreat. Only the remnants of the armored and motorized units could be extricated. The foot soldiers, mostly Italian, were left behind to surrender. Within 15 days Rommel had fallen back 700 miles to beyond Benghazi.

Worse news was to follow almost immediately. Anglo-American troops under General Dwight Eisenhower hit the beaches of Morocco and Algeria at 1:30 a.m. on November 8, 1942. Hitler poured nearly a quarter of a million German and Italian troops in to hold Tunis. If he had sent one fifth as many to Rommel a few months before, the Desert Fox most probably would have been beyond the Nile by now, the Anglo-American landing in Northwest Africa could not have taken place, and any opportunity in the Mediterranean would have been irretrievably lost to the Allies. As it was, every soldier and tank and gun rushed by Hitler to Tunisia that winter, as well as the remnants of the Afrika Korps, would be lost by the end of the spring.

Above: German propaganda photograph showing the "Caucasus to Stalingrad" Railroad, August 6, 1942.

Stalingrad – The Turning Point

Left: A German-occupied area of the city.

Below left: German motorcycle despatch riders during the advance to Stalingrad.

Bottom: Russian civilians sheltering from the fighting at Stalingrad. One feature of the city was the number of low hills near the river which often provided good positions for the Russian defenders.

Right: German infantry preparing for a street battle in Stalingrad. Even specially trained police battalions were employed in an attempt to overcome Russian skill in this type of battle.

Below right: German troops in action in the Stalingrad Tractor Factory, one of the key Russian defense positions.

Below: German prisoners shuffle into captivity, February 1943.

The Holocaust at Stalingrad

Below: German troops pick their way through a destroyed factory at Stalingrad. Some of the fiercest fighting in Stalingrad took place in and around the city's industrial areas, notably in the Red October factory and the tractor factory.

Just eleven days after the Allied landings in North Africa, an overwhelming Russian armored force had broken clean through the Axis lines just northwest of Stalingrad. The Russians were clearly driving in great strength to cut off Stalingrad and to force the German Sixth Army there either to retreat or see itself surrounded. The mere suggestion of retreat threw the Fuehrer into a tantrum.

"I won't leave the Volga! I won't go back from the Volga!" he shouted, and that was that. This decision, taken in a fit of frenzy, led promptly to disaster.

On November 22 a wireless message arrived from General Paulus, commander of the Sixth Army, confirming that his troops were surrounded. Hitler promptly radioed back, telling Paulus that the army would be supplied by air until it could be relieved.

But this was futile talk. There were now twenty German and two Rumanian divisions cut off at Stalingrad. Paulus radioed that they would need a minimum of 750 tons of supplies a day flown in. This was far beyond the capacity of the Luftwaffe, which lacked the required number of transport planes. Even if they had been available, not all of them could have got through in the blizzardy weather and over an area where the Russians had

Right: A German officer gives orders to his soldiers.

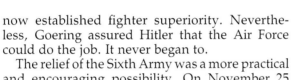

now established fighter superiority. Nevertheless, Goering assured Hitler that the Air Force could do the job. It never began to.

The relief of the Sixth Army was a more practical and encouraging possibility. On November 25 Hitler had recalled Field Marshal von Manstein, the most gifted of his field commanders, from the Leningrad front and put him in charge of a newly created formation, Army Group Don. His assignment was to push through from the southwest and relieve the Sixth Army at Stalingrad.

But now the Fuehrer imposed impossible conditions on his new commander. Manstein tried to explain to him that the only chance of success lay in the Sixth Army's breaking out of Stalingrad to the west while his own forces, led by the Fourth Panzer Army, pressed northeast against the Russian armies which lay between the two German forces. But once again Hitler refused to draw back from the Volga. The Sixth Army must remain in Stalingrad and Manstein must fight his way to it there.

This, as Manstein tried to argue with the supreme warlord, could not be done. The Russians were too strong. Nevertheless, with a heavy heart, Manstein launched his attack on December 12. It was called, appropriately, "Operation Winter Gale," for the full fury of the Russian winter had now hit the southern steppes, piling up the snow in drifts and dropping the temperature below zero. At first the offensive made good progress, the Fourth Panzer Army, under General Hoth, driving northeast up both sides of the railroad from Kotelnikovski toward Stalingrad, some seventy-five miles away. By December 19 it had advanced to within some forty miles of the southern perimeter of the city; by the twenty-first it was within thirty miles, and across the snowy steppes the besieged troops of the Sixth Army could see at night the signal flares of their rescuers. At this

moment, according to the later testimony of the German generals, a breakout from Stalingrad of the Sixth Army toward the advancing lines of the Fourth Panzer Army would almost certainly have succeeded. But once again Hitler forbade it. On December 21, Zeitzler had wrung permission from the Leader for the troops of Paulus to break out *provided* they also held on to Stalingrad. This piece of foolishness, the General Staff Chief says, nearly drove him insane.

"On the following evening," Zeitzler related later, "I begged Hitler to authorize the breakout. I pointed out that this was absolutely our last chance to save the two hundred thousand men of Paulus' army." Hitler would not give way. In vain I described to him conditions inside the so-called fortress: the despair of the starving soldiers, their loss of confidence in the Supreme Command, the wounded expiring for lack of proper attention while thousands froze to death. He remained as impervious to arguments of this sort as to those others which I had advanced."

In the face of increasing Russian resistance in front of him and on his flanks General Hoth lacked the strength to negotiate that last thirty miles to Stalingrad. He believed that if the Sixth Army broke out he could still make a junction with it and then both forces could withdraw to Kotelnikovski. This at least would save a couple of hundred thousand German lives. Probably for a day or two – between December 21 and 23 – this could have been done, but by the latter date it had become impossible. For unknown to Hoth the Red Army had struck farther north and was now endangering the left flank of Manstein's whole Army Group Don. On the night of December 22, Manstein telephoned Hoth to prepare himself for drastic new orders. The next day they came. Hoth was to abandon his drive on Stalingrad, dispatch one of his three panzer divisions to the Don front on

the north, and defend himself where he was and with what he had left as well as he could.

The attempt to relieve Stalingrad had failed.

Manstein's drastic new orders had come as the result of alarming news that reached him on December 17. On the morning of that day a Soviet army had broken through the Italian Eighth Army farther up the Don at Boguchar and by evening opened a gap twenty-seven miles deep. Within three days the hole was ninety miles wide, the Italians were fleeing in panic and the Rumanian Third Army to the south, which already had been badly pummeled on the opening day of the Russian offensive on November 19, was also disintegrating. No wonder Manstein had had to take part of Hoth's armored forces to help stem the gap. A chain reaction followed.

Not only the Don armies fell back but also Hoth's forces, which had come so close to Stalingrad. These retreats in turn endangered the German Army in the Caucasus, which would be cut off if the Russians reached Rostov on the Sea of Azov. A day or two after Christmas Zeitzler pointed out to Hitler, "Unless you order a withdrawal from the Caucasus now, we shall soon have a second Stalingrad on our hands." Reluctantly the Supreme Commander issued the necessary instructions on December 29 to Kleist's Army Group A, which comprised the First Panzer and Seventeenth armies, and which had failed in its mission to grab the rich oil fields of Grozny. It too began a long retreat after having been within sight of its goal.

The reverses of the Germans in Russia and of the Italo-German armies in North Africa stirred Mussolini to thought. Hitler had invited him to come to Salzburg for a talk around the middle of December and the ailing Duce, now on a strict diet for stomach disorders, had accepted, though, as he told Ciano, he would go on one condition only: that he take his meals alone "because he does not want a lot of ravenous Germans to notice that he is compelled to live on rice and milk."

The time had come, Mussolini decided, to tell Hitler to cut his losses in the East, make some sort of deal with Stalin and concentrate Axis strength on defending the rest of North Africa, the Balkans and Western Europe. "Nineteen forty-three will be the year of the Anglo-American effort," he told Ciano. Hitler was unable to leave his Eastern headquarters in order to meet Mussolini, so Ciano made the long journey to Rastenburg on December 18 on his behalf, repeating to the Nazi leader the Duce's proposals. Hitler scorned them and assured the Italian Foreign Minister that without at all weakening the Russian front he could send additional forces to North Africa, which must, he said, be held. Ciano found German spirits at a low ebb at headquarters, despite Hitler's confident assurances. "The atmosphere is heavy. To the bad news there should perhaps be added the sadness of that humid forest and the boredom of collective living in the barracks . . . No one tries to conceal from me the unhappiness over the news of the breakthrough on the Russian front. There were open attempts to put the blame on us."

At that very moment the survivors of the Italian Eighth Army on the Don were scurrying for their lives, and when one member of Ciano's party asked an OKW officer whether the Italians had suffered heavy losses he was told "No losses at all: they are running."

The German troops in the Caucasus and on the Don, if not running, were getting out as quickly as they could to avoid being cut off. Each day, as the year 1943 began, they withdrew a little farther from Stalingrad. The time had now come for the Russians to finish off the Germans there. But first they gave the doomed soldiers of the Sixth Army an opportunity to save their lives.

On the morning of January 8, 1943, three young Red Army officers, bearing a white flag, entered

Above: Post orderly delivering mail to the troops on the Eastern Front.

Below: Wintry scenes on a Luftwaffe airfield in Russia.

the German lines on the northern perimeter of Stalingrad and presented General Paulus with an ultimatum from General Konstantin Rokossovski, commander of the Soviet forces on the Don front. After reminding him that his army was cut off and could not be relieved or kept supplied from the air, the note said: "The situation of your troops is desperate. They are suffering from hunger, sickness and cold. The cruel Russian winter has scarcely yet begun. Hard frosts, cold winds and blizzards still lie ahead. Your soldiers are unprovided with winter clothing and are living in appalling sanitary conditions . . . Your situation is hopeless, and any further resistance senseless. In view of [this]

and in order to avoid unnecessary bloodshed, we propose that you accept the following terms of surrender . . ."

They were honorable terms. All prisoners would be given "normal rations." The wounded, sick and frostbitten would receive medical treatment. All prisoners could retain their badges of rank, decorations and personal belongings. Paulus was given twenty-four hours to reply.

He immediately radioed the text of the ultimatum to Hitler and asked for freedom of action. His request was curtly dismissed by the supreme warlord. Twenty-four hours after the expiration of the time limit on the demand for surrender, on the morning of January 10, the Russians opened the last phase of the Battle of Stalingrad with an artillery bombardment from five thousand guns.

The fighting was bitter and bloody. Both sides fought with incredible bravery and recklessness over the frozen wasteland of the city's rubble – but not for long. Within six days the German pocket had been reduced by half, to an area fifteen miles long and nine miles deep at its widest. By January 24 it had been split in two and the last small emergency airstrip lost. The planes which had brought in some supplies and which had flown out 29,000 hospital cases, could no longer land.

Once more the Russians gave their courageous enemy a chance to surrender. Soviet emissaries arrived at the German lines on January 24 with a new offer. Again Paulus, torn between his duty to obey the mad Fuehrer and his obligation to save his own surviving troops from annihilation, appealed to Hitler. "Troops without ammunition [he radioed on the twenty-fourth] or food. Effective command no longer possible . . . 18,000 wounded without any supplies or dressings or drugs . . . Further defense senseless. Collapse inevitable. Army requests immediate permission to surrender in order to save lives of remaining troops."

Hitler's answer has been preserved. "Surrender is forbidden. Sixth Army will hold their positions to the last man and the last round and by their heroic endurance will make an unforgettable contribution toward the establishment of a defensive front and the salvation of the Western world."

The Western world! It was a bitter pill for the men of the Sixth Army who had fought against that world in France but a short time ago.

Further resistance was not only senseless and futile but impossible, and as the month of January 1943 approached its end the epic battle wore itself out, expiring like the flame of an expended candle which sputters and dies. By January 28 what was left of a once great army was split into three small pockets, in the southern one of which General Paulus had his headquarters in the cellar of the ruins of the once thriving Univermag department store. According to one eyewitness the commander in chief sat on his camp bed in a darkened corner in a state of near collapse.

He was scarcely in the mood, nor were his soldiers, to appreciate the flood of congratulatory radiograms that now began to pour in. Goering, who had whiled away a good part of the winter in sunny Italy, strutting about in his great fur coat and fingering his jewels, sent a radio message on January 28. "The fight put up by the Sixth Army will go down in history, and future generations will speak proudly of a Langemarck of daredevilry, an Alcázar of tenacity, a Narvik of courage and a Stalingrad of self-sacrifice."

Nor were they cheered when on the last evening, January 30, 1943, the tenth anniversary of the Nazis' coming to power, they listened to the Reich Marshal's bombastic broadcast. "A thousand years hence Germans will speak of this battle [of Stalingrad] with reverence and awe, and will remember that in spite of everything Germany's ultimate victory was decided there . . . In years to come it will be said of the heroic battle on the

Above: Rumania infantry supporting German troops at Stalingrad.

Left: A ruined village near Stalingrad.

Volga: When you come to Germany, say that you have seen us lying at Stalingrad, as our honor and our leaders ordained that we should, for the greater glory of Germany."

The glory and the horrible agony of the Sixth Army had now come to an end. On January 30, Paulus radioed Hitler: "Final collapse cannot be delayed more than twenty-four hours."

This signal prompted the Supreme Commander to shower a series of promotions on the doomed officers in Stalingrad, apparently in the hope that such honors would strengthen their resolve to die gloriously at their bloody posts. "There is no record in military history of a German Field Marshal being taken prisoner," Hitler remarked to Jodl, and thereupon conferred on Paulus, by radio, the coveted marshal's baton. Some 117 other officers were also jumped up a grade. It was a macabre gesture.

The end itself was anticlimactic. Late on the last day of January Paulus got off his final message to headquarters. "The Sixth Army, true to their oath and conscious of the lofty importance of their mission, have held their position to the last man and the last round for Fuehrer and Fatherland unto the end."

At 7:45 P.M. the radio operator at Sixth Army headquarters sent a last message on his own: "The Russians are at the door of our bunker. We are destroying our equipment." He added the letters "CL" – the international wireless code signifying "This station will no longer transmit."

There was no last-minute fighting at headquarters. Paulus and his staff did not hold out to the last man. A squad of Russians led by a junior officer peered into the commander in chief's darkened hole in the cellar. The Russians demanded surrender and the Sixth Army's chief of staff, General Schmidt accepted. Paulus sat dejected on his camp bed. When Schmidt addressed him – "May I ask the Field Marshal if there is anything more to be said?" – Paulus was too weary to answer.

Farther north a small German pocket, containing all that was left of two panzer and four infantry divisions, still held out in the ruins of a tractor factory. On the night of February 1 it received a message from Hitler's headquarters. "The German people expect you to do your duty exactly as

did the troops holding the southern fortress. Every day and every hour that you continue to fight facilitates the building of a new front."

Just before noon on February 2, this group surrendered after a last message to Hitler: " . . . Have fought to the last man against vastly superior forces. Long live Germany!"

Silence at last settled on the snow-covered, blood-spattered shambles of the battlefield. At 2:46 P.M. on February 2 a German reconnaissance plane flew high over the city and radioed back: "No sign of any fighting at Stalingrad."

By that time 91,000 German soldiers, including twenty-four generals, half-starved, frostbitten, many of them wounded, all of them dazed and broken, were hobbling over the ice and snow, clutching their blood-caked blankets over their heads against the 24-degree-below-zero cold toward the dreary, frozen prisoner-of-war camps of Siberia. Except for some 20,000 Rumanians and the 29,000 wounded who had been evacuated by air they were all that was left of a conquering army

Right: Goebbels calling for total war in the Berlin Sportpalast, February 18, 1943.

Below: "Our fanatical oath: Retribution." The headline in a Nazi newspaper following the surrender of Stalingrad.

Below right: "One struggle, one victory." Nazi commemorative poster of the tenth anniversary of the Seizure of Power.

that had numbered 285,000 men two months before. The rest had been slaughtered. And of those 91,000 Germans who began the weary march into captivity that winter day, only 5,000 were destined ever to see the Fatherland again.

"Stalingrad," wrote one German historian, "was certainly the greatest defeat a German army had ever undergone."

It was more than that. Coupled with El Alamein and the British-American landings in North Africa, it marked the great climax in World War II. The high tide of Nazi conquest which had rolled over most of Europe to the frontier of Asia and in Africa almost to the Nile had now begun to ebb, and it would never flow back again. The initiative had passed from Hitler's hands, never to return.

And finally, in the snows of Stalingrad and in the burning sands of the North African desert, a great and terrible Nazi dream was destroyed. Not only the Third Reich was doomed by the disasters to Paulus and Rommel but also the gruesome and grotesque so-called New Order which Hitler and his S.S. thugs had been busy setting up in the conquered lands. It might be well now to pause and see what this New Order was like – in theory and in barbarous practice – and what the ancient and civilized continent of Europe barely escaped after a nightmare of experiencing its first horrors.

Horror Unparalleled

Although the Nazi New Order was mercifully short-lived, it sank to a level of degradation seldom experienced by man in all his time on earth. Millions of decent, innocent men and women were driven into forced labor; millions more tortured and tormented in the concentration camps; millions more still, of whom there were 4,500,000 Jews alone, were massacred in cold blood or deliberately starved to death and their remains – in order to remove the traces – burned. This incredible story of horror would be unbelievable were it not fully documented and testified to by the perpetrators themselves.

No comprehensive blueprint for the New Order was ever drawn up, but it is clear from captured documents and from what took place that Hitler knew very well what he wanted it to be: a Nazi-ruled Europe whose resources would be exploited for the profit of Germany, whose people would be made the slaves of the German master race and whose "undesirable elements" – above all, the Jews, but also many Slavs in the East, especially the intelligentsia among them – would be exterminated.

The Jews and the Slavic peoples were the *Untermenschen* – subhumans. To Hitler they had no right to live, except as some of them, among the Slavs, might be needed to toil in the fields and the mines as slaves of their German masters. Not only were the great cities of the East, Moscow, Leningrad and Warsaw, to be permanently erased but the culture of the Russians and Poles and other Slavs was to be stamped out and formal education denied them. Their thriving industries were to be dismantled and shipped to Germany and the people themselves confined to the pursuits of agriculture so that they could grow food for Germans, being allowed to keep for themselves just enough to subsist on. Europe itself, as the Nazi leaders put it, must be made "Jew-free."

"What happens to a Russian, to a Czech, does not interest me in the slightest," declared Heinrich Himmler on October 4, 1943, in a confidential address to his S.S. officers at Posen. By this time Himmler, as chief of the S.S. and the entire police apparatus of the Third Reich, was next to Hitler in importance, holding the power of life and death not only over eighty million Germans but over twice that many conquered people. "What the nations [Himmler continued] can offer in the way of good blood of our type, we will take, if necessary by kidnaping their children and raising them here with us. Whether nations live in prosperity or starve to death like cattle interests me only in so far as we need them as slaves to our *Kultur*; otherwise it is of no interest to me. Whether 10,000 Russian females fall down from exhaustion while digging an antitank ditch interests me only in so far as the antitank ditch for Germany is finished."

Long before Himmler's Posen speech in 1943, the Nazi chiefs had laid down their thoughts and plans for enslaving the people of the East.

By October 15, 1940, Hitler had decided on the future of the Czechs, the first Slavic people he had conquered. One half of them were to be "assimilated," mostly by shipping them as slave labor to Germany. The other half, "particularly" the intellectuals, were simply to be, in the words of a secret report on the subject, "eliminated."

A fortnight before, on October 2, the Fuehrer had clarified his thoughts about the fate of the Poles, the second of the Slavic peoples to be conquered. His faithful secretary, Martin Bormann, has left a long memorandum on the Nazi plans, which Hitler outlined to Hans Frank, the Governor General of rump Poland, and to other officials. "The Poles are especially born for low labor . . . There can be no question of improvement for them. It is necessary to keep the standard of life low in Poland and it must not be permitted to rise . . . The Poles are lazy and it is necessary to use compulsion to make them work . . . The Government General [of Poland] should be used by us merely as a source of unskilled labor . . . Every year the laborers needed by the Reich could be procured from there."

This obsession of the Germans with the idea that they were the master race and that the Slavic peoples must be their slaves was especially virul-

Below: An S.S. recruiting poster for Norway. Although in the end the Nazis tried to recruit soldiers throughout Occupied Europe, they particularly favored "racially pure" "Nordic types" like the Norwegians.

There were a few in Berlin who believed that if Hitler played his cards shrewdly, treating the population with consideration and promising relief from Bolshevik practices (by granting religious and economic freedom and making true cooperatives out of the collectivized farms) and eventual self-government, the Russian people could be won over. They might then not only cooperate with the Germans in the occupied regions but in the unoccupied ones strive for liberation from Stalin's harsh rule. If this were done, it was argued, the Bolshevik regime itself might collapse and the Red Army disintegrate, as the Czarist armies had done in 1917.

But the savagery of the Nazi occupation and the obvious aims of the German conquerors, often publicly proclaimed, to plunder the Russian lands, enslave their peoples and colonize the East with Germans soon destroyed any possibility of such a development.

No one summed up this disastrous policy and all the opportunities it destroyed better than a German himself, Dr. Otto Bräutigam, a career diplomat and the deputy leader of the Political Department of Rosenberg's newly created Ministry for the Occupied Eastern Territories. In a bitter confidential report to his superiors on October 25,

Left: The S.S. Jewish "expert" and organiser of the final solution, S. S. Sturmbannfuehrer Adolf Eichmann.

Below: Vichy *milice* arrest resisters in France, 1943. The milice was a paramilitary police organisation established in the non-occupied, Vichy, zone of France to support the pro-Nazi policies of the government and combat resistance.

ent in regard to Russia. Erich Koch, the roughneck Reich Commissar for the Ukraine, expressed it in a speech at Kiev on March 5, 1943. "We are the Master Race and must govern hard but just . . . I will draw the very last out of this country. I did not come to spread bliss . . . The population must work, work, and work again . . . We definitely did not come here to give out manna. We have come here to create the basis for victory. We are a master race, which must remember that the lowliest German worker is racially and biologically a thousand times more valuable than the population here."

Nearly a year before, on July 23, 1942, when the German armies in Russia were nearing the Volga and the oil fields of the Caucasus, Martin Bormann, Hitler's party secretary and, by now, right-hand man, wrote a long letter to Rosenberg reiterating the Fuehrer's views on the subject. The letter was summed up by an official in Rosenberg's ministry: "The Slavs are to work for us. In so far as we don't need them, they may die. Therefore compulsory vaccination and German health services are superfluous. The fertility of the Slavs is undesirable. They may use contraceptives or practice abortion – the more the better. Education is dangerous. It is enough if they can count up to 100. . . . Every educated person is a future enemy. Religion we leave to them as a means of diversion. As for food they won't get any more than is absolutely necessary. We are the masters. We come first."

When the German troops first entered Russia they were in many places hailed as liberators by a population long ground down and terrorized by Stalin's tyranny. There were, in the beginning, wholesale desertions among the Russian soldiers. Especially in the Baltic, which had been under Soviet occupation but a short time, and in the Ukraine, where an incipient independence movement had never been quite stamped out, many were happy to be freed from the Soviet yoke – even by the Germans.

1942, Bräutigam dared to pinpoint the Nazi mistakes in Russia. "In the Soviet Union we found on our arrival a population weary of Bolshevism, which waited longingly for new slogans holding out the prospect of a better future for them. It was Germany's duty to find such slogans, but they remained unuttered. The population greeted us with joy as liberators and placed themselves at our disposal."

Actually, there was a slogan but the Russian people soon saw through it. "With the inherent instinct of Eastern peoples," Bräutigam continued, "the primitive man soon found out that for Germany the slogan 'Liberation from Bolshevism' was only a pretext to enslave the Eastern peoples according to her own methods . . . The worker and peasant soon perceived that Germany did not regard them as partners of equal rights but considered them only as the objective of her political and economic aims . . ."

There were two other developments, Bräutigam declared, which had turned the Russians against the Germans: the barbaric treatment of Soviet prisoners of war and the shanghaiing of Russian men and women for slave labor. "It is no longer a secret from friend or foe that hundreds of thousands of Russian prisoners of war have died of hunger or cold in our camps . . . We now experience the grotesque picture of having to recruit millions of laborers from the occupied Eastern territories after prisoners of war have died of hunger like flies . . . In the prevailing limitless abuse of the Slavic humanity, 'recruiting' methods were used which probably have their origin only in the blackest periods of the slave traffic. A regular man hunt was inaugurated. Without consideration of health or age the people were shipped to Germany. . . ."

German policy and practice in Russia had "brought about the enormous resistance of the Eastern peoples," this official concluded. "Our policy has forced both Bolshevists and Russian nationalists into a common front against us. The Russian fights today with exceptional bravery and self-sacrifice for nothing more or less than recognition of his human dignity."

Closing his thirteen-page memorandum on a positive note Dr. Bräutigam asked for a complete change of policy. "The Russian people," he argued, "must be told something concrete about their future."

But this was a voice in the Nazi wilderness. Hitler, as we have seen, already had laid down, before the attack began, his directives on what would be done with Russia and the Russians and he was not a man who could be persuaded by any living German to change them by one iota.

On July 16, 1941, less than a month after the commencement of the Russian campaign but when it was already evident from the initial German successes that a large slice of the Soviet Union would soon be within grasp, Hitler convoked Goering, Keitel, Rosenberg, Bormann and Lammers (the last, head of the Reich Chancellery) to his headquarters in East Prussia to remind them of his aims in the newly conquered land. At last his goal so clearly stated in *Mein Kampf* of securing a vast German *Lebensraum* in Russia was in sight and it is clear from the confidential memorandum of the meeting drawn up by Bormann (which showed up at Nuremberg) that he wanted his chief lieuten-

Left: Money printed for use in the Theresienstadt ghetto. Conditions there were much less harsh than in every other camp and neutral reporters were even allowed to see for themselves. It was only a brief reprieve and later in the war the ghetto was closed and the inmates sent to the gas chambers.

Below: Map of the principal POW and concentration camps.

ants to understand well what he intended to do with it. His intentions, he admonished, must however not be "publicized." There is no need for that but the main thing is that we ourselves know what we want . . . Nobody must be able to recognize that it initiates a final settlement. This need not prevent our taking all necessary measures – shooting, resettling, etc. – and we shall take them."

In principle, Hitler continued, "we now have to face the task of cutting up the cake according to our needs in order to be able: first, to dominate it; second, to administer it; third, to exploit it."

He did not mind, he said, that the Russians had ordered partisan warfare behind the German

lines; "it enables us to eradicate everyone who opposes us."

In general, Hitler explained, Germany would dominate the Russian territory up to the Urals. None but Germans would be permitted to carry weapons in that vast space. Then Hitler went over specifically what would be done with various slices of the Russian cake. "The entire Baltic country will have to be incorporated into Germany . . . The Crimea has to be evacuated by all foreigners and settled by Germans only, [becoming] Reich territory . . . The Kola Peninsula will be taken by Germany because of the large nickel mines there. The annexation of Finland as a federated state should be prepared with caution . . . The Fuehrer will raze Leningrad to the ground and then hand it over to the Finns."

The Baku oil fields, Hitler ordered, would become a "German concession" and the German colonies on the Volga would be annexed outright. When it came to a discussion as to which Nazi leaders would administer the new territory a violent quarrel broke out. "Rosenberg states he intends to use Captain von Petersdorff, owing to his special merits; general consternation; general rejections. The Fuehrer and the Reich Marshal [Goering] both emphasize there was no doubt that Von Petersdorff was insane."

There was also an argument on the best methods of policing the conquered Russian people. Hitler suggested the German police be equipped with armored cars. Goering doubted that they would be necessary. His planes could "drop bombs in case of riots," he said.

Goering, as head of the Four-Year Plan, was also put in charge of the economic exploitation of Russia. "Plunder" would be a better word, as Goering made clear in a speech to the Nazi commissioners for the occupied territories on August 6, 1942. "It used to be called plundering," he said. "But today things have become more humane. In spite of that, I intend to plunder and to do it thoroughly." On this, at least, he was as good as his word, not only in Russia but throughout Nazi-conquered Europe.

By the end of September 1944, 7,500,000 civilian foreigners were toiling for the Third Reich. Nearly all of them had been rounded up by force, deported to Germany in boxcars, usually without food or water or any sanitary facilities, and there put to work in the factories, fields, mines. They were not only put to work but degraded, beaten and starved, and often left to die for lack of food, clothing and shelter.

In addition, two million prisoners of war were added to the foreign labor force. The treatment of Western prisoners of war, especially of the British and Americans, was comparatively milder than that meted out by the Germans to the Russians. There were occasional instances of murder and massacre of them, but this was due usually to the excessive sadism and cruelty of individual commanders. Such a case was the slaughter in cold blood of seventy-one American prisoners near Malmédy, Belgium, on December 17, 1944, during the Battle of the Bulge.

Nevertheless, it seemed to be deliberate German policy to encourage the killing of Allied airmen who bailed out over Germany; civilians were encouraged to lynch the fliers as soon as they had parachuted to the ground.

The inhabitants of the conquered lands fared little better. On October 22, 1941, a French newspaper, *Le Phare*, published the following notice:

"Cowardly criminals in the pay of England and Moscow killed the Feldkommandant of Nantes on the morning of October 20. Up to now the assassins have not been arrested.

"As expiation for this crime I have ordered that 50 hostages be shot, to begin with. Fifty more hostages will be shot in case the guilty should not be arrested between now and October 23 by midnight."

This became a familiar notice in the pages of the newspapers or on red posters edged with black in France, Belgium, the Netherlands, Norway, Poland and Russia. The proportion, publicly proclaimed by the Germans, was invariably 100 to 1 – a hundred hostages shot for every German killed.

Again, the Germans were more ruthless in the East, where the *Einsatzgruppen* – Special Action Groups, or what might better be termed, in view of their performance, Extermination Squads – followed the armies into Poland and Russia.

Asked on the stand at Nuremberg what instructions it received, Otto Ohlendorf, chief of one of the *Einsatzgruppen*, answered, "The instructions were that the Jews and the Soviet political commissars were to be liquidated; the Jewish population should be totally exterminated."

The judge: "Including the children?"

Ohlendorf: "Yes."

The judge: "Were all the Jewish children murdered?"

Ohlendorf: "Yes."

An eyewitness report by a German of how a comparatively minor mass execution was carried out in the Ukraine brought a hush of terror over the Nuremberg courtroom when it was read.

"My foreman and I," the German witness deposed, "went directly to the pit. The people – men, women and children of all ages – had to undress upon the order of an S.S. man, who carried a whip. They had to put down their clothes in

a fixed place, sorted according to shoes, top clothing and underclothing.

"Without screaming or weeping these people undressed, stood around in family groups, kissed one another, said farewells and waited for a sign from another S.S. man. During the 15 minutes that I stood near the pit I heard no complaint or plea for mercy.

"An old woman with snow-white hair was holding a one-year-old child in her arms and singing to it. The child was cooing with delight. The parents were looking on with tears in their eyes. The father was holding the hand of a boy about ten years old and speaking to him softly; the boy was fighting his tears. The father pointed to the sky, stroked his head and seemed to explain something to him.

"At that moment the S.S. man at the pit shouted

Above: The new, Nazi map of Europe.

Left: In 1943 German and Red Cross officials inspect the exhumed bodies of Polish officers murdered by the Soviets at Katyn, one atrocity the Nazis were keen to publicize.

Left: Jewish women about to be shot by the S.S. in Latvia, 1941. A photo taken by one of the S.S. men.

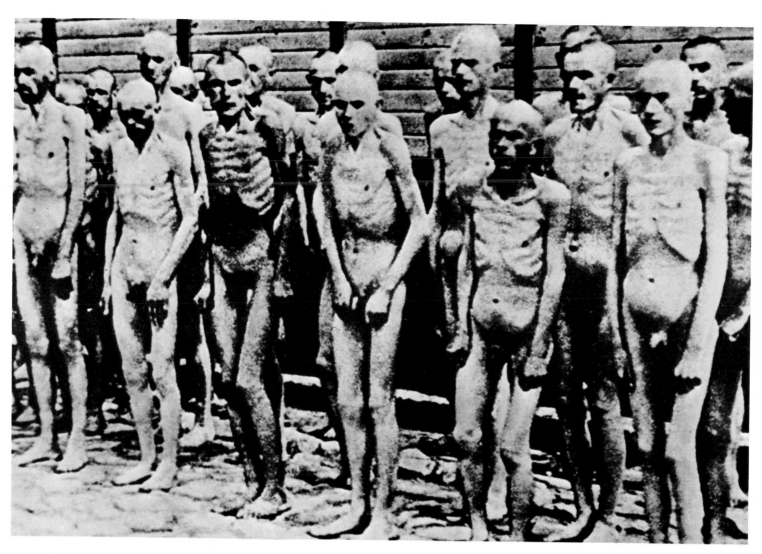

something to his comrade. The latter counted off about 20 persons and instructed them to go behind the earth mound. I well remember a girl, slim and with black hair, who, as she passed close to me, pointed to herself and said, 'Twenty-three years old.'

"I walked around the mound and found myself confronted by a tremendous grave. People were closely wedged together and lying on top of one another so that only their heads were visible. The pit was already two thirds full. I estimated that it contained about a thousand people. An S.S. man sat at the edge, his feet dangling into the pit. He had a tommy gun on his knees and he was smoking a cigarette.

"The people went down some steps and clambered over the heads of the people lying there to the place to which the S.S. man directed them. They lay down, then I heard a series of shots. The next batch was approaching already. They went down into the pit, lined themselves up against the previous victims and were shot."

And so it went, batch after batch.

All in all, according to Adolf Eichmann, the head of the Jewish Office of the Gestapo, two million persons, almost all Jews, were liquidated by the *Einsatzgruppen* in the East. Even though this is almost certainly an exaggeration, it is small compared with the number of Jews who were done to death in Himmler's extermination camps where the "final solution" came to be carried out.

It was in the death camps that the "final solution" achieved its most ghastly success. All the 30-odd principal Nazi concentration camps were

death camps, and millions of tortured, starved inmates perished in them. But it was in the extermination camps, the *Vernichtungslager*, where most progress was made toward the "final solution." The greatest and most renowned of these was Auschwitz, whose four huge gas chambers and adjoining crematoria gave it a capacity for death and burial far beyond that of the others – Treblinka, Belsec, Sobibor and Chelmno, all in Poland. Speed was an important factor, especially at Auschwitz, where toward the end the camp was setting records by gassing 6000 victims a day.

"We had," Auschwitz commandant Rudolf Hoess explained at Nuremberg, "two S.S. doctors on duty to examine the incoming prisoners. These would be marched by one of the doctors, who would make spot decisions. Those who were fit to work were sent into the camp. Others were sent immediately to the extermination plants. Children of tender years were invariably exterminated, since by reason of their youth they were unable to work."

Always Herr Hoess kept making improvements in the art of mass killing.

"Still another improvement we made over Treblinka was that at Treblinka the victims almost always knew that they were to be exterminated, while at Auschwitz we endeavored to fool the victims into thinking that they were to go through a delousing process. We were required to carry out these exterminations in secrecy, but of course the foul and nauseating stench from the continuous burning of bodies permeated the entire area, and all of the people living in the surrounding communities knew that exterminations were going on at Auschwitz."

Above: Croat soldiers molesting an elderly Serbian woman in occupied Yugoslavia.

Above left: Concentration camp inmates.

Left: Jewish women and children being evicted from the Warsaw Ghetto and sent to Auschwitz for extermination, 1943.

Right: Transport of Jewish women and children on the ramp at Auschwitz extermination camp before the selection of those to go to the gas chambers.

The Tables Begin to Turn

For three successive war years when summer came, it had been the Germans who launched the great offensives on the continent of Europe. Now in 1943 the tables turned.

With the capture in early May of that year of the Axis forces in North Africa, it was obvious that General Eisenhower's Anglo-American armies would next move on Italy itself. Mussolini was now ill, disillusioned and frightened. Defeatism was rife among his people, and the discredited and corrupt Fascist regime was fast crumbling. The Allied conquest of Tunisia in May was followed by the successful Anglo-American landings in Sicily on July 10. The Italians had little stomach for battle in their own homeland. Reports soon reached Hitler that the Italian army was "in a state of collapse." Benito Mussolini, tired and senile though he was only going on 60, he who had strutted so arrogantly across Europe's stage for two decades, was at the end of his rope.

On July 25 he was summoned to the royal palace by the King, summarily dismissed from office and carted off under arrest in an ambulance to a police station. Not a gun was fired – not even by the Fascist militia – to save him; not a voice was raised in his defense. On the contrary, there was general rejoicing in his fall. Fascism itself collapsed as easily as its founder. Marshal Pietro Badoglio formed a nonparty government of generals and civil servants, and the Fascist Party was dissolved.

On September 3 Allied troops landed on the boot of southern Italy, and on September 8 public announcements were made of the armistice (secretly signed on September 3) between Italy and the Western powers.

For a day or two the situation of the German forces in central and south Italy was critical. Five Italian divisions faced two German divisions in the vicinity of Rome. If the powerful Allied invasion fleet which had appeared off Naples on September 8 moved north and landed near the capital, eight German divisions and all of southern Italy would be lost.

But the Allied army landed not near Rome, but south of Naples, and the Italian divisions surrendered almost without firing a shot. This gave the Germans possession of two thirds of Italy, including the industrial north, whose factories were put to work turning out arms for Germany. Almost miraculously Hitler had received a new lease on life.

He followed up his good fortune by executing a daring stroke – the kidnapping of Mussolini from his Italian captors. The Duce was then installed as the premier of the new Italian Social Republic.

It never amounted to anything. He and his "Fascist Republican Government" had no power except what the Fuehrer gave them in Germany's interests. There was no disputing that Hitler's fortunes in the south had been considerably restored by his daring and resourcefulness and by the prowess of his troops.

Elsewhere his fortunes continued to fall.

Below: German glider used to rescue Mussolini, September 12, 1943.

On July 5, 1943, he had launched his last great offensive of the war against the Russians. The flower of the German army – some 500,000 men – was hurled against a large Russian salient west of Kursk.

It led to a decisive defeat. The Russians were prepared for the attack. By July 22 the Germans were brought to a complete halt and started to fall back. So confident of their strength were the Russians that without waiting for the outcome of the offensive they launched one of their own, which soon spread along the entire front. Kharkov fell on August 23. On September 25, 300 miles to the northwest, the Germans were driven out of Smolensk. And by the end of the year the Soviet armies in the south were approaching the Polish and Rumanian frontiers, past the battlefields where the soldiers of Hitler had achieved their early victories in the summer of 1941 as they romped toward the interior of the Russian land.

There were two other setbacks to Hitler's fortunes that year which also marked the turning of the tide: the loss of the Battle of the Atlantic and the intensification of the devastating air war day and night over Germany itself.

In 1942, as we have seen, German submarines sank 6,250,000 tons of Allied shipping, most of it bound for Britain or the Mediterranean, a tonnage which far outstripped the capacity of the shipyards in the West to make good. But by the beginning of 1943 the Allies had gained the upper hand over the U-boats, thanks to an improved technique of using long-range aircraft and aircraft carriers and, above all, of equipping their surface vessels with radar which spotted the enemy submarines before the latter could sight them. Admiral Karl Doenitz, the new commander of the Navy and the top U-boat man in the service, at first suspected treason when so many of his underwater craft were ambushed and destroyed before they could even approach the Allied convoys. He quickly learned that it was not treason but radar which was causing the disastrous losses. In the three months of February, March and April they had amounted to exactly fifty vessels; in May alone, thirty-seven U-boats were sunk. This was a rate of loss which the German Navy could not long sustain, and before the end of May Doenitz, on his own authority, withdrew all submarines from the North Atlantic.

They returned in September but in the last four months of the year sank only sixty-seven Allied vessels against the loss of sixty-four more submarines – a ratio which spelled the doom of U-boat warfare and definitely settled the Battle of the Atlantic. In 1917 in the First World War, when her armies had become stalled, Germany's submarines had almost brought Britain to her knees. They were threatening to accomplish this in 1942, when Hitler's armies in Russia and North Africa had also been stopped, and when the United States and Great Britain were straining themselves not only to halt the drive of the Japanese in Southeast Asia but to assemble men and arms and supplies for the invasion of Hitler's European empire in the West.

Their failure to seriously disrupt the North Atlantic shipping lanes during 1943 was a bigger disaster than was realized at Hitler's headquarters, depressing though the actual news was. For it was during the twelve months of that crucial

year that the vast stocks of weapons and supplies were ferried almost unmolested across the Atlantic which made the assault of Fortress Europe possible in the following year.

And it was during that period too that the horrors of modern war were brought home to the German people – brought home to them on their own doorsteps. The public knew little of how the U-boats were doing. And though the news from Russia, the Mediterranean and Italy grew increasingly bad, it dealt after all with events that were transpiring hundreds or thousands of miles distant from the homeland. But the bombs from the

Above: German paratroopers fighting in Italy.

Below: Mussolini and on his right Otto Skorzeny the S.S. tough who led the force which freed Mussolini from the captivity of the new Italian government.

Right: Recruiting poster for women auxiliaries for the Luftwaffe.

British planes by night and the American planes by day were now beginning to destroy a German's home, and the office or factory where he worked.

Hitler himself declined ever to visit a bombed-out city; it was a duty which seemed simply too painful for him to endure. Goebbels was much distressed at this, complaining that he was being flooded with letters "asking why the Fuehrer does not visit the distressed air areas and why Goering isn't to be seen anywhere." The Propaganda Minister's diary authoritatively describes the growing damage to German cities and industries from the air.

"*May 16, 1943.* . . . The day raids by American bombers are creating extraordinary difficulties. At Kiel . . . very serious damage to military and technical installations of the Navy.

"*May 25.* The night raid of the English on Dortmund was extraordinarily heavy, probably the worst ever directed against a German city . . . Reports from Dortmund are pretty horrible . . . Industrial and munition plants have been hit very hard . . . Some eighty to one hundred thousand inhabitants without shelter.

"*July 26.* During the night a heavy raid on Hamburg . . . with most serious consequences both for the civilian population and for armaments production . . . It is a real catastrophe.

"*July 29.* During the night we had the heaviest raid yet made on Hamburg . . . with 800 to 1,000 bombers . . . Kaufmann [the local Gauleiter] gave me a first report . . . He spoke of a catastrophe the extent of which simply staggers the imagination. A city of a million inhabitants has been destroyed in a manner unparalleled in history. We are faced with problems that are almost impos-

Below: German civilian dead after an Allied air raid.

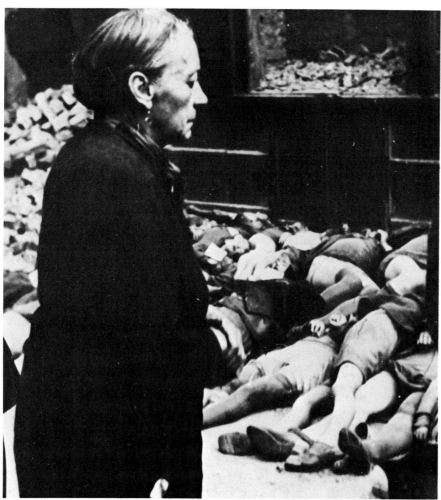

sible of solution. Food must be found for this population of a million. Shelter must be secured. The people must be evacuated as far as possible. They must be given clothing. In short, we are facing problems there of which we had no conception even a few weeks ago . . . Kaufmann spoke of some 800,000 homeless people who are wandering up and down the streets not knowing what to do."

Although considerable damage was done to specific German war plants, especially to those turning out fighter planes, ball bearings, naval ships, steel, and fuel for the new jets, and to the vital rocket experimental station at Peenemunde on which Hitler had set such high hopes, and though rail and canal transport were continually disrupted, over-all German armament production was not materially reduced during the stepped-up Anglo-American bombings of 1943. This was partly due to the increased output of factories in the occupied zones – above all, those in Czechoslovakia, France, Belgium and northern Italy, which escaped bombing.

The greatest damage inflicted by the Anglo-American air forces, as Goebbels makes clear in his diary, was to the homes and the morale of the German people. In the first war years they had been buoyed up, as this writer remembers, by the lurid reports of what Luftwaffe bombing had done to the enemy, especially to the British. They were sure it would help bring the war to an early – and victorious – end. Now, in 1943, they themselves began to bear the full brunt of air warfare far more devastating than any the Luftwaffe had dealt to others, even to the populace of London in 1940-41. The German people endured it as bravely and as stoically as the British people had done. But after four years of war it was all the more a severe strain, and it is not surprising that as 1943 approached its end, with all its blasted hopes in

Russia, in North Africa and in Italy, and with their own cities from one end of the Reich to the other being pulverized from the air, the German people began to despair and to realize that this was the beginning of the end that could only spell their defeat.

"Toward the end of 1943 at the latest," the now unemployed General Halder would later write, "it had become unmistakably clear that the war was militarily lost."

As 1944 came, it appeared certain that Anglo-American armies would soon launch an invasion across the Channel, that the Red armies would be approaching the frontiers of the Reich itself, and that the great and ancient cities of Germany would soon be reduced to rubble by the Allied bombing. A small group of anti-Nazi plotters, which included high-ranking army officers, some of them on the general staff, girded themselves for a desperate attempt to murder the Nazi dictator and overthrow his regime before it dragged Germany over the precipice to complete disaster.

They knew there was not much time.

Invasion and Rebellion

Throughout most of his regime, there were German underground conspiracies against Hitler. But for all the conspirators' idealism and undoubted courage in the face of constant Gestapo hounding, the movement suffered from one fatal defect: an inability to organize forceful, direct action. For years small groups talked and plotted, laid elaborate plans for coups and the overthrow of the Nazi government, but somehow at the last minute they always found some reason for not acting.

As the war progressed, however, and the Fuehrer's fanaticism became more pronounced, they gradually overcame their hesitations, and during 1943 they made at least half a dozen attempts to assassinate Hitler, one of which miscarried only when a time bomb planted in the warlord's airplane during a flight behind Russian lines failed to explode. By now they knew they *had* to succeed soon, if they were to achieve any meaningful results from their daring efforts.

As it was, their most dramatic attempt came almost too late. On June 6, 1944, a vast Allied armada slipped across the English Channel in weather that the Germans thought too inclement to permit an invasion attempt, and began disgorging thousands upon thousands of troops on the beaches of Normandy.

If the Germans were in the dark about the date of the invasion, they were also ignorant of where it would take place. Rundstedt and Rommel were

Left: Foreign forced laborers at bomb disposal work in Germany.

Below: Berlin burning during an Allied air raid.

Right: A German V-1 flying bomb being prepared for launch against Britain, 1944.

certain it would be in the Pas-de-Calais area, where the Channel was at its narrowest. There they had concentrated their strongest force, the Fifteenth Army, whose strength during the spring was increased from ten to fifteen infantry divisions. But by the end of March Adolf Hitler's uncanny intuition was telling him that the *Schwerpunkt* of the invasion probably would be in Normandy, and during the next few weeks he ordered considerable reinforcements to the region between the Seine and the Loire. "Watch Normandy!" he kept warning his generals.

Still, the overwhelming part of German strength, in both infantry and panzer divisions, was retained north of the Seine, between Le Havre and Dunkirk. Rundstedt and his generals were watching the Pas-de-Calais rather than Normandy and they were encouraged in this by a number of deceptive maneuvers carried out during April and May by the British-American High Command which indicated to them that their calculations were correct.

The day of June 5, then, passed in relative quiet, so far as the Germans were concerned. Severe Anglo-American air attacks continued to disrupt German depots, radar stations, V-1 sites, communications and transport, but these had been going on night and day for weeks and seemed no more intense on this day than on others.

Shortly after dark [on June 5] Rundstedt's headquarters was informed that the BBC in London was broadcasting an unusually large number of coded messages to the French resistance and that the German radar stations between Cherbourg and Le Havre were being jammed. At 10 P.M. the Fifteenth Army intercepted a code message from the BBC to the French resistance which it believed meant that the invasion was about to begin. This army was alerted, but Rundstedt did not think it necessary to alert the Seventh Army, on whose sector of the coast farther west, between Caen and

Cherbourg, the Allied forces were now – toward midnight – approaching on a thousand ships.

It was not until eleven minutes past 1 A.M., June 6, that the Seventh Army – its commander Friedrich Dollmann absent on a map exercise at Rennes – realized what was happening. Two American and one British airborne divisions had begun landing. The alarm sounded at 1:30 A.M.

Forty-five minutes later Major General Max Pemsel, chief of staff of the Seventh Army, called General Speidel at Rommel's headquarters (Rommel was on leave) and told him that it looked like "a large-scale operation." Speidel did not believe it but passed on the report to Rundstedt, who was equally skeptical. Both generals believed the dropping of parachutists was merely an Allied feint to cover their main landings around Calais. At 2:40 A.M. Pemsel was advised that Rundstedt "does not consider this to be a major operation." Not even when the news began to reach him shortly after dawn on June 6 that on the Normandy coast between the rivers Vire and Orne a huge Allied fleet was disembarking large bodies of troops, under cover of a murderous fire from the big guns of an armada of warships, did the Commander in Chief West believe that this was to be the main Allied assault. It did not become apparent, Speidel says, until the afternoon of June 6. By that time the Americans had a toehold on two beaches and the British on a third and had penetrated inland for a distance of from two to six miles.

Speidel had telephoned Rommel at 6 A.M. at his home and the Field Marshal had rushed back by car without going on to see Hitler, but he did not arrive at Army Group B headquarters until late that afternoon. In the meantime Speidel, Rundstedt and the latter's chief of staff, General Blumentritt, had been on the telephone to OKW, which was then at Berchtesgaden. Due to an idiotic order of Hitler's not even the Commander in Chief in the West could employ his panzer divisions without the specific permission of the Fuehrer. When the three generals early on the morning of the sixth begged for permission to rush two tank divisions to Normandy, Jodl replied that Hitler wanted first to see what developed. Whereupon the Fuehrer went to bed and could not be disturbed by the frantic calls of the generals in the West until 3 P.M. When he woke up, the bad news which had in the meantime arrived finally stirred the Nazi warlord to action. He gave – too late, as it turned out – permission to engage the Panzer Lehr and 12th S.S. Panzer divisions in Normandy. He also issued a famous order which has been preserved for in the log of the Seventh Army:

16:55 hours. June 6, 1944

Chief of Staff Western Command emphasizes the desire of the Supreme Command to have the enemy in the bridgehead annihilated by the evening of June 6 since there exists the danger of additional sea- and airborne landings for support . . . The beachhead must be cleaned up by not later than tonight.

In the eerie mountain air of the Obersalzberg, from which Hitler was now trying to direct the most crucial battle of the war up to this moment – he had been saying for months that Germany's destiny would be decided in the West – this fantastic order seems to have been issued in all seriousness, concurred in by Jodl and Keitel. Even

Below: D-Day – the Anglo-American invasion of Normandy, June 6, 1944.

Rommel, who passed it on by telephone shortly before 5 o'clock that afternoon, an hour after his return from Germany, seems to have taken it seriously, for he ordered Seventh Army headquarters to launch an attack by the 21st Panzer Division, the only German armored unit in the area, "immediately regardless of whether reinforcements arrive or not."

This the division had already done, without waiting for Rommel's command. General Pemsel, who was on the other end of the line when Rommel called Seventh Army headquarters, gave a blunt reply to Hitler's demand that the Allied beachhead – there were actually now three – "be cleaned up by not later than tonight."

"That," he replied, "would be impossible."

Hitler's much-propagandized Atlantic Wall had been breached within a few hours. The once vaunted Luftwaffe had been driven completely from the air and the German Navy from the sea,

and the Army taken by surprise. The battle was far from over, but its outcome was not long in doubt. "From June 9 on," says Speidel, "the initiative lay with the Allies."

The successful landings threw the conspirators, led by Lieutenant Colonel Klaus Philip Schenk, Count von Stauffenberg; former General Staff Chief General Ludwig Beck; and politician Carl Goerdeler, into great confusion. Was there any point, they wondered now, in going ahead with any further attempt to assassinate Hitler? Or would they merely be blamed by their countrymen for bringing on the final catastrophe for Germany? Finally, one of the senior members of the conspiracy provided the inspired answer:

"The assassination must be attempted at any cost. We must prove to the world that the men of the German resistance dared to take the decisive step and to hazard their lives upon it. Compared with this object, nothing else matters."

Below: The decline in Germany's fortunes, 1943-44.

The Coup of July 20, 1944

Toward the end of June the plotters received one good stroke of fortune. Stauffenberg was promoted to full colonel and appointed chief of staff to General Fromm, the commander in chief of the Home Army. This post not only enabled him to issue orders to the Home Army under Fromm's name but gave him direct and frequent access to Hitler. Indeed, the Fuehrer began to summon the chief of the Replacement Army, or his deputy, to headquarters two or three times a week to demand fresh replacements for his decimated divisions in Russia. At one of these meetings Stauffenberg intended to plant his bomb.

Stauffenberg had now become the key man in the conspiracy. On his shoulders alone rested its only chance for success. As the one member of the plot who could penetrate the heavily guarded Fuehrer headquarters it was up to him to kill Hitler. As chief of staff of the Replacement Army it would have to be left to him – since Fromm had not been won over completely and could not be definitely counted on – to direct the troops that were to seize Berlin after Hitler was out of the way. And he had to carry out both objectives on the same day and at two spots separated by two or three hundred miles – the Fuehrer's headquarters, whether on the Obersalzberg or at Rastenburg, and Berlin. Between the first and the second acts there must be an interval of two or three hours while his plane returned to the capital during which he could do nothing but hope that his plans were being energetically initiated by his confederates. That was one trouble, as we shall shortly see.

There were others. One seems to have been an almost unnecessary complication that sprang up in the minds of the now desperate conspirators. They came to the conclusion that it would not suffice to kill Adolf Hitler. They must at the same time kill Goering and Himmler, thus ensuring that the military forces under the command of these two men could not be used against them. They thought too that the top generals at the front who had not yet been won over would join them more quickly if Hitler's two chief lieutenants were also done away with. Since Goering and Himmler usually attended the daily military conferences at the Fuehrer headquarters, it was believed that it would not be too difficult to kill all three men with one bomb. This foolish resolve led Stauffenberg to miss two golden opportunities.

He was summoned to the Obersalzberg on July 11 to report to the Fuehrer on the supply of badly needed replacements. He carried with him on the plane down to Berchtesgaden one of the Abwehr's English-made bombs. It had been decided at a meeting of the plotters in Berlin the night before that this was the moment to kill Hitler – and Goering and Himmler as well. But Himmler was not present at the conference that day and when Stauffenberg, leaving the meeting for a moment, rang up fellow conspirator General Friedrich Olbricht in Berlin to tell him so, stressing that he could still get Hitler and Goering, the General urged him to wait for another day when he could get all three. That night, on his return to Berlin, Stauffenberg met with Beck and Olbricht and insisted that the next time he must attempt to kill Hitler, regardless of whether Goering and Himmler were present or not. The others agreed that this was best.

The next time was soon at hand. On July 14 Stauffenberg was ordered to report the next day to the Fuehrer on the replacement situation – every available recruit was needed to help fill the gaps in Russia, where Army Group Center, having lost twenty-seven divisions, had ceased to exist as a fighting force. That day – the fourteenth – Hitler had moved his headquarters back to Wolfsschanze at Rastenburg to take personal charge of trying to restore the central front, where Red Army troops had now reached a point but sixty miles from East Prussia.

Again, on the morning of July 15, Colonel Stauffenberg set out by plane for the Fuehrer's headquarters with a bomb in his briefcase. This time the conspirators were so certain of success that it was agreed that the first Valkyrie signal – for the troops to start marching in Berlin and for the tanks from the panzer school at Krampnitz to begin rolling toward the capital – should be given two hours before Hitler's conference, scheduled for 1 P.M., began. There must be no delay in taking over.

At 11 A.M. on Saturday, July 15, General Olbricht issued Valkyrie I for Berlin and before noon troops were moving toward the center of the capital with orders to occupy the Wilhelmstrasse quarter. At 1 P.M. Stauffenberg, briefcase in hand, arrived at the Fuehrer's conference room, made his report on replacements, and then absented himself long enough to telephone Olbricht in Berlin to say – by prearranged code – that Hitler was present and that he intended to return to the meeting and set off his bomb. Olbricht informed him that the troops in Berlin were already on the march. At last success in the great enterprise seemed at hand. But when Stauffenberg returned to the conference room Hitler had left it and did not return. Disconsolate, Stauffenberg hurriedly rang up Olbricht with the news. The General frantically canceled the Valkyrie alarm and the troops

Below: Hitler with Himmler at Rastenberg following the unsuccessful attempt to kill him on July 20, 1944.

were marched back to their barracks as quickly and as inconspicuously as possible.

The news of still another failure was a heavy blow to the conspirators, who gathered in Berlin on Stauffenberg's return to consider what next to do. Goerdeler was for resorting to the so-called "Western solution." He proposed to Beck that both of them fly to Paris to confer with Field Marshall von Kluge on getting an armistice in the West whereby the Western Allies would agree not to push farther than the Franco-German border, thus releasing the German armies in the West to be shunted to the Eastern front to save the Reich from the Russians and their Bolshevism. Beck had a clearer head. The idea that they could now get a separate peace with the West, he knew, was a pipe dream. Nevertheless the plot to kill Hitler and overthrow Nazism must be carried out at all costs, Beck argued, if only to save Germany's honor. Stauffenberg agreed. He swore he would not fail the next time. General Olbricht, who had received a dressing down from Keitel for moving his troops in Berlin, declared that he could not risk doing it again, since that would unmask the whole conspiracy. He had barely got by, he said, with an explanation to Keitel and Fromm that this was a practice exercise. This fear of again setting the troops in motion until it was known definitely that Hitler was dead was to have disastrous consequences on the crucial following Thursday.

Left: Oberst Klaus Schenk von Stauffenberg.

Below: Hitler showing Mussolini the aftermath of the bomb explosion in the conference room. The force of the blast and Hitler's lucky escape are evident.

Above: Members of the anti-Nazi "White Rose" group in Munich 1943. Left to right, Hans Scholl, Sophie Scholl and Christoph Probst.

On Sunday evening, July 16, Stauffenberg invited to his home at Wannsee a small circle of his close friends and relatives: his brother, Berthold, a quiet, introspective, scholarly young man who was an adviser on international law at naval headquarters; Lieutenant Colonel Caesar von Hofacker, a cousin of the Stauffenbergs and their liaison man with the generals in the West; Count Fritz von der Schulenburg, a former Nazi who was still deputy police president of Berlin; and Trott zu Solz. Hofacker had just returned from the West, where he had conferred with a number of generals – Falkenhausen, Stuelpnagel, Speidel, Rommel and Kluge. He reported an imminent German breakdown on the Western front but, more impor-

Right: Carl Goerdeler, on trial before the People's Court, 1944.

tant, that Rommel would back the conspiracy regardless of which way Kluge jumped, though he still opposed killing Hitler. After a long discussion the young conspirators agreed, however, that ending Hitler's life was now the only way out. They had no illusions by this time that their desperate act would save Germany from having to surrender unconditionally. They even agreed that this would have to be done to the Russians as well as to the Western democracies. The important thing, they said, was for Germans – and not their foreign conquerors – to free Germany from Hitler's evil tyranny.

They were terribly late. The Nazi despotism had endured for eleven years and only the certainty of utter defeat in a war which Germany had launched, and which they had done little to oppose – or, in many cases, not opposed at all – had roused them to action. But better late than never. There remained, however, little time. The generals at the front were advising them that collapse in both the East and the West was probably only a matter of weeks.

For the plotters there seemed to be only a few more days left to them to act. The premature march of the troops in Berlin on July 15 had aroused the suspicions of OKW. On that day came news that General von Falkenhausen, one of the leaders of the plot in the West, had been suddenly dismissed from his post as military governor of Belgium and northern France. Someone, it was feared, must be giving them away. On July 17 they learned that Rommel had been so seriously wounded that he would have to be left out of their plans indefinitely. The next day Goerdeler was tipped off by his friends at police headquarters that Himmler had issued an order for his arrest. At Stauffenberg's insistence Goerdeler went, protesting, into hiding. That same day a personal friend in the Navy, Captain Alfred Kranzfelder, one of the very few naval officers in on the conspiracy, informed Stauffenberg that rumors were spreading in Berlin that the Fuehrer's headquarters were to be blown up in the next few days. Again it seemed that someone in the conspiracy must have been indiscreet. Everything pointed to the Gestapo's closing in on the inner ring of the conspiracy.

On the afternoon of July 19 Stauffenberg was again summoned to Rastenburg, to report to Hitler on the progress being made with the new *Volksgrenadier* divisions which the Replacement Army was hurriedly training to be thrown in on the dissolving Eastern front. He was to make his report at the first daily conference at Fuehrer headquarters in the next day, July 20, at 1 P.M. Field Marshal von Witzleben and General Hoepner, who lived some distance outside Berlin, were notified by Stauffenberg to appear in the city in good time. General Beck made his last-minute preparations for directing the coup until Stauffenberg could return by air from his murderous deed. The key officers in the garrisons in and around Berlin were apprised that July 20 would be *Der Tag*.

Stauffenberg worked at the Bendlerstrasse on his report for Hitler until dusk, leaving his office shortly after 8 o'clock for his home at Wannsee. On his way he stopped off at a Catholic church in Dahlem to pray. He spent the evening at home quietly with his brother, Berthold, and retired early. Everyone who saw him that afternoon and

evening remembered that he was amiable and calm and was behaving as if nothing unusual was in the offing.

Shortly after 6 o'clock on the warm, sunny summer morning of July 20, 1944, Colonel Stauffenberg, accompanied by his adjutant, Lieutenant Werner von Haeften, drove out past the bombed-out buildings of Berlin to the airport at Rangsdorf. In his bulging briefcase were papers concerning the new *Volksgrenadier* divisions on which at 1 P.M. he was to report to Hitler at the "Wolf's Lair" at Rastenburg in East Prussia. In between the papers, wrapped in a shirt, was a time bomb. Of English make, it was set off by breaking a glass capsule, whose acid then ate away a small wire, which released the firing pin against the percussion cap. The thickness of the wire governed the time required to set off the explosion. On this morning the bomb was fitted with the thinnest possible wire. It would dissolve in a bare ten minutes.

At the airport Stauffenberg met General Stieff, who had produced the bomb the night before. There they found a plane waiting, the personal craft of General Eduard Wagner, the First Quartermaster General of the Army and a ringleader in the plot, who had arranged to put it at their disposal for this all-important flight. By 7 o'clock the plane was off, landing at Rastenburg shortly after 10 A.M. Haeften instructed the pilot to be ready to take off for the return trip at any time after twelve noon.

From the airfield a staff car drove the party to the Wolfsschanze headquarters, set in a gloomy, damp, heavily wooded area of east Prussia. It was not an easy place to get into or, as Stauffenberg undoubtedly noted, out of. It was built in three rings, each protected by mine fields, pillboxes and an electrified barbed-wire fence, and was patrolled day and night by fanatical S.S. troops.

To get into the heavily guarded inner compound, where Hitler lived and worked, even the highest general had to have a special pass, good for one visit, and pass the personal inspection of S.S. Oberfuehrer Rattenhuber, Himmler's chief of security and commander of the S.S. guard, or of one of his deputies. However, since Hitler himself had ordered Stauffenberg to report, he and Haeften, though they were stopped and their passes examined, had little trouble in getting through the three check points. After breakfast with Captain von Moellendorff, adjutant to the camp commander, Stauffenberg sought out General Fritz Fellgiebel, Chief of Signals at OKW.

Fellgiebel was one of the key men in the plot. Stauffenberg made sure that the General was ready to flash the news of the bombing to the conspirators in Berlin so that action there could begin immediately. Fellgiebel was then to isolate the Fuehrer headquarters by shutting off all telephone, telegraph and radio communications. No one was in such a perfect position to do this as the head of the OKW communications network, and the plotters counted themselves lucky to have won him over. He was indispensable to the success of the entire conspiracy.

After calling on General Buhle, the Army's representative at OKW, to discuss the affairs of the Replacement Army, Stauffenberg walked over to Keitel's quarters, hung up his cap and belt in the anteroom and entered the office of the Chief of OKW. There he learned that he would have to act with more dispatch than he had planned. It was now a little after 12 noon, and Keitel informed him that because Mussolini would be arriving by train at 2:30 P.M. the Fuehrer's first daily conference had been put forward from 1 P.M. to 12:30. The colonel, Keitel advised, must make his report brief. Hitler wanted the meeting over early.

Before the bomb could go off? Stauffenberg

must have wondered if once again, and on what was perhaps his last try, fate was robbing him of success. Apparently he had hoped too that this time the conference with Hitler would be held in the Fuehrer's underground bunker, where the blast from the bomb would be several times more effective than in one of the surface buildings. But Keitel told him the meeting would be in the *Lagebaracke* – the conference barracks. This was far from being the flimsy wooden hut so often described. During the previous winter Hitler had had the original wooden structure reinforced with concrete walls eighteen inches thick to give protection against incendiary and splinter aerial bombs that might fall nearby. These heavy walls would add force to Stauffenberg's bomb.

He must soon set it to working. He had briefed Keitel on what he proposed to report to Hitler and toward the end had noticed the OKW Chief glancing impatiently at his watch. A few minutes before 12:30 Keitel said they must leave for the conference immediately or they would be late. They emerged from his quarters, but before they had taken more than a few steps Stauffenberg remarked that he had left his cap and belt in the anteroom and quickly turned to go back for them before Keitel could suggest that his adjutant, a Lieutenant von John, who was walking alongside, should retrieve them for him.

In the anteroom Stauffenberg swiftly opened his briefcase, seized the tongs and broke the capsule. In just ten minutes, unless there was another mechanical failure, the acid would do its work and the bomb would explode.

Keitel, as much a bully with his subordinates as he was a toady with his superiors, was aggravated at the delay and turned back to the building to shout to Stauffenberg to get a move on. They were late, he yelled. Stauffenberg apologized for the delay . . . As they walked over to Hitler's hut Stauffenberg seemed to be in a genial mood and

Keitel's petty annoyance – he had no trace of suspicion as yet – was dissipated.

Nevertheless, as Keitel had feared, they were late. The conference had already begun. As Keitel and Stauffenberg entered the building the latter paused for a moment in the entrance hall to tell the sergeant major in charge of the telephone board that he expected an urgent call from his office in Berlin, that it would contain information he needed to bring his report up to the minute (this was for Keitel's ear), and that he was to be summoned immediately when the call came. This too, though it must have seemed most unusual – even a field marshal would scarcely dare to leave the Nazi warlord's presence until he had been dismissed or until the conference was over and the Supreme Commander had left *first* – did not arouse Keitel's suspicions.

The two men entered the conference room. About four minutes had ticked by since Stauffenberg reached into his briefcase with his tongs and broke the capsule. Six minutes to go. The room was relatively small, some thirty by fifteen feet, and it had ten windows, all of which were wide open to catch the breezes on this hot, sultry day. So many open windows would certainly reduce the effect of any bomb blast. In the middle of the room was an oblong table, eighteen by five feet, made of thick oak planks. It was a peculiarly constructed table in that it stood not on legs but on two large heavy supports, or socles, placed near the ends and extending to nearly the width of the table. This interesting construction was not without its effect on subsequent history.

When Stauffenberg entered the room, Hitler was seated at the center of the long side of the table, his back to the door. On his immediate right were General Heusinger, Chief of Operations and Deputy Chief of Staff of the Army, General Korten, Air Force Chief of Staff, and Colonel Heinz Brandt, Heusinger's chief of staff. Keitel took his

Right: Field Marshal von Rundstedt attending Rommel's funeral service in Ulm. Rommel was buried with full military honors with an announcement he had died of wounds but in fact he had been compelled to commit suicide after being implicated in the anti-Hitler plots.

Left: Goering making the memorial address for a Luftwaffe officer killed by the Bomb Plot explosion.

place immediately to the left of the Fuehrer and next to him was General Jodl. There were eighteen other officers of the three services and the S.S. standing around the table, but Goering and Himmler were not among them. Only Hitler, playing with his magnifying glass – which he now needed to read the fine print on the maps spread before him – and two stenographers were seated.

Heusinger was in the midst of a lugubrious report on the latest breakthrough on the central Russian front and on the perilous position, as a consequence, of the German armies not only there but on the northern and southern fronts as well. Keitel broke in to announce the presence of Colonel von Stauffenberg and its purpose. Hitler glanced up at the one-armed colonel with a patch over one eye, greeted him curtly, and announced that before hearing his report he wanted to have done with Heusinger's.

Stauffenberg thereupon took his place at the table between Korten and Brandt, a few feet to the right of Hitler. He put his briefcase on the floor, shoving it under the table so that it leaned against the *inside* of the stout oaken support. It was about six feet distant from the Fuehrer's legs. The time was now 12:37. Five minutes to go. Heusinger continued to talk, pointing constantly to the situation map spread on the table. Hitler and the officers kept bending over to study it.

No one seems to have noticed Stauffenberg stealing away. Except perhaps Colonel Brandt. This officer became so absorbed in what his General was saying that he leaned over the table the better to see the map, discovered that Stauffenberg's bulging briefcase was in his way, tried to shove it aside with his foot and finally reached down with one hand and lifted it to the *far side* of the heavy table support, which now stood be-

tween the bomb and Hitler. This seemingly insignificant gesture probably saved the Fuehrer's life; it cost Brandt his.

Keitel, who was responsible for the summoning of Stauffenberg, glanced down the table to where the colonel was supposed to be standing. Heusinger was coming to the end of his gloomy report and the OKW Chief wanted to indicate to Stauffenberg that he should make ready to report next. Perhaps he would need some aid in getting his papers out of his briefcase. But the young colonel, he saw to his extreme annoyance, was not there. Recalling what Stauffenberg had told the telephone operator on coming in, Keitel slipped out of the room to bring him back.

Below: Nazi propaganda linking Hitler with Bismarck and Frederick the Great.

Stauffenberg was not at the telephone. The sergeant at the board said he had hurriedly left the building. Nonplused. Keitel turned back to the conference room. Heusinger was concluding, at last, his report on the day's catastrophic situation. *"The Russian,"* he was saying, *"is driving with strong forces west of the Duna toward the north. His spearheads are already southwest of Dunaburg. If our army group around Lake Peipus is not immediately withdrawn, a catastrophe . . ."*

It was a sentence that was never finished.

At that precise moment, 12:42 P.M., the bomb went off.

Stauffenberg saw what followed. He was standing with General Fellgiebel before the latter's office in Bunker 88 a couple of hundred yards away, glancing anxiously first at his wrist watch as the seconds ticked off and then at the conference barracks. He saw it go up with a roar in smoke and flame, as if, he said later, it had been hit directly by a 155-mm. shell. Bodies came hurtling out of the windows, debris flew into the air. There was not the slightest doubt in Stauffenberg's excited mind that every single person in the conference room was dead or dying. He bade a hasty farewell to Fellgiebel, who was now to telephone the conspirators in Berlin that the attempt had succeeded and

then cut off communication until the plotters in the capital had taken over the city and proclaimed the new government.

Stauffenberg's next task was to get out of the Rastenburg headquarters camp alive and quickly. The guards at the check points had seen or heard the explosion at the Fuehrer's conference hall and immediately closed all exits. At the first barrier, a few yards from Fellgiebel's bunker, Stauffenberg's car was halted. He leaped out and demanded to speak with the duty officer in the guardroom. In the latter's presence he telephoned someone – whom is not known – spoke briefly, hung up and turned to the officer, saying, "Herr Leutnant, I am allowed to pass."

This was pure bluff, but it worked, and apparently, after the lieutenant had dutifully noted in his log: *"12:44: Col. Stauffenberg passed through,"* word was sent along to the next check point to let the car through. At the third and final barrier, it was more difficult. Here an alarm had already been received, the rail had been lowered and the guard doubled, and no one was to be permitted to enter or leave. Stauffenberg and his aide, Lieutenant Haeften, found their car blocked by a very stubborn sergeant major named Kolbe. Again Stauffenberg demanded the use of the telephone

Below: German infantry in Caen, France 1944.

Left: Panzers and infantry in eastern France, September 1944.

Below: Hitler decorating S.S. Oberstgruppenführer Sepp Dietrich in August 1944.

and rang up Captain von Moellendorff, adjutant to the camp commander. He complained that "because of the explosion," the guard would not let him through. "I'm in a hurry. General Fromm is waiting for me at the airfield." This also was bluff. Fromm was in Berlin, as Stauffenberg well knew.

Hanging up, the colonel turned to the sergeant. "You heard, Sergeant, I'm allowed through." But the sergeant was not to be bluffed. He himself rang through to Moellendorff for confirmation. The captain gave it.

The car then raced to the airport while Lieutenant Haeften hurriedly dismantled a second bomb that he had brought along in *his* briefcase, tossing out the parts on the side of the road, where they were later found by the Gestapo. The airfield commandant had not yet received any alarm. The pilot had his engines warming up when the two men drove on to the field. Within a minute or two the plane took off.

It was now shortly after 1 P.M. The next three hours must have seemed the longest in Stauffenberg's life. There was nothing he could do as the slow Heinkel plane headed west over the sandy, flat German plain but to hope that Fellgiebel had been able to get through to Berlin with the all-important signal, that his fellow plotters in the capital had swung immediately into action in taking over the city and sending out the prepared messages to the military commanders in Germany and in the West, and that his plane would not be forced down by alerted Luftwaffe fighters or by prowling Russian craft, which were increasingly active over East Prussia. His own plane had no long-distance radio which might have enabled him to tune in on Berlin and hear the first thrilling broadcasts which he expected the conspirators would be making before he landed. Nor, for this lack, could he himself communicate with his confederates in the capital and give the signal that General Fellgiebel might not have been able to flash.

His plane droned on through the early summer

afternoon. It landed at Rangsdorf at 3:45 P.M. and Stauffenberg, in high spirits, raced to the nearest telephone at the airfield to put through a call to General Olbricht to learn exactly what had been accomplished in the fateful three hours on which all depended. To his utter consternation he found that nothing had been accomplished. Word about the explosion had come through by telephone from Fellgiebel shortly after 1 o'clock but the connection was bad and it was not quite clear to the conspirators whether Hitler had been killed or not. Therefore nothing had been done. The Valkyrie orders had been taken from Olbricht's safe but not sent out. Everyone in the Bendlerstrasse had been standing idly by waiting for Stauffenberg's return. General Beck and Field Marshal von Witzleben, who as the new head of state and Commander in Chief of the Wehrmacht, respectively,

Left: German transport destroyed by Allied air power in Normandy.

Below: French crowds take cover from snipers during the entry of Allied troops into Paris, August 26, 1944.

were supposed to have started issuing immediately the already-prepared proclamations and commands and to have gone on the air at once to broadcast the dawn of a new day in Germany, had not yet showed up.

Hitler, contrary to Stauffenberg's firm belief, which he imparted to Olbricht on the telephone from Rangsdorf, had not been killed. Colonel Brandt's almost unconscious act of shoving the briefcase to the far side of the stout oaken table support had saved his life. He had been badly shaken but not severely injured. His hair had been singed, his legs burned, his right arm bruised and temporarily paralyzed, his eardrums punctured and his back lacerated by a falling beam. He was, as one eyewitness later recalled, hardly recognizable as he emerged from the wrecked and burning building on the arm of Keitel, his face blackened, his hair smoking and his trousers in shreds. Keitel, miraculously, was uninjured. But most of those who had been at the end of the table where the bomb had exploded were either dead, dying or badly wounded.

In the first excitement there were several guesses as to the origin of the explosion. Hitler thought at first it might have been caused by a sneak attack of an enemy fighter-bomber. Jodl, nursing a blood-spattered head – the chandelier, among other objects, had fallen on him – was convinced that some of the building laborers had planted a time bomb under the floor of the building. The deep hole which Stauffenberg's bomb had blown in the floor seemed to confirm this. It was some time before the colonel became suspected. Himmler, who came running to the scene on hearing the explosion, was completely puzzled and his first act was to telephone – a minute or two before Fellgiebel shut down communications – Artur Nebe, the head of the criminal police in Berlin, to dispatch by plane a squad of detectives to carry out the investigation.

In the confusion and shock no one at first remembered that Stauffenberg had slipped out of the conference room shortly before the explosion. It was at first believed that he must have been in the building and was one of those severely hurt who had been rushed to the hospital. Hitler, not yet suspicious of him, asked that the hospital be checked.

Some two hours after the bomb went off the clues began to come in. The sergeant who operated the telephone board at the *Lagebaracke* reported that "the one-eyed colonel," who had informed him he was expecting a long-distance call from Berlin, had come out of the conference room and, without waiting for it, had left the building in a great hurry. Some of the participants at the conference recalled that Stauffenberg had left his briefcase under the table. The guardhouses at the check points revealed that Stauffenberg and his aide had passed through immediately after the explosion.

Hitler's suspicions were now kindled. A call to the airfield at Rastenburg supplied the interesting information that Stauffenberg had taken off from there in great haste shortly after 1 P.M., giving as his destination the airport at Rangsdorf. Himmler immediately ordered that he be arrested on landing there, but his order never got through to Berlin because of Fellgiebel's courageous action in closing down communications. Up to this minute no one at headquarters seems to have suspected that anything untoward might be happening in Berlin. All now believed that Stauffenberg had acted alone. It would not be difficult to apprehend him unless, as some suspected, he had landed behind the Russian lines. Hitler, who, under the circumstances, seems to have behaved calmly enough, had something else on his mind. He had to greet Mussolini, who was due to arrive at 4 P.M., his train having been delayed.

There is something weird and grotesque about

this last meeting of the two fascist dictators on the afternoon of July 20, 1944, as they surveyed the ruins of the conference hall and tried to fool themselves into thinking that the Axis which they had forged, and which was to have dominated the continent of Europe, was not also in shambles. The once proud and strutting Duce was now no more than a Gauleiter of Lombardy, rescued from imprisonment by Nazi thugs, and propped up by Hitler and the S.S. Yet the Fuehrer's friendship and esteem for the fallen Italian tyrant had never faltered and he greeted him with as much warmth as his physical condition permitted, showed him through the still smoking debris of the *Lagebaracke* where his life had almost been snuffed out a few hours before, and predicted that their joint cause would soon, despite all the setbacks, triumph.

Dr. Schmidt, who was present as interpreter, has recalled the scene. "Mussolini was absolutely horrified. He could not understand how such a thing could happen at Headquarters. . . . 'I was standing here by this table, [Hitler recounted]: 'the bomb went off just in front of my feet . . . It is obvious that nothing is going to happen to me; undoubtedly it is my fate to continue on my way and bring my task to completion . . . What happened here today is the climax! Having now escaped death . . . I am more than ever convinced that the great cause which I serve will be brought through its present perils and that everything can be brought to a good end.'"

Mussolini, carried away as so often before by Hitler's words, says Schmidt, agreed.

The two dictators, with their entourages, then went to tea, and there now ensued – it was about 5 P.M. – a ludicrous scene that gives a revealing, if

Above: General von Manteuffel at a front line command post in Rumania, May 1944.

Then someone brought up the subject of an earlier "revolt" against the Nazi regime, the Roehm "plot" of June 30, 1934. Mention of this aroused Hitler – who had been sitting morosely sucking brightly colored medicinal pills supplied by his quack physician, Dr. Theodor Morell – to a fine fury. Eyewitnesses say he leaped from his chair, foam on his lips, and screamed and raged. What he had done with Roehm and his treasonable followers was nothing, he shouted, to what he would do to the traitors of this day. He would uproot them all and destroy them. 'I'll put their wives and children into concentration camps," he raved, "and show them no mercy!" In this case, as in so many similar ones, he was as good as his word.

Partly because of exhaustion but also because the telephone from Berlin began to bring in details of the conspirators' uprising there, Hitler broke off his mad monologue, but his temper did not subside. When told at about six o'clock that the putsch had not yet been squelched, he grabbed the telephone and shrieked orders to the S.S. in Berlin to shoot everyone who was the least suspect.

Because of the Fuehrer's survival, the long and carefully prepared rebellion in Berlin was a failure. Too many wavering officers, who would have gladly arrested the other Nazi bigwigs if they had known that Hitler was dead, failed to join the uprising once they learned that their hypnotic Fuehrer was still alive.

By some time after midnight it was all over. Stauffenberg and other leading conspirators had been shot. The revolt, the only serious one ever made against Hitler in the 11½ years of the Third Reich, had been snuffed out in 11½ hours.

The barbarism of the Nazis toward their fellow Germans now reached its zenith. There was a wild wave of arrests followed by gruesome torture, drumhead trials, and death sentences carried out, in many cases, by slow strangling while the victims were suspended by piano wire from meathooks. The death roll, according to one source, numbered some 4,980 names.

From now on there was to be no more opposition to Hitler, not even any criticism of him. The once mighty army, like every other institution in the Third Reich, would go down with him, its leaders too benumbed now to stay the hand of the man they fully realized was leading them and the German people to the most awful catastrophe in the history of their beloved Fatherland. For by now the generals knew the evil of the man before whom they groveled. Guderian later recalled Hitler as he was after July 20:

"What had been hardness became cruelty, while a tendency to bluff became plain dishonesty. He lied without hesitation and assumed that others lied to him. It had already been difficult enough dealing with him; it now became a torture that grew steadily worse from month to month."

Nevertheless, it was this man alone, half mad, rapidly deteriorating in body and mind, who now, as he had done in the snowy winter of 1941 before Moscow, rallied the beaten, retreating armies and put new heart into the battered nation. By an incredible exercise of will power which all the others in Germany – in the army, in the government and among the people – lacked, he was able almost singlehandedly to prolong the agony of war for well nigh a year.

not surprising, picture of the shabby, tattered Nazi chiefs at the moment of one of the supreme crises in the Third Reich. By this time the communications system of Rastenburg had been restored by the direct order of Hitler and the first reports from Berlin had begun to come in indicating that a military revolt had broken out there and perhaps one on the Western front. Mutual recriminations, long suppressed, broke out between the Fuehrer's captains, their shouting echoing through the rafters though at first Hitler himself sat silent and brooding while Mussolini blushed with embarrassment.

Admiral Doenitz, who had rushed by air to Rastenburg at the news of the *attentat* and arrived after the tea party had begun, lashed out at the treachery of the Army. Goering, on behalf of the Air Force, supported him. Then Doenitz lit on Goering for the disastrous failures of the Luftwaffe, and the fat Reich Marshal, after defending himself, attacked his pet hate, Ribbentrop, for the bankruptcy of Germany's foreign policy, at one point threatening to smack the arrogant Foreign Minister with his marshal's baton. "You dirty little champagne salesman! Shut your damned mouth!" Goering cried, but this was impossible for Ribbentrop, who demanded a little respect, even from the Reich Marshal. "I am still the Foreign Minister," he shouted, "and my name is *von* Ribbentrop!"

Above: Germans retreating in the Ukraine, 1944.

Left: A powerful "King Tiger" tank in Budapest in late 1944.

The Wehrmacht's Last Offensive

Scarcely had Hitler recovered from the shock of the July 20 bombing when he was faced with the loss of France and Belgium and of the great conquests in the East. Enemy troops in overwhelming numbers were converging on the Third Reich.

By the middle of August 1944, the Russian summer offensives had brought the Red Army to the border of East Prussia, penetrated Finland, and brought an advance of 400 miles in six weeks to the Vistula, opposite Warsaw, while in the south a new attack had resulted in the conquest of Rumania and the Ploesti oilfields, the only major source of natural oil for the German armies. On August 26 Bulgaria formally withdrew from the war, and the Germans began hastily to clear out of that country. In September Finland gave up and turned against the German troops who refused to evacuate its territory.

In the West, France was liberated quickly. By the end of August the German armies in the West had lost 500,000 men, and almost all of their tanks, artillery and trucks. There was little left to defend the Fatherland. "As far as I was concerned," Field Marshal Rundstedt told Allied interrogators after the war, "the war was ended in September."

But not for Adolf Hitler. The Fuehrer was planning to launch a mighty new offensive through the Ardennes, where the great breakthrough in 1940 had begun, and which German intelligence knew to be weakly defended.

It was a daring plan. It would, Hitler believed, almost certainly catch the Allies by surprise and overcome them before they had a chance to recover. But there was one drawback. Not only was the German army weaker than it had been in 1940 but it was up against a much more resourceful and far better armed enemy. The German generals lost no time in bringing this to the Fuehrer's attention.

"When I received this plan early in November," Rundstedt later declared, "I was staggered. Hitler had not troubled to consult me. It was obvious that the available forces were far too small for such an extremely ambitious plan."

But it was useless to argue with Hitler. The generals who assembled at the Fuehrer's headquarters on December 12 found the Nazi warlord, as one of them later recalled, "a stooped figure with a pale and puffy face, hunched in his chair, his hands trembling, his left arm subject to a violent twitching. A sick man. When he walked, he dragged one leg behind him."

Hitler's spirits, however, were as fiery as ever. "It is essential," he insisted, "to deprive the enemy of his belief that victory is certain. We must allow no moment to pass without showing the enemy that, whatever he does, he can never reckon on our capitulation. Never! Never!"

With this pep talk resounding in their ears the generals dispersed, none of them – or at least so they said afterward – believing that the Ardennes blow would succeed but determined to carry out their orders to the best of their ability.

This they did. The night of December 15 was dark and frosty, and a thick mist hung over the rugged, snow-laden hills of the Ardennes Forest as the Germans moved up to their assault positions. Their meteorologists had predicted several days of such weather, during which the Allied air forces would be grounded. For five days Hitler's luck with the weather held, and the Germans, catching the Allied high command completely by surprise, scored several significant breakthroughs after their initial penetrations on the morning of December 16.

The definite turning point in Hitler's Ardennes gamble came the day before Christmas. A reconnaissance battalion of the German 2nd Panzer Division had reached the heights three miles east of the Meuse the day before, and had waited for gasoline for its tanks and some reinforcements before plunging down the slopes to the river. Neither the gasoline nor the reinforcements ever arrived. The U.S. 2nd Armored Division suddenly struck from the north. And two days before Christmas the weather finally cleared, and the Anglo-American air forces launched massive attacks on German supply lines. For the Germans it now became a question of extricating their forces from the narrow corridor of the advance before they were cut off and annihilated.

Once again Hitler would not listen to any withdrawal being made. He appealed to the generals to support new attacks "with all your fire. We shall smash the Americans completely. We shall yet master fate!"

It was too late. Germany lacked the military force to make good his words. By January 16, just a month after the beginning of the offensive on which Hitler had staked his last reserves in men and guns and ammunition, the German forces were back to the line from which they had set out. This was the last major offensive of the German army in World War II. Its failure not only made defeat inevitable in the West; it doomed the German armies in the East, where the effect of Hitler's throwing his last reserves into the Ardennes became immediately felt.

On January 12, 1945, Konev's Russian army group broke out of its bridgehead at Baranov on the upper Vistula south of Warsaw and headed for Silesia. Farther north Zhukov's armies crossed the Vistula north and south of Warsaw, which fell on

Right: The end of Hitler's Germany.

Below: US troops with two young S.S. prisoners captured near Bastogne during the Battle of the Bulge.

Below right: Red Army units street fighting in Berlin, April 1945.

January 17. Farther north still, two Russian armies overran half of East Prussia and drove to the Gulf of Danzig.

This was the greatest Russian offensive of the war. Stalin was throwing in 180 divisions, a surprisingly large part of them armored, in Poland and East Prussia alone. There was no stopping them.

"By January 27 [only fifteen days after the Soviet drive began] the Russian tidal wave," says Guderian, "was rapidly assuming for us the proportions of a complete disaster." By that date East and West Prussia were cut off from the Reich. Zhukov that very day crossed the Oder near Lueben after an advance of 220 miles in a fortnight, reaching German soil only 100 miles from Berlin. Most catastrophic of all, the Russians had overrun the Silesian industrial basin.

Albert Speer, in charge of armament production, drew up a memorandum to Hitler on January

30 – the twelfth anniversary of Hitler's coming to power – pointing out the significance of the loss of Silesia. "The war is lost," his report began, and he went on in his cool and objective manner to explain why. The Silesian mines, ever since the intensive bombing of the Ruhr, had supplied 60 per cent of Germany's coal. There was only two weeks' supply of coal for the German railways, power plants and factories. Henceforth, now that Silesia was lost, Speer could supply, he said, only one quarter of the coal and one sixth of the steel which Germany had been producing in 1944. This augured disaster for 1945.

The Fuehrer, Guderian later related, glanced at Speer's report, read the first sentence and then ordered it filed away in his safe. He refused to see Speer alone, saying to Guderian: "I refuse to see anyone alone any more . . . [He] always has something unpleasant to say to me. I can't bear that."

On the afternoon of January 27, the day Zhukov's troops crossed the Oder a hundred miles from Berlin, there was an interesting reaction at Hitler's headquarters, which had now been transferred to the Chancellery in Berlin, where it was to remain until the end. On the twenty-fifth the desperate Guderian had called on Ribbentrop and urged him to try to get an immediate armistice in the West so that what was left of the German armies could be concentrated in the East against the Russians. The Foreign Minister had quickly tattled to the Fuehrer, who that evening upbraided his General Staff Chief and accused him of committing "high treason."

But two nights later, under the impact of the disaster in the East, Hitler, Goering and Jodl were in such a state that they thought it would not be necessary to ask the West for an armistice. In the end these German architects of the Nazi-Soviet Pact against the West would reach a point where they could not understand why the British and Americans did not join them in repelling the Russian invaders.

The end came quickly for the Third Reich in the spring of 1945. On February 8 Eisenhower's armies began to close in on the Rhine. They had expected that the Germans would fight only a delaying action, but here, as elsewhere, Hitler would not listen to a withdrawal.

It was becoming apparent that Hitler, his mission as world conqueror having failed, was determined to go down, like Wotan at Valhalla, in a torrent of blood – not only the enemy's but that of his own people. He was fast becoming a physical wreck, and this helped to poison his view. The strain of conducting the war, the shock of defeats, the unhealthy life without fresh air and exercise in the underground bunkers which he rarely left had undermined his health. More and more, as the news from the fronts in 1945 grew worse, he gave way also to hysterical rage, accompanied by an uncontrollable trembling of his hands and feet.

General Guderian later described him at these moments: "His fist raised, his cheeks flushed with rage, his whole body trembling, the man stood there in front of me, beside himself with fury and having lost all self-control. He was almost screaming, his eyes seemed to pop out of his head and the viens stood out in his temples."

The end now approached for the German army. On April 16, the day American troops reached Nuremberg, Zhukov's Russian armies broke loose from their bridgeheads over the Oder, and on the afternoon of April 21 they reached the outskirts of Berlin. Vienna had already fallen on April 13. At 4:40 on the afternoon of April 25, patrols of the U.S. 69th Infantry Division met forward elements of the Russian 58th Guards Division at Torgau on the Elbe, some 75 miles south of Berlin. North and South Germany were severed. Adolf Hitler was cut off in Berlin. The last days of the Third Reich had come.

Right: Hitler at a military conference in January 1945 to discuss the defense of Silesia. By that time Hitler's military schemes had little backing in reality.

A Macabre Wedding

Above: Hitler congratulating members of the Hitler Youth for their exploits in meeting Soviet attacks. A photo taken at the Reich Chancellery, March 1945.

On April 15 Eva Braun arrived in Berlin to join Hitler. Very few Germans knew of her existence and even fewer of her relationship to Adolf Hitler. For more than 12 years she had been his mistress. Now in April she had come for her wedding and her ceremonial death. Hitler, although he undoubtedly found relaxation in her unobtrusive company, had always kept her out of sight, refusing to allow her to come to his various headquarters, where he spent almost all of his time during the war years, and rarely permitting her even to come to Berlin. She remained immured at the Berghof on the Obersalzberg, passing her time in swimming and skiing, seeing trashy films and endlessly grooming herself, pining away for her absent loved one.

"She was," the Fuehrer's chauffeur said, "the unhappiest woman in Germany. She spent most of her life waiting for Hitler." Eva couldn't endure the long separations and twice tried to kill herself in the early years of their friendship. But gradually she accepted her frustrating and ambiguous role – acknowledged neither as wife nor as mistress – content to be sole woman companion of the great man and making the most of their rare moments together.

Hitler's birthday on April 20 passed quietly enough, although, as General Karl Koller, the Air Force Chief of Staff, who was present at the celebration in the bunker, noted in his diary, it was a day of further catastrophes on the rapidly disintegrating fronts. All the Old Guard Nazis, Goering, Goebbels, Himmler, Ribbentrop and Bormann, were there, as well as the surviving military leaders, Doenitz, Keitel, Jodl and Krebs – the last-named the new, and last, Chief of the Army General Staff. They offered the Fuehrer birthday congratulations.

The warlord was not unusually cast down, despite the situation. He was still confident, as he had told his generals three days before, that "the Russians were going to suffer their bloodiest defeat of all before Berlin." The generals knew better, and at the regular military conference after the birthday party they urged Hitler to leave Berlin for the south. In a day or two, they explained, the Russians would cut off the last escape corridor in that direction. Hitler hesitated; he would not say

Left: "The Big Three," Stalin, Roosevelt and Churchill.

yes or no. Apparently he could not quite face the appalling fact that the capital of the Third Reich was now about to be captured by the Russians, whose armies, he had announced years before, were as good as destroyed. As a concession to the generals he consented to setting up two separate commands in case the Americans and Russians made their junction on the Elbe. Admiral Doenitz would head that in the north and perhaps Kesselring the one in the south – he was not quite sure about the latter appointment.

That night there was a general getaway from Berlin. Two of the Fuehrer's most trusted and veteran aides got out: Himmler and Goering, the latter in a motor caravan whose trucks were filled with booty from his fabulous estate, Karinhall. Each of these Old Guard Nazis left convinced that his beloved Leader would soon be dead and that he would succeed him.

They never saw him again. Nor did Ribbentrop, who also scurried for safer parts late that night.

But Hitler had not yet given up. On the day after his birthday he ordered an all-out counterattack on the Russians in the southern suburbs of Berlin by S.S. General Felix Steiner. Every available soldier in the Berlin area was to be thrown into the attack, including the Luftwaffe ground troops.

"Any commander who holds back his forces," Hitler shouted to General Koller, who had remained behind to represent the Air Force, "will forfeit his life in five hours. You yourself will guarantee with your head that the last man is thrown in."

All through the day and far into the next Hitler waited impatiently for the news of Steiner's counterattack. It was a further example of his loss of contact with reality. There was no Steiner attack. It was never attempted. It existed only in the feverish mind of the desperate dictator. When he was finally forced to recognize this the storm broke.

April 22 brought the last turning point in Hitler's road to ruin. From early morning until 3 P.M. he had been on the telephone, as he had been the day before, trying to find out from the various command posts how the Steiner counterattack was going. No one knew. General Koller's planes could not locate it, nor could the ground commanders, though it was supposed to be rolling only two or three miles south of the capital. Not even Steiner, though he existed, could be found, let alone his army.

The blowup came at the daily military conference in the bunker at 3 P.M. Hitler angrily demanded news of Steiner. Neither Keitel nor Jodl nor anyone else had any. But the generals had other news. The withdrawal of troops from the north of Berlin to support Steiner had so weakened the front there that the Russians had broken through and their tanks were now within the city limits.

This was too much for the Supreme Warlord.

Below: Red Army tanks in Berlin, April 1945.

All the surviving witnesses testify that he completely lost control of himself. He flew into the greatest rage of his life. This was the end, he shrieked. Everyone had deserted him. There was nothing but treason, lies, corruption and cowardice. All was over. Very well, he would stay on in Berlin. He would personally take over the defense of the capital of the Third Reich. The others could leave, if they wished. In this place he would meet his end.

The others protested. There was still hope, they said, if the Fuehrer retired to the south, where Field Marshal Ferdinand Schoerner's army group in Czechoslovakia and considerable forces of Kesselring were still intact. Doenitz, who had left for the northwest to take over command of the troops there, and Himmler, who, as we shall see, was up to his own game, telephoned to urge the Leader not to remain in Berlin. Even Ribbentrop called up to say he was about to spring a "diplomatic coup" which would save everything. But Hitler had no more faith in them, not even in his "second Bismarck," as he once, in a moment of folly, had called his Foreign Minister. He had made his decision, he said to all. And to show them that it was irrevocable, he called for a secretary and in their presence dictated an announcement that was to be read immediately over the radio. The Fuehrer, it said, would stay in Berlin and defend it to the end.

Hitler then sent for Goebbels and invited him, his wife and their six young children to move into the *Fuehrerbunker* from their badly bombed house in the Wilhelmstrasse garden. He knew that at least this fanatical and faithful follower, and his family, would stick by him to the end. Next Hitler turned to his papers, sorted out those he wished

to be destroyed, and turned them over to one of his adjutants, Julius Schaub, who took them up to the garden and burned them.

April 28 was a trying day in the bunker. The Russians were getting close. No news of any counterattack had come through. Desperately the besieged had asked for radio news of developments outside the encircled city.

The radio listening post of the Propaganda Ministry had picked up from a BBC broadcast one piece of sensational, incredible news. Heinrich Himmler – *der treue Heinrich* – had deserted the sinking ship of state! The Reuters dispatch told of

Above: Hitler and Eva Braun.

Below: Field Marshal Montgomery accepts the German surrender in northwest Europe, May 4, 1945.

Above: Field Marshal Keitel signs the unconditional surrender in Berlin, May 8, 1945.

mally married her. He had always said that marriage would interfere with his complete dedication to leading his party and his nation. Now that there was no more leading to do and his life was at an end, he could safely enter into a marriage which could last only a few hours.

After the brief ceremony there was a macabre wedding breakfast in the Fuehrer's private apartment. For a time the talk gravitated to the good old times and the party comrades of better days. As was his custom, even to the very last, the bridegroom talked on and on, reviewing the high points in his dramatic life. Now it was ended, he said, and so was National Socialism. It would be a release for him to die, since he had been betrayed by his oldest friends and supporters. The wedding party was plunged into gloom, and some of the guests stole away in tears. Hitler finally slipped away himself. In an adjoining room he summoned one of his secretaries and began to dictate his last will and testament.

These documents confirm that the man who had ruled Germany for more than 12 years, and most of Europe for four, had learned nothing from his experience; not even his reverses and shattering failure had taught him anything. Indeed, in the last hours of his life, he reverted to the young man he had been in the gutter days in Vienna and in the early rowdy beer-hall period in Munich, cursing the Jews for all the ills of the world, spinning his half-baked theories about the universe and whining that fate once more had cheated Germany of victory and conquest.

In this valedictory Hitler dredged up all the empty claptrap of *Mein Kampf* and added his final falsehoods. It was a fitting epitaph of a power-drunk tyrant whom absolute power had corrupted absolutely and destroyed. The Supreme Warlord remained true to character to the very end. The great victories had been due to him. The defeats and final failure had been due to others – to their "disloyalty and betrayal."

All the millions of German dead, all the millions of German homes crushed under the bombs, even the destruction of the German nation had not convinced him that his vision of German supremacy was a futile Teutonic dream.

his offer to surrender the German armies in the West to Eisenhower.

To Hitler, who had never doubted Himmler's absolute loyalty, this was the heaviest blow of all. "He raged like a madman," says an eyewitness. "His color rose to a heated red, and his face was virtually unrecognizable. After the outburst Hitler sank into a stupor, and for a time the entire bunker was silent."

Goering, who had already deserted his Fuehrer, at least had asked the Leader's permission to take over. But the *treue* S.S. chief and Reichsfuehrer had not bothered to ask; he had treasonably contacted the enemy without saying a word. This, Hitler told his followers when he had somewhat recovered, was the worst act of treachery he had ever known.

This blow – coupled with the news received a few minutes later that the Russians were nearing the Potsdamerplatz, but a block away, and would probably storm the chancellery on the morning of April 30, a few hours hence – was the signal for the end. It forced Hitler to make immediately the last decisions of his life. Sometime between 1 a.m. and 3 a.m. on April 29, as a crowning reward for her loyalty, he accorded Eva Braun's wish and formally married her.

Right: Banner headline of *The New York Times*, May 8, 1945.

The New York Times.

Copyright. 1945, by The New York Times Company.

VOL. XCIV....No. 31,881.   Entered as Second-Class Matter, Postoffice, New York, N. Y.   NEW YORK, TUESDAY, MAY 8, 1945.   THREE CENTS IN NEW YORK CITY

THE WAR IN EUROPE IS ENDED! NAZIS SIGN SURRENDER TERMS; V-E WILL BE PROCLAIMED TODAY; LAST FIGHTING IN CZECH POCKET

GAINS ON OKINAWA

Island-Wide Advance Is Made as U. S. Troops Use Flame-Throwers

7 MORE SHIPS SUNK

Search Planes Again Hit

Pulitzer Awards For 1944 Revealed

The Pulitzer Prize awards announced yesterday by the trustees of Columbia University included: For a distinguished novel, to "A Bell for Adano," by John Hersey; for an original American play of the current season, to "Harvey," by Mary Chase, and for "distinguished reporting on national affairs," to James B. Reston of THE NEW YORK TIMES for his reporting of the Dumbarton Oaks Security Conference.

GERMANY SURRENDERS: NEW YORKERS MASSED UNDER SYMBOL OF LIBERTY

GERMANS CAPITULATE UNCONDITIONALLY

American, Russian and French Generals Accept Surrender in Reims Schoolhouse Used as Eisenhower's Headquarters

REICH CHIEF OF STAFF ASKS FOR MERCY

Götterdämmerung

During the afternoon of April 29 came one of the last pieces of news to reach the bunker from the outside world. Mussolini, Hitler's fellow Fascist dictator and partner in aggression, had been caught by Italian partisans and executed, with his mistress, the day before. The bodies were brought to Milan and strung up by the heels from lampposts.

It is not known how many of the details of the Duce's shabby end were communicated to the Fuehrer. One can only speculate that if he heard many of them he was only strengthened in his resolve not to allow himself or his bride to be made a "spectacle."

Shortly after receiving the news of Mussolini's death Hitler began to make the final preparations for his. He had his favorite Alsatian dog, Blondi, poisoned and two other dogs in the household shot. Then he called in his two remaining women secretaries and handed them capsules of poison to use if they wished to when the barbarian Russians broke in. He was sorry, he said, not to be able to give them a better farewell gift, and he expressed his appreciation for their long and loyal service.

Evening had now come, the last of Adolf Hitler's life. He instructed Frau Junge, one of his secretaries, to destroy the remaining papers in his files and he sent out word that no one in the bunker was to go to bed until further orders. This was interpreted by all as meaning that he judged the time had come to make his farewells. But it was not until long after midnight, at about 2:30 A.M. of April 30, as several witnesses recall, that the Fuehrer emerged from his private quarters and appeared in the general dining passage, where some twenty persons, mostly the women members of his entourage, were assembled. He walked down the line shaking hands with each and mumbling a few words that were inaudible. There was a heavy film of moisture on his eyes and, as Frau Jung remembers, "they seemed to be looking far away, beyond the walls of the bunker."

After he retired, a curious thing happened. The tension which had been building up to an almost unendurable point in the bunker broke, and several persons went to the canteen – to dance. The weird party soon became so noisy that word was sent from the Fuehrer's quarters requesting more quiet. The Russians might come in a few hours and kill them all – though most of them were already thinking of how they could escape – but in the meantime for a brief spell, now that the Fuehrer's strict control of their lives was over, they would seek pleasure where and how they could find it. The sense of relief among these people seems to have been enormous and they danced on through the night.

Not Bormann. This murky man still had work to do. His own prospects for survival seemed to be diminishing. There might not be a long enough interval between the Fuehrer's death and the arrival of the Russians in which he could escape to Doenitz. If not, while the Fuehrer still lived and thus clothed his orders with authority, Bormann could at least exact further revenge on the "traitors." He dispatched during this last night a further message to Doenitz.

Left: A German prisoner identifies Goebbel's burned body for a group of Soviet officers.

"DOENITZ!

Our impression grows daily stronger that the divisions in the Berlin theater have been standing idle for several days. All the reports we receive are controlled, suppressed, or distorted by Keitel . . . The Fuehrer orders you to proceed at once, and mercilessly, against all traitors."

And then, though he knew that Hitler's death was only hours away, he added a postscript, "The Fuehrer is alive, and is conducting the defense of Berlin."

But Berlin was no longer defensible. The Russians already had occupied almost all of the city. It was now merely a question of the defense of the Chancellery. It too was doomed, as Hitler and Bormann learned at the situation conference at noon on April 30, the last that was ever to take place. The Russians had reached the eastern end of the Tiergarten and broken into the Potsdamerplatz. They were just a block away. The hour for Adolf Hitler to carry out his resolve had come.

His bride apparently had no appetite for lunch that day and Hitler took his repast with his two secretaries and with his vegetarian cook, who perhaps did not realize that she had prepared his last meal. While they were finishing their lunch at about 2:30 P.M., Erich Kempka, the Fuehrer's chauffeur, who was in charge of the Chancellery garage, received an order to deliver immediately 200 liters of gasoline in jerricans to the Chancellery garden. Kempka had some difficulty in rounding up so much fuel but he managed to collect some

180 liters and with the help of three men carried it to the emergency exit of the bunker.

While the oil to provide the fire for the Viking funeral was being collected, Hitler, having done with his last meal, fetched Eva Braun for another and final farewell to his most intimate collaborators: Dr. Goebbels, Generals Krebs and Burgdorf, the secretaries and Fräulein Manzialy, the cook. Frau Goebbels did not appear. This formidable and beautiful blond woman had, like Eva Braun, found it easy to make the decision to die with her husband, but the prospect of killing her six young children, who had been playing merrily in the underground shelter these last days without an inkling of what was in store for them, unnerved her.

"My dear Hanna," she had said to Fräulein Reitsch two or three evenings before, "when the end comes you must help me if I become weak about the children . . . They belong to the Third Reich and to the Fuehrer, and if these two cease to exist there can be no further place for them. My greatest fear is that at the last moment I will be too weak." Alone in her little room she was now striving to overcome her greatest fear.

Hitler and Eva Braun had no such problem. They had only their own lives to take. They finished their farewells and retired to their rooms. Outside in the passageway, Dr. Goebbels, Bormann and a few others waited. In a few moments a revolver shot was heard. They waited for a second one, but there was only silence. After a

Below: German refugees in a town captured by the Americans.

Left: German POWs wait to have their papers checked.

Below: German civilians emerging from a cellar in Berlin at the end of the fighting.

decent interval they quietly entered the Fuehrer's quarters. They found the body of Adolf Hitler sprawled on the sofa dripping blood. He had shot himself in the mouth. At his side lay Eva Braun. Two revolvers had tumbled to the floor, but the bride had not used hers. She had swallowed poison.

It was 3:30 P.M. on Monday, April 30, 1945, ten days after Adolf Hitler's fifty-sixth birthday, and twelve years and three months to a day since he had become Chancellor of Germany and had instituted the Third Reich. It would survive him but a week.

The Viking funeral followed. There were no words spoken; the only sound was the roar of Russian shells exploding in the garden of the Chancellery and on the shattered walls around it. Hitler's valet, S.S. Sturmbannfuehrer Heinz Linge, and an orderly carried out the Fuehrer's body, wrapped in an Army field-gray blanket, which concealed the shattered face. Kempka identified it in his own mind by the black trousers and shoes which protruded from the blanket and which the warlord always wore with his field-gray jacket. Eva Braun's death had been cleaner, there was no blood, and Bormann carried out her body just as it was to the passage, where he turned it over to Kempka. "Frau Hitler" [the chauffeur later recounted] "wore a dark dress . . . I could not recognize any injuries to the body."

The corpses were carried up to the garden and during a lull in the bombardment placed in a shell hole and ignited with gasoline. The mourners, headed by Goebbels and Bormann, withdrew to the shelter of the emergency exit and as the flames mounted stood at attention and raised their right hands in a farewell Nazi salute. It was a brief ceremony, for Red Army shells began to spatter the garden again and the survivors retired to the safety of the bunker, leaving the gasoline-fed flames to complete the work of eradicating the last earthly remains of Adolf Hitler and his wife.

End of the Nightmare

The Third Reich survived the death of its founder by seven days.

A little after ten o'clock on the evening of May 1, the Hamburg radio interrupted the playing of a recording of Bruckner's solemn Seventh Symphony. There was a roll of military drums, and then an announcer spoke:

"Our Fuehrer, Adolf Hitler, fighting to the last breath against Bolshevism, fell for Germany this afternoon in his operational headquarters in the Reich chancellery. On April 30 the Fuehrer appointed Grand Admiral Doenitz his successor."

The Third Reich was expiring, as it had begun, with a shabby lie. Aside from the fact that Hitler had not died that afternoon but the previous one, which was not important, he had not fallen fighting "to the last breath." But the broadcasting of this falsehood was necessary if the inheritors of his mantle were to perpetuate a legend and hold control of the troops who were still offering some resistance.

Doenitz knew that German resistance was at an end, however. On April 29, the day before Hitler took his life, the German armies in Italy had surrendered unconditionally. On May 4 the German high command surrendered to British General Bernard Montgomery all German forces in northwest Germany, Denmark and Holland. The next day Field Marshal Albert Kesselring's armies north of the Alps capitulated.

The game was up.

In a little red schoolhouse at Reims, where Eisenhower had made his headquarters, Germany surrendered unconditionally at 2:41 on the morning of May 7, 1945.

The guns in Europe ceased firing and the bombs ceased dropping at midnight on May 8-9, 1945, and a strange but welcome silence settled over the Continent for the first time since September 1, 1939. In the intervening five years, eight months and seven days millions of men and women had been slaughtered on a hundred battlefields and in a thousand bombed towns, and millions more done to death in the Nazi gas chambers or on the edge of the S.S. Einsatzgruppen pits in Russia and Poland – as the result of Adolf Hitler's lust for German conquest. A greater part of most of Europe's ancient cities lay in ruins, and from their rubble, as the weather warmed, there was the stench of the countless unburied dead.

No more would the streets of Germany echo to the jack boot of the goose-stepping storm troopers or the lusty yells of the brown-shirted masses or the shouts of the Fuehrer blaring from the loudspeakers.

After twelve years, four months and eight days, an Age of Darkness to all but a multitude of Germans and now ending in a bleak night for them too, the Thousand-Year Reich had come to an end. It had raised, as we have seen, this great nation and this resourceful but so easily misled people to heights of power and conquest they had never before experienced and now it had dissolved with a suddenness and a completeness that had few, if any, parallels in history.

In 1918, after the last defeat, the Kaiser had fled, the monarchy had tumbled, but the other traditional institutions supporting the State had remained, a government chosen by the people had continued to function, as did the nucleus of a German Army and a General Staff. But in the spring of 1945 the Third Reich simply ceased to exist. There was no longer any German authority on any level. The millions of soldiers, airmen and sailors were prisoners of war in their own land. The millions of civilians were governed, down to the villages, by the conquering enemy troops, on whom they depended not only for law and order but throughout that summer and bitter winter of 1945 for food and fuel to keep them alive. Such was the state to which the follies of Adolf Hitler – and their own folly in following him so blindly and with so much enthusiasm – had brought them, though I found little bitterness toward him when I returned to Germany that fall.

The people were there, and the land – the first dazed and bleeding and hungry, and, when winter came, shivering in their rags in the hovels which the bombings had made of their homes; the second a vast wasteland of rubble. The German people had not been destroyed, as Hitler, who had tried to destroy so many other peoples and, in the end, when the war was lost, themselves, had wished.

But the Third Reich had passed into history.

Right: Josef Kramer, Commandant of Belsen Concentration Camp, tried and executed for War Crimes.

Far right: An S.S. Guard from Dachau Concentration Camp is identified by a former inmate at a War Crimes Trial.

Below right: Leading Nazis in the dock at the War Crimes Trials at Nuremberg.

Below: A liberated concentration camp inmate. The scenes in the liberated camps finally brought home to the world the crimes and cruelty of Hitler's regime.

Index

Page numbers in *italics* refer to illustrations

Acknowledgments

The publisher would like to thank, David Eldred who designed this book, Rolf Steinberg who helped with the picture research and Pat Coward who compiled the index.

We would also like to thank the following picture agencies and institutions for supplying illustrations on the pages noted:

Archiv Gerstenberg: pages 16 (bottom), 19 (top), 20, 27 (top & bottom), 28 (bottom), 36 (bottom), 37, 39 (bottom), 40 (bottom), 44 (both), 45 (bottom), 47 (bottom), 49 (top left), 50, 51 (both), 56 (right), 59 (bottom), 64 (both), 67 (bottom), 70, 81 (left), 83 (top), 86 (both), 89 (top), 91 (top), 92 (both), 94-5, 96, 97 (top), 98, 99 (top), 100, 107 (top) 110, 112 (top), 115 (inset), 118-9 (top), 119, 121 (top), 130, 131 (bottom), 148 (both), 170 (bottom), 178 (top), 187 (both), 190, 191, 196 (top), 204 (center left), 210 (top), 213 (inset left), 215 (top), 216 (top), 218, 219, 220 (both) 221 (bottom), 229 (top), 230 (both), 231, 245 (top), 246 (bottom), 251 (top left)

Archiv Fur Kunst Und Geschichte, Berlin: pages 13 (bottom), 14, 21 (top), 26, 88, 101 (bottom), 114-5, 118 (bottom), 125 (bottom), 183, 196 (bottom), 204 (top & bottom), 205 (both), 208 (both), 209, 211 (bottom), 246 (top), 251 (bottom)
BBC Hulton Picture Library: pages 103 (bottom), 104 (top), 132 (both), 133, 167
Bundesarchiv: pages 10-11, 12 (both), 15 (all 3), 16 (top), 17 (both), 21 (bottom), 22 (both), 24 (bottom), 25 (bottom), 27 (middle), 28 (top), 29, 30, 31 (both), 32 (both), 33 (both), 34, 35 (both), 36 (top), 38, 39 (top), 40 (top), 41, 42, 43 (both), 45 (top), 46, 48, 49 (bottom), 52 (top), 54 (bottom), 55 (bottom), 57 (top), 59 (top left), 60-1, 62, 63 (both), 66 (both), 67 (top), 69 (top), 71, 73, 74, 75 (top), 76 (bottom), 77 (bottom), 78 (both), 79, 81 (right), 83 (bottom), 87 (bottom), 89 (bottom), 90 (bottom), 91 (bottom), 93 (top), 97 (bottom), 99 (bottom), 103 (top), 104 (bottom), 107 (bottom), 108, 111, 112 (bottom), 120, 121 (bottom), 123 (top), 124, 126 (both), 127 (both), 128 (top), 129, 131 (top), 135 (both), 138, 139 (top), 141 (both), 142 (bottom), 143, 144, 146 (top), 147, 149 (top), 150 (both), 143, 144, 146 (top), 147, 149 (top), 150 (both), 151, 154, 155 (all 4), 156,

157, 158 (both), 164 (bottom), 165 (both), 166 (both), 168 (bottom), 169, 172 (top), 174, 175, 176 (both), 177, 178, 180, 181 (top), 185, 188, 189, 192, 194, 198 (top), 199, 200, 201 (both), 202 (both), 203, 210 (bottom), 212 (top), 213 (top), 215 (bottom), 221 (top), 222, 223 (bottom), 226 (bottom), 228, 233 (top), 234, 235 (both), 236, 238, 239 (both), 242, 243 (top)
Robert Hunt Picture Library: pages 122, 123 (bottom), 125 (top), 139 (bottom), 152, 163, 179, 226 (top)
Imperial War Museum: pages 76 (top), 82, 84 (top), 87 (top), 93 (bottom), 105, 146 (bottom), 162, 171 (bottom), 181 (bottom), 184, 198 (bottom), 204 (center right), 207, 224 (bottom left), 229 (bottom), 232, 240, 245 (bottom)
Landesbildstelle Berlin: pages 13 (top), 18 (both), 19 (bottom), 23 (both), 24 (top), 54 (top), 75 (bottom), 81 (bottom), 84 (bottom), 85, 90 (top), 160-1, 225 (both), 241, 244, 247, 249 (bottom)
TPS/Central Press Agency: page 168 (top)
TPS/Keystone: pages 106, 117 (bottom), 206, 248, 249 (top)
TPS/3 Lions: pages 116 (top), 251 (top right)
US Signal Corps: page 237